THE NEGOTIATOR

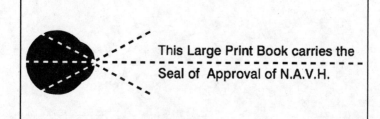

This Large Print Book carries the
Seal of Approval of N.A.V.H.

THE NEGOTIATOR

A MEMOIR

GEORGE J. MITCHELL

THORNDIKE PRESS
A part of Gale, Cengage Learning

GALE
CENGAGE Learning

Farmington Hills, Mich • San Francisco • New York • Waterville, Maine
Meriden, Conn • Mason, Ohio • Chicago

GALE
CENGAGE Learning®

LIBRARY OF CONGRESS CATALOGING-IN-PUBLICATION DATA

Mitchell, George J. (George John), 1933–
   The negotiator : a memoir / by George J. Mitchell. — Large print edition.
    pages cm. — (Thorndike Press large print biographies and memoirs)
   Include bibliographical references.
   ISBN 978-1-4104-8102-3 (hardcover) — ISBN 1-4104-8102-6 (hardcover)
   1. Mitchell, George J. (George John), 1933– 2. Legislators—United States—Biography. 3. United States. Congress. Senate—Biography. 4. United States—Politics and government—20th century. 5. Conduct of life. 6. Maine—Biography. I. Title.
   E840.8.M545A3 2015b
   328.73'092—dc23
   [B]   2015014268

Published in 2015 by arrangement with Simon & Schuster, Inc.

Printed in the United States of America
1 2 3 4 5 6 7 19 18 17 16 15

For my parents
Mary and George Mitchell

CONTENTS

AUTHOR'S NOTE

In the summer of 2011, with relief and a renewed sense of appreciation, I returned with my family to our home on Mount Desert Island, just off the coast of Maine. I had just completed my service as the U.S. envoy for Middle East peace after two and a half difficult and disappointing years. Although I had for years summered on the island, it now seemed new and fresh and comforting.

Going through familiar routines and attending events as I had in the past was also comforting. One such event was a meeting with Maine students at which I was asked to talk about my life. "You don't have to prepare anything, just get up and talk from your heart," I was told. That's what I did. Without any notes or preparation of any kind, I told stories and answered questions about my life, mostly about growing up in Maine. The next morning I woke up early, sat at my desk, and wrote down some of those stories. Over the next few months I wrote some more. The result is this book.

This is not a complete biography. It is rather a telling of some favorite stories about my very fortunate life. It's also about the lessons I've learned along the way about negotiation, lessons that have been central to my ability to get things done in law, in business, in the Senate, and in Northern Ireland.

After I retired from the U.S. Senate in 1995, I spent five years working on the peace process in Northern Ireland and did two tours of duty in the Middle East. These assignments, and others earlier in my life, took me to war-torn countries and exposed me to death and destruction on a scale that I had difficulty comprehending. The more I experienced of life outside the United States and away from Maine, the more I appreciated and longed for both.

In this book I mention only briefly two events that were an important part of my public life, the Iran-Contra investigation and the Northern Ireland peace process, because I have already written books about them. I also mention my work in the Middle East, but that deserves a full accounting in a separate book, which I hope to write in the near future. And although I describe some of the legislative efforts in which I engaged while in the Senate, they represent only a small part of my fifteen years of service there.

I am fortunate to be an American, a citizen of what I believe to be, despite its many serious imperfections, the most open, the most free, the most just society in all of human history. In America no one should be guaranteed success, but everyone should have a fair chance to succeed. This is the story of how I came to have that chance.

Mount Desert Island
2014

■ ■ ■ ■

FAMILY

■ ■ ■ ■

HEAD OF FALLS

"Right over there, just across the tracks, in what used to be Head of Falls, the senator was born."

As he said those words, Tom Nale, the mayor of Waterville, pointed to his left. The few people in the crowd, standing in the November cold, instinctively turned to look. From the square in front of City Hall, where the Veterans Day ceremony was taking place, they could see little: a railroad track, across it a parking lot, and then a short, grassy slope down to the Kennebec River. As I too looked toward the river, I thought about living "right over there" many years ago.

Head of Falls, usually pronounced "hedda falls," was the informal name given to a small triangle of land along the banks of the Kennebec River in Waterville, Maine. Bounded roughly by a railroad track, the river, and a textile mill, it consisted of about two acres of land onto which were crammed dozens of buildings, most of them apartment houses. Inside were jammed scores of families, almost all of them immigrants. It was the lowest rung on the American ladder of success.

Prior to 1900 most of them were French Canadian from Quebec. As families established themselves, they moved up and out of Head of Falls and were replaced by more recent immigrants. After the turn of the century, as the number of immigrants from what is now known as Lebanon grew, they gradually displaced the French Canadians, who in turn moved to a section of Waterville called The Plains. By 1933, when I was born, almost all of the families living there were Lebanese immigrants; a few French Canadian families remained, in homes adjacent to the textile mill.

The Head of Falls has since been cleared and turned into a parking lot. If it still existed, it would be described as a slum. But to me and the many children who lived there it was just home. On one side was the Kennebec River, rising in northern Maine and flowing southerly to the coast. The river is now clean, used by rafters, boaters, fishermen, and even some swimmers. Seventy years ago it was a stinking, open sewer; the towns located on the river dumped their sewage into it, and many industries added their wastes. Directly across and just up the river from Head of Falls, in the neighboring town of Winslow, the Hollingsworth and Whitney paper mill daily discharged huge volumes of wastes, as did the textile mill on the Waterville side. As a result the river usually was covered with scum and foam. It looked terrible and smelled worse.

The name Head of Falls comes from a nearby point in the river where it drops sharply. A dam now marks the spot. Just above the dam, a railroad bridge spans the river. It carries a main track of what was then the Maine Central Railroad. As it crossed into Waterville, that track formed one long boundary of Head of Falls, separating it from the town center. In the 1930s Waterville was a rail center, with a large repair shop located less than a mile to the north of the bridge. Large trains regularly rumbled past, shaking every building and covering the area with soot.

The third, short side of the triangle, across Temple Street, was a large textile mill, the Wyandotte Worsted Factory. Since its discharges occurred on the Waterville side, just a few feet up river, the water directly adjacent to Head of Falls was particularly foul. The Wyandotte mill, also since torn down to make way for a parking lot, was noisy, the clatter of its looms filling the air around the clock. Combined with the whine of the paper mill's huge saws cutting trees into wood chips and the rumble of the trains, it made Head of Falls a very noisy place.

It sounds bad now, but it didn't seem so then. That was just the way it was. Not until I left home to go to college, at the age of seventeen, did I realize what it's like to sleep through the night without the sound and feel of a passing train.

Baby Joe and Mintaha Become George and Mary

My mother was born in 1902 in Bkassine, a small village in the mountains of south central Lebanon. Her father, Ameen Saad, and his wife, Hilda, already had three children — Marium, Rose, and Tamem — when Hilda again became pregnant. Ameen desperately wanted a boy. Disappointed at the birth of his fourth daughter, he called it quits, so he named his fourth daughter Mintaha, "the end" in Arabic. Hilda died soon thereafter, and Ameen took a second wife. The oldest daughter, Marium, married a man named Thomas Boles and had a daughter, Eugenie. Tom and Marium decided to emigrate to the United States, and, as was common at the time, they left their daughter behind until they could establish themselves. In 1920, by now settled in Waterville, they sent for her. Eugenie was nine years old and could not make the trip alone, so Mintaha was chosen to accompany her. She was eighteen and had never before left Lebanon. She could not read, speak, or understand a word of English.

Mintaha and Eugenie traveled first to Marseilles, then made their way to Paris. According to Eugenie, who later described the trip to my sister and brother Paul, one purpose of the trip was for my mother to meet a prospective husband for an arranged marriage; the man was a Lebanese immigrant living in Paris where he was a practicing dentist. After the meeting, Mintaha and Eugenie traveled to Le Havre, where on June 5, 1920, they boarded the SS *Leopoldina,* arriving in New York eleven days later, two of 1,169 immigrants on board, part of the human tide that passed through Ellis Island. But Mintaha did not return to Paris as planned, and she never again lived in Lebanon. She did not tell Eugenie what happened at that meeting in Paris, but based on her later life and words, it's clear that all along what she wanted was to get to America, where she would join her sisters and be free to make her own decisions. Soon after she got to Maine she became Mary, and she stayed.

After arriving in Waterville and moving in with her sister and brother-in-law, Mary found work as a dishwasher in a local restaurant. But she soon learned the trade she would ply for the rest of her working life. Throughout central Maine textile mills were running around the clock, spinning out thousands of yards of cotton and woolen goods. In the previous half century they had become, in the aggregate, the largest employer in the state, hiring thousands of immigrants. By all accounts Mary became a skilled weaver. For several decades she worked the night shift, from eleven o'clock in the evening until seven in the morning. The textiles mills of the time were noisy, the clatter of the looms so deafening that conversation was impossible. The air inside the mill was hot and heavy, dense with suffocating lint that filled the workers' lungs, hair, nostrils, and ears and covered their clothing. The floors were slick with many years' accumulation of lubricating oil, so the workers shuffled around, their feet always in contact with the floor so as not to slip. It was (and still is, although conditions in modern mills are much improved, particularly the reduction of lint) hot, hard, demanding work. Mary did it for most of her adult life so her children would never have to.

My father was born in 1900 in Boston.

Known as "Baby Joe," he was the youngest son of Irish immigrants. He never knew his parents and was raised in an orphanage in Boston. It was common practice at the time for the nuns who operated the orphanage to take the children on weekends to Catholic churches throughout northern New England. After Mass the children were lined up in the front of the church. Any person attending Mass who wanted to adopt a child could do so simply by taking one by the hand and walking out. In that way, when he was four years old, my father was adopted by an elderly, childless couple from Bangor, John and Mary Mitchell.

The Mitchells had emigrated from their native Lebanon to Egypt, where they lived for several years before coming to the United States. Once here they assumed their new surname. So when they walked out of a Bangor church after Mass on a Sunday in 1904, Baby Joe became George Mitchell. Soon after, the family moved to Waterville, fifty-five miles southwest of Bangor, where they operated a small store in the Head of Falls. George attended a parochial elementary school where many of the students were of French ancestry, and he soon learned their language. But his childhood was short; he left school after the fourth grade to begin a long life of hard work and low wages.

In his early teens he went to the Portland area, where he worked as a laborer on the railroad. From there he traveled to northern Maine to find work as a logger. Despite his lack of formal education he was an avid reader. A friend of his told my sister about one of their early trips into the woods. It was a cold winter. They took the train to Farmington, about thirty miles to the northwest of Waterville. From the station they walked several miles through the snow into the woods to a logging camp. Throughout the trip young George struggled with two large suitcases. One of them was especially heavy because, as his friend learned when they unpacked, it was full of books. The loggers slept in a big one-room building that held about sixty men. Near the center of the building was a large opening in the ceiling for ventilation. Because my father was one of the youngest men, he got the least desirable bunk: an upper, right under what his friend called "the big hole in the ceiling." There he spent a miserable winter, working all day, cold and coughing all night. No wonder he so much enjoyed being a janitor in his later years. At least then he was inside, keeping warm.

Sometime between 1920 and 1924 George Mitchell and Mary Saad met, fell in love, and married. I was born on August 20, 1933, the fourth of their five children.

My mother worked at several mills in central Maine. Despite the strenuous demands of working all night in a textile mill, she was home in time to get us off to school and be ready with supper when we returned home. After putting us to bed in the evening, she left for work. She slept briefly during the day, but to her children she seemed tireless and energetic, full of life and love. My father worked too, of course, but in the manner of the time, his working day ended when he got home. For my mother home was another workplace; she cooked, cleaned, and did the wash, the daily shopping, and many other chores. She often must have been exhausted, and surely she complained in private. But none of that was apparent to her children. To us she was always there, always ready, always supportive, always loving. She was a strong and very determined woman and she knew how to enforce discipline in her children, but it was always within a context of such total love, and often good humor, that it was impossible to feel put upon or to doubt her good intentions. She was the most impressive and influential person in my life.

My mother could not read or write English and spoke with a thick accent, mispronouncing words and fracturing sentences. She especially had trouble with the "th" sound, so *smooth* came out as "smool" and *thirty* as "sirty." When any of us kidded her about it, she would laughingly mispronounce the words even worse, for comic effect. She loved to cook and did so constantly. I can still recall the warm smell of freshly baked bread; it filled the house, sweeter than the most expensive perfume.

My mother was raised in a society in which hospitality to guests is mandatory and she carried that practice to an extreme. Every person who entered our home was required to sit and have a meal, no matter the time of day. She simply would not take no for an answer. The most modest offering — the last resort for those not able to eat a full meal — was freshly baked bread and coffee. So the plumber, the electrician, the family doctor — all sat at our kitchen table and ate and ate, until they could eat no more. I remember the plumber saying that he made a mistake on his first visit to our house because he came just after lunch; he was full, so he couldn't eat much. He never made that mistake again, always arriving in the late morning or late afternoon.

She also welcomed complete strangers into her kitchen. One year, two young men rented an apartment in the rear of a neighbor's house. They were Mormons, performing their service to their faith. Unluckily for them, the poor immigrant families in our neighborhood, most of them French or Lebanese, were deeply dedicated Catholics, so there were no converts. When the two young missionaries first visited our home, my mother understood their purpose, but couldn't comprehend their arguments. That made no difference to her. She sat them at the kitchen table and fed them a full, warm meal. As they left, she invited them to return, which they did. Their visits became regular and more frequent and a ritual developed — they talked about religion, which she ignored, and she talked about food, which they ate. Consistent with her belief that everyone is a good person, she liked and admired them. Once, when my father criticized our town's newly elected Republican mayor, my mother reproached him, saying, "He's a good person."

"How do you know that?" my father asked.

"Because I see him at Mass on Sunday,"

she answered. To her, that was proof enough.

She was totally devoted to her husband, but her dependence on him did not become evident until after his death, when it became clear that life had been taken from her too. She began to shrink, physically and mentally. She became irritable and unpredictable. Worst of all, my mother, who had been so open, warm, and trusting, became mistrustful. Within a few years she had to enter a nursing home. There, despite good and warm care, she declined rapidly. Seeing her near the end — pale, eyes shut tight, murmuring incoherently — was the most painful experience of my life, far more painful than her death. Gradually that image has faded and I recall the strong woman of my youth, looking across the table at me and saying, laughing as she spoke, "You want to grow up strong and smart? Drink this goat's milk and do your homework!" She was worried about my lack of size and strength and believed that goat's milk would help me grow faster. It became a standing joke in our family: if I succeeded in anything — a good test score in school; getting a law degree; becoming a federal judge; entering the Senate — it was the goat's milk!

For many years my father worked as a

laborer at a division of the local utility company. In 1950 the utility discontinued the division and he lost his job. The ensuing crisis nearly destroyed him. He was fifty years old and had worked steadily since he was ten. For nearly a year he was out of work. My mother's income barely supported us. As the year stretched on, my father's depression intensified and his mood darkened. I was sixteen, in my last year in high school. Immature, insensitive to the poison of despair that was consuming him, I didn't comprehend what my father was going through. We argued often, to my mother's dismay. He tried very hard, but he couldn't get a job, and each failure drove the downward cycle of despair and deepened his loss of self-esteem. It was by far the worst year of my life. After months of discord we were both emotionally worn out, and a gloomy, sullen silence descended on us. He withdrew even deeper into himself and seemed to physically shrink as well. For a long time we didn't speak. Our eyes rarely met. Finally, just as his self-esteem had all but vanished, he found a job as a janitor at Colby College in Waterville. For him, and for our family, it was a life-saving reprieve.

To this day I have difficulty restraining my anger when I hear someone engage in blanket condemnation of the unemployed. Having lived through the tragedy of unemployment, I know that most of those out of work would prefer to be working. Yet without precisely saying so, the message of many who seek to exploit the issue is to the contrary: they're lazy, dependent, and don't want to work. Those critics without any conscience equate all of the unemployed with welfare cheats. Whenever I hear such remarks, I angrily think (and often, if the situation permits, say), "My father wasn't like that. He wanted to work, he tried very hard to find a job, and I'm sure that most of those who are out of work now are like him. They are human beings, many of them living through the despair and the wrenching and soul-killing loss of self-esteem that nearly destroyed my father."

Fortunately Colby College needed a janitor. It didn't seem like much of a job, but it suited my father. He loved books and magazines, so just being at an institution of higher learning all day was a pleasure for him. His intelligence was soon recognized and he was put in charge of all the janitors and maids and then of most of the grounds crew as well. As a result he thoroughly enjoyed the last fifteen years of his working life, even though he earned very little money during that time.

I learned from my father's experience that there is dignity in every human being and in every form of work. My father took pride in his work as a janitor and as a groundskeeper. He brought excellence to the job, which in turn gave him back his dignity and self-esteem. In fact it saved his life. Once he started to work at Colby, his despair gradually gave way to optimism. After a year of slouching and stooping he stood straight again. The mist vanished from his blue eyes and they regained their sparkle. The difficult times were fewer and fewer and finally disappeared. He again laughed and joked and took an interest in what and how I was doing. I felt as though we had come out of a long dark tunnel into bright sunshine.

Although he was not a learned man, when my father became interested in a subject, he pursued it avidly. Perhaps because he could rarely travel, he was fascinated by geography. I can still recall as a small boy sitting with him at the kitchen table, poring over maps of the world. There I first learned about the Alps and the Himalayan Mountains; the Nile, the Amazon, and the great rivers of Russia; the Straits of Magellan and Malacca. Because of him I became interested in the subject. After he retired from Colby, and for the next seven years until his death, whenever I returned to Waterville to visit, I prepared a geography quiz for him. I studied maps and atlases, trying to stump him. But I never did. I remember clearly the quiz I gave him on my last visit before his sudden death in July 1972. I asked him three questions, of increasing difficulty: Which country has the most cities with a population of more than one million? How many such cities are there in that country? Name them. Without hesitation he answered: China (obviously); fourteen (not so obvious); and then, methodically, with brief pauses, Peking, Shanghai, Canton, Chungking, Mukden, and so on down the list. Perfect! I told him I'd stump him the next time. We both laughed, and he gave me a long, close hug when I left to return to Washington. I never saw him alive again.

My parents knew little of history or political science, but they understood the meaning of America because they valued freedom and opportunity. They conveyed their values to their children by example more than by words. Though it was not often expressed aloud, their message was clear. Their values were simple, universal in reach, and enduring in strength: faith, family, work, country.

My mother's faith was total and unquestioning, an integral part of her life. After she stopped working, she attended church every day. But her faith involved more than ritual, more than just listening to the gospel or reciting it; it meant living its message in daily life. She integrated faith, love, and charity into a life of meaning, even though she lacked education, wealth, or status. Often in my life, when facing a difficult challenge, I, with my college and law school degrees, tried to figure out what my mother would do. She had more common sense and good moral judgment than anyone I've ever known.

My parents' commitment to family was deep and unwavering. Nothing came before their children. Ever. My father's goal in life was to see that all of his children graduated from college. And we all did. By current standards we were poor, but we never felt poor; we lived the way everyone we knew lived. Not once, ever, did we go hungry; our home never lacked heat in the winter; though there were lots of hand-me-downs we were always adequately dressed. To us it was a normal life: family, church, school, work, sports.

THE TWO PENNY BRIDGE

A favorite pastime of children in Head of Falls was trying to sneak across the Two Penny Bridge. From the time the paper mill in Winslow opened, just prior to the turn of the century, many men from Waterville worked at the mill. Because they had to make a long trip across the only bridge that spanned the river, an especially difficult trip in the winter, a petition was presented to the Waterville City Council in 1898 urging the construction of a footbridge. The council rejected the proposal as too expensive. Two local businessmen then obtained a charter from the state legislature and proceeded to build a private, toll footbridge. On the Winslow side it was located near the paper mill; on the Waterville side it was located at the foot of Temple Street, right next to the Head of Falls. I could see the bridge from the back window of our house, just a few feet away.

The bridge opened in April 1901, and the toll was two cents. It did a brisk business. Unfortunately in that December there occurred on the Kennebec one of the worst floods in nearly a century and the bridge was washed away. Undaunted, the owners rebuilt and reopened it in 1903. The new bridge was 570 feet long and six feet wide. The toll was still two cents, where it remained until 1960, when it was raised to five cents. The bridge was in operation until 1973, when declining traffic forced its closure. It has since been listed on the National Register of Historic Landmarks, renovated and re-opened to the public, toll free.

The toll booth was located near the Waterville end of the bridge. Since the bridge is only six feet wide, the bridge keeper could easily see anyone walking in either direction. His only blind spot was right below the door to the toll booth. By crawling along the side of the bridge and just below the booth, it was sometimes possible to sneak across without paying the toll, especially if other people were crossing at the same time. So it became a challenge to the kids in our neighborhood to get across the bridge for free.

I was not quite five in the summer of

1938, when I made my first trip across the bridge. It was a windy day and the bridge was swaying. Many times from a distance I had seen it sway, but I had never before *felt* it. Needless to say, it felt like it was swinging high enough to throw me off. I was frightened and wanted to turn back, but I was even more afraid of being called a sissy. I was with four older boys, all of whom had done it before, so I kept going. We crawled past the toll booth and then stood up and ran across. It felt good to have made it, even better to get off that swaying bridge. Now we were in Winslow. We had nothing to do there, of course. The point of it all was to cross the bridge, not to get to Winslow. We had no money, nowhere to go, nothing to do. So we got ready to do the only thing we could think of: go back across. That called for a different strategy. Since the booth was near the Waterville end, it made no sense to crawl all the way across from the Winslow end. The return strategy was to wait until adults were crossing, walk behind them as casually as possible, and then run full speed off the other end. It was midafternoon and there weren't many people using the bridge, so we just waited for the next shift change at the mill, when there would be lots of workers crossing back to Waterville. We got

37

back easily. As we ran off the bridge, one of the older boys paid me what was then the ultimate compliment: he told the others, "He's okay."

That winter was long and difficult for me. Some of the homes on Head of Falls were built at the top of a small hill that sloped sharply down to the river; the others were at the very bottom, right on the riverbank. Connecting the two groups was a gravel footpath. When it snowed, the path was used for sliding by children from both groups. One particularly heavy snowstorm was followed by a clear, cold, sunlit day. My brother Paul, then twelve years old, was sliding with a friend. I heard their laughter and wanted to be part of the fun, so I asked if I could join them. There was only one sled, so Paul hesitated. I pleaded and he gave in. There wasn't enough room for the three of us to sit comfortably on the sled, so Paul sat in the middle, and I sat in front, snuggled close to him; his feet were on the steering pedals in the front, while my legs were spread wide, on top of and outside of his. It took a while to get settled, but once the sled started it quickly picked up speed. About two-thirds of the way down the hill the sled veered to the left, directly into a large post holding up a wooden fence that lined the side of the path. My left leg, sticking out the side of the sled, took the full force of the collision; several bones were broken. After the sharp pain the only thing I remember is my mother carrying me in her arms down the hill to our home. I spent months in a full leg cast and "baby crutches," filled with regret at how much trouble I'd caused Paul. As the firstborn he was plainly our mother's favorite; her nickname for him was "Sunshine." But on that day, and several more afterward, there was no sunshine for Paul. Gradually I recovered; there were no permanent effects, and in time sunshine returned.

FRONT STREET

In 1938 we made what was for my family a major move: we crossed the railroad tracks. After the birth of my sister, Barbara, all five children slept in one tiny bedroom, Paul and John in one bed, Robbie and me in another, and Barbara's crib crammed in between. Once Barbara grew out of the crib, we had to move. My father bought an old house on Front Street, which runs directly adjacent and parallel to the tracks, so we were now actually closer to the tracks than we had been in Head of Falls. But the move was symbolic because we were, literally and figuratively, out of Head of Falls and on *the right side* of the tracks. My father took great pride in being able to move us there. That September I started school at St. Joseph's Maronite Parochial School, located just off Front Street, about three blocks from our house. The school was operated by the parish. The instructors were nuns of the

Ursuline Order, deeply religious and dedicated teachers. Strict discipline was maintained, and heavy emphasis was placed on learning the basics. We attended Mass daily. Then, as now, the young boys assisted in the Masses as altar boys. There I learned early the value of knowing more than one language.

Maron was a priest and hermit who lived in the early part of the fifth century in the mountains of what is now central Lebanon. He devoted his life to prayer and good works, living simply and frugally. Eventually the Maronite Church was created in his name. In the sixteenth century it permanently joined with and became part of the Roman Catholic Church. Although its liturgy and practices were once significantly different from those of the Roman Catholic faith, over time the differences have diminished and the two are now virtually indistinguishable, especially as they operate in the United States.

In 1938 one difference was that all Masses at St. Joseph's were held in Arabic, the language of Syria and Lebanon, while Masses at most Roman Catholic churches were in Latin. Now, except for one Arabic Mass a week, all Masses at St. Joseph's and other Catholic churches in the United

States are in English. Although my mother and father both spoke Arabic, they rarely did so when we children were around, as they, like many immigrants, were anxious that we be Americanized as quickly and completely as possible. Thus to this day I can say and understand only a few words in Arabic.

The first time I served as an altar boy I was paired with Henry Nagem, a happy-go-lucky older boy. He knew even less Arabic than I did. The priest was the church pastor, Father Joseph Awad, a stern, intimidating figure. Both Henry and I were nervous as the Mass began. Things went well until near the end, when one of us was supposed to get Father Awad's cap, which he had placed at the side of the altar at the beginning of the Mass. We both forgot, and a long, motionless silence occurred. Then Father Awad, in a low, stern voice said something neither of us understood. He repeated it three or four times in a voice rising with anger. I looked at Henry; he looked at me. My legs were shaking. He was sweating. Finally an exasperated parishioner yelled out, "His hat, he wants you to get his hat, you dumbbells!" We collided and nearly fell, scrambling to get Father Awad's cap. Afterward, in the rectory, he reprimanded us and made us stay there and memorize the Arabic words necessary to serve Mass, including the word for *cap,* pronounced "boor-nite-ah." I will never forget it.

Serving as an altar boy was my introduction to public speaking. The church was usually full at Sunday Mass, and one of us always read the epistle; it was an honor and a challenge. My father insisted that I learn to speak in public and encouraged my reading of the epistle. To make sure I could be heard and understood throughout the church, he made me practice at home: I would stand in the back hallway while he sat in the living room at the far end of our house. There were three rooms between us and I couldn't see him, but I read the epistle over and over, louder and louder, pronouncing every syllable clearly, until he could hear and understand every word. Although I objected at first, once I found that I could do it well, I looked forward to the Sunday readings.

My brother Robbie and I shared a bedroom, as did my two older brothers. My sister, Barbara, the youngest, had her own bedroom, as did my parents. In retrospect the only real inconvenience came from seven people sharing a single, very tiny bathroom. That led to occasional waiting lines, but we learned to take our turn. Over time, as Paul and then Johnny went off to college, the waiting time decreased.

Barbara, the youngest of five children, and the only girl, didn't have a natural playmate in the family, but she handled it well, becoming highly successful and fiercely independent; she now tends to lead, and occasionally to dominate, family discussions. As one of my brothers once said, "The four of us against Barbara: an even battle."

SPORTS

I got into politics because of basketball. In Waterville one of the most important things in life was high school basketball, and my three older brothers were all great players. Then I came along. I was not as good as they were. In fact I was not as good as anyone else's brother. When I was fourteen I began to be known as Johnny Mitchell's kid brother, the one who isn't any good. As you might expect, I developed a massive inferiority complex and a highly competitive attitude toward my brothers. I hoped it would just be a passing phase. But it wasn't. Even after high school and college, I continued to be known as the Mitchell brother who wasn't any good. So I resolved to outdo my brothers, to become more famous than my brother Johnny, nicknamed "the Swisher" for his prowess on the basketball court. As proof that I've succeeded, one of the high points in my life

45

was the day after my election to a full term in the Senate. The Portland paper ran a big picture of the victory celebration the night before. It showed me waving to the cheering crowd, and draped over me, mugging for the camera, is my brother Johnny. The caption read, "Senator George Mitchell, celebrating his surprise election victory, being cheered on by an unidentified supporter."

Our lives revolved around team sports: baseball all summer, some football, and especially basketball. While in high school I could not have named either of Maine's U.S. senators, but I knew exactly what Ted Williams's batting average was every day. We played sports almost daily, for as long as possible. Right after school, from early fall to late spring, if work didn't interrupt, we went to the Boys Club. There boys of all ages played basketball until the Club closed at nine o'clock.

I was younger and smaller than most of my classmates — sixteen when I graduated from high school, twenty when I graduated from college. My father explained to me over and over again that the reason I didn't seem to be as good an athlete as my brothers was that I was always playing against boys older than I was; in the meantime, he said, I was actually better off because I was getting through school faster. What he said may have been logical, but it did nothing to ease the hurt and constant embarrassment.

My two oldest brothers' teams won the State and New England championships, and Robbie's won the State Championship. I played on the junior varsity in my sophomore and junior years and made the varsity in my senior year, but I started only one game (and played poorly) and played little in the others. I couldn't even make the tournament team. That was the low point, the final humiliation. The best teams in the state are divided into the eastern and western Maine tournaments of eight teams each; then the winners of the two regional tournaments meet for the State Championship. When tournament time came, our squad had to be cut to ten, down from the twelve that were carried during the year. The coach gave me and one other sad boy the bad news. As a consolation he asked us to come to the tournament with the team as ball boys. Ball boys! I was so surprised, hurt, and angry I was afraid I'd cry if I opened my mouth. So I didn't say anything. Neither did the other boy (I assume for the same reason). The coach took our silence for acquiescence, and we went to the tournament as ball boys. Fortunately all of my brothers were away. If they had been at home, they would have made fun of me and made me even more miserable than I was.

My father handled the situation well. He encouraged my brothers without discouraging me. He kept sports in the proper perspective and emphasized scholastic achievement. He urged me to study, to read, to get the education he never had but that he was determined his children would have. I didn't really listen, didn't read or study much. But every time I attended a game or a practice and heard other fathers yelling at their kids, at the opposing team, at the coaches, at the referees, I silently thanked God for my father. He attended some games, but by no means all the ones in which we played, and when he did attend he sat quietly, never raising his voice.

Not so my mother. She attended many more games than did my father. Although she didn't understand any of the sports involved, her point of view was simple: her boys were playing and she was there for them. In 1949, when I was a junior in high school and Robbie a senior, Waterville won the Eastern Maine Championship and played South Portland for the state title. Robbie was the star of the team and had a great night in the championship game, scoring twenty-one points and leading Waterville to victory. According to several eyewitnesses, my mother was seated directly in front of a man who throughout the game made loud and abusive remarks about Robbie. Finally, during a timeout, unable to stand it any longer, she stood up, wheeled around, swung her handbag, and belted the man on the side of the head. As she did so, she shouted, "That's my son you're talking about!" The crowd around her cheered. The man, obviously embarrassed, sat silently through the rest of the game.

While supportive of her sons, she understood the meaning of team effort. In the fall of Johnny's junior year in high school, he refused to report when the basketball team started practice. He was angry at the coach because in the last game of the recently concluded football season, the coach had used Johnny for only a few minutes. The same man coached both football and basketball, and Johnny fancied himself a star in both sports. He was sitting around the house one afternoon after school, sulking. My mother was baking bread at the time. She asked him why he wasn't at basketball practice. She was holding a large wooden spatula that she used for baking bread. When Johnny told her why he wasn't at practice, she hit him with the spatula, which broke apart. "You *psynee!*" she said, using the Arabic word for *kitten,* or *pussycat,* which she frequently called Johnny. "You're going to practice right now." She grabbed him by the ear and started for the door. He, fearing the embarrassment of having his mother drag him into practice, pleaded with her to let him go alone. She made him call the coach and tell him he'd be there in fifteen minutes. He didn't miss another practice. That year Waterville was undefeated and became the first (and still only) Maine team to win the New England High School Basketball Championship when all six states participated. In the final game, held at Brown University in Providence, Rhode Island, Johnny excelled and was named the Most Valuable Player. It was his eighteenth birthday.

Our mother didn't understand anything about baseball, but because her children listened to the games on the radio, so did she. Because her children loved the Red Sox and idolized Ted Williams, so did she. She had great fun talking back to the radio, arguing with the announcer, all in fractured English that kept everybody laughing, and when Williams hit a home run she led the cheers. Although I didn't think of her in such terms at the time, she was a lot of fun to be around, especially when she was in her jovial, self-deprecating moods.

By my senior year in high school my relative lack of athletic ability was evident to everyone. But I wouldn't admit it. I went to college determined to play basketball and prove to my brothers that I could keep pace with them. Although I played more in college than I did in high school, and even more later while in the army, I gradually came to realize and accept the truth. It was a hard but useful lesson.

EVERYONE WORKED

Although I did not understand how or why, and still cannot fully explain it, my father insisted that I move rapidly through the school system. As a result I entered high school two weeks after I turned thirteen and graduated when I was sixteen. My father was proud of my brothers' achievements, of course, but he had not gone beyond the fourth grade, so to him learning was everything. Whenever I was in tears or dejected (or both) at not having done well in a sport, he always tried to console me: "Don't worry about it, it's not that important. You study hard and someday your brothers will look up to you, just like you look up to them now." I didn't believe him, but he did increase my incentive to do well in school.

As far back as I can remember, everyone in our family worked: delivering newspapers, mowing lawns, washing cars, sweeping floors, shoveling snow, in textile mills and paper mills, self-employed and for others. We never talked about it; it was expected and we just did it. I still remember clearly the two most difficult jobs I had, one because it was too cold, the other too hot. I hated waking up early to deliver morning newspapers. It was dark, extremely cold in the winter, and the pile of papers we loaded into our delivery bags was heavy. I could just barely lift the bag when it was full, so the early deliveries were the hardest. Although just a few blocks long, the route seemed endless. It was a joy to get back home to a steaming cup of hot chocolate. For a few years I also delivered afternoon papers, then published in Portland and Lewiston. That was much easier; there were no home deliveries. Sales were made directly, in places like Bill's Bar, just off Front Street, where workers returning home would stop for a beer. We newsboys would burst into the bar yelling, "Portland Evening Express!" or "Lewiston Evening Journal!" as we scrambled for sales from the friendly workers.

The other job that was difficult was picking beans in the summer. Large farms (or so they seemed at the time) outside of Waterville grew green beans, which were harvested in August. Kids from Waterville were bused to the farms in the morning and spent the day picking. Pay was based on the volume of beans picked, so speed was of the essence. The fastest way was to stand with your legs upright, one foot on either side of the row of beans, your back bent at a ninety-degree angle as you stooped to pick the beans and move quickly down each row. But after a short time the back pain was severe. The alternative was to crawl up and down the space between the rows on your hands and knees; that was easier on your back but much slower and less profitable. So, depending on your individual tolerance, you would stoop as long as you could, then crawl for as short a time as necessary. Inevitably the amount of stooping was greatest early in the morning; as the sun rose and the day got hotter, we (especially the younger kids like me) tired quickly and ended the day crawling ever more slowly. It was difficult work, but the few dollars we earned made a difference at home. We were fortunate that the harvest season was only a few weeks long. Many years later, as a lawyer on a business trip, I found myself standing in truly large agricultural fields in western Arizona and southern California watching migrant laborers pick vegetables under a brutally hot sun. I thought of how fortunate I was to have had to do such work for just a couple of weeks over a few summers, and I wondered if any of the children I was watching would have the same luck in their lives as I had in mine.

I worked my way through college as a truck driver, an advertising salesman, a dormitory proctor, and a fraternity steward. I then worked full time as an insurance adjuster while attending law school at night. To me this was not remarkable. It was the way of life I learned from my parents.

ELVIRA WHITTEN

Those who know me know that my mother, my father, and Edmund Muskie were three of the most influential persons in my life. Few know who the fourth person was.

I have read accounts that describe me in early youth as studious and always with a book in my hand, but those accounts are inaccurate. Before high school I had done no meaningful reading. If I did have a book in my hand, it was a comic book (or, as we called them at the time, a funny book). Otherwise I read only the bare minimum of textbooks necessary to get through school.

Then I met Elvira Whitten, who taught English at Waterville High School. I was in her class in my junior year. I was fifteen years old, naïve, lacking in confidence and self-esteem. She was elderly, intelligent, kind, formal, and erect. With her gray hair swept up on her head she was attractive in a dignified, straitlaced way. She was strict, but she had a calm and gentle manner that effectively banished fear and intimidation from her classroom. One day she asked me to come back to her class after school. I did, not knowing what to expect.

She pulled a chair up beside her desk and asked me to sit down. I did so, nervously. She looked directly at me and, after a slight pause, asked, "What do you read?" I heard and understood her but instinctively answered, "What do you mean?" She asked again, "What do you read?" Then she added, "Books. Do you read any books? Or magazines, or newspapers?" I told her, truthfully, that the only books I read were textbooks and that I read those only to the extent needed to get by. I was too embarrassed to add that most of my reading was of comic books.

She smiled and said, "I think you're ready for more serious reading." She lifted a book from her desk and handed it to me. "Start with this. When you finish it come back and tell me about it." I took the book and scanned the cover. *The Moon Is Down* by John Steinbeck. It was a short book, a novella. Mrs. Whitten said, "You don't have to do this, it won't affect your grade one way or the other, but I hope you will. I think you'll enjoy it."

I admired her so much that I would have done just about anything to gain her approval. "I'll read it. I want to read it," I responded. That evening I started reading. The story is a fictionalized account of the Nazi occupation of Norway during World War II. I found it riveting and, interrupted only by my chores at the Boys Club and the office building next door, read it straight through, finishing that night. The next school day passed slowly for me, eager as I was to report to Mrs. Whitten. After her class, nervous and excited, I told her about it, delivering an emotional book report that was almost as long as the book. She smiled and in her reassuring manner took back the book and handed me another one, *Parnassus on Wheels.* "This one is different," she said, "but I think you'll like it." She was right.

From November to late May I read fiction, history, biography, long books, short books. She picked them out; I read and reported to her on them. I wasn't conscious of it, but my life was changing. Then in May, after one of my reports, I waited for her to hand me the next book. Her smile and tone of voice were the same as she said, "I think you're ready to choose your own books." I was surprised, and my face must have betrayed my disappointment at the prospect of no longer being able to meet with her after class, so she quickly added, "Of course if you read something really interesting and want to tell me about it I hope you'll do so." Relieved, but still sad, I left.

I spent weeks pondering my choice. I wanted to keep reading, but I had no basis for decision. I had enjoyed reading every book Mrs. Whitten gave me, in part because they came from her. For days I wandered through both the school library and the public library, browsing, looking through stacks and lists, wondering what Mrs. Whitten would think of my choice. Finally I settled on three books, known collectively as *The Bounty Trilogy.* That summer I raced through *Mutiny on the Bounty, Men Against the Sea,* and *Pitcairn's Island.* Fletcher Christian and Captain Bligh came alive for me. For the first summer of my life baseball had competition. It was an unsettling surprise to me that by mid-August I looked forward to my next book as much as I did to my next ball game.

One of the great regrets of my life is that I never returned as an adult to thank Mrs. Whitten in person. I'm certain that my life would have been different, far less meaningful, had I not been one of her students.

My early failure to comprehend and thank her for her role in my life is consistent with our society's failure to properly recognize and value the contributions made daily by thousands of Elvira Whittens. All across America, extraordinary and devoted men and women teach, and also shape and inspire, our children. We should do much more to raise their status and compensation. We all benefit if in our society as many young Americans as possible reach their full potential.

A half century later I tried to make up for my failure. After I retired from the Senate I established a scholarship fund to help young students in need to attend and graduate from college. At the first event the guest speaker was Mrs. Whitten's daughter. At my request she had traveled from New Hampshire, where she lives, to Maine. As I introduced her, I told the large crowd in attendance about the huge contribution her mother had made to my life. It was gratifying to be able to describe that contribution to her daughter.

ROBBIE

It started early in life. Paul and John competed, and occasionally fought, as did Robbie and I. My father nailed a backboard with an attached hoop to the backside of the house. The driveway was dirt but smooth enough to dribble on. There was one drawback: right next to the basket, the house angled back to the garage. Someone driving for a layup, if not careful, could run into a sharp corner of the house. Robbie, my friend Ron Stevens, and I were playing there one day, alternating one-on-one. Robbie was older, bigger, and a better athlete than Ron or I. He was outscoring us and elbowing, pushing, and knocking us around. Angry at losing and taking a physical beating in the process, I let him drive past me for a layup, and, just as he started up to take it, I shoved him from behind, right into the corner of the house. He hit it hard, bounced off, and fell heavily to the ground.

I immediately regretted what I'd done and, thinking he was seriously hurt, started toward him. Just before I got to him, he jumped up and came at me, swearing and swinging. His first punch hit me square in the face and knocked me backward, over a low wire fence that separated the driveway from the garden. He jumped over the fence, landed on top of me, and started slugging away. Fortunately for me, Ron began yelling, "He's killing him! He's killing him!" My mother ran out of the house and pulled Robbie off me, thereby saving, if not my honor, at least my teeth.

The competition continued in other ways, and in most of them Robbie scored heavily. We were close in age, born just twenty months apart, separated by one year in school. We grew up together, he the older brother who was a prominent athlete, who always had money and a girlfriend, I the younger, frail brother who was not good in sports, hardly ever had a date, and worked for him to earn spending money. In his senior year Robbie led Waterville High School to the state title in basketball and was voted the Most Valuable Player in the championship game. In my senior year I was unable to make the varsity team. That accurately summed up the difference in our status. Yet I loved and admired him.

While still in high school he was already a successful entrepreneur, engaged in several business ventures. On most afternoons and evenings during the school year we and many of our classmates went to the Boys Club to play, mostly basketball. One evening Robbie approached me with a proposition. He said he had gotten "the concession" to do the janitorial work at the Boys Club; if I were willing to help he would split the fee with me. I didn't know what it meant to get a concession, but it sounded important, so I quickly accepted his offer. I had worked for Robbie before; he was a good source of spending money. At nine o'clock, when the Club closed, he handed me a broom and told me to sweep all of the floors, dust the desks and chairs, empty the wastebaskets, and clean the bathrooms. While I was working he went into the director's office, sat in the director's chair, put his feet up on the director's desk, and talked on the telephone with Janet Fraser, then his girlfriend, later his wife. When I cleaned the director's office I had to be quiet so as not to disturb him. At ten-thirty I reported to him that I had finished. He said good night to Janet, hung up the phone, and we went home.

At the end of the first week he paid me

$2.50. I thanked him and thought about how lucky I was to have such a smart and generous brother. A few weeks later he told me he had gotten "the concession" to do the janitorial work at a small office building next door to the Boys Club, and he offered me the same deal. I couldn't believe my luck. I already had two other jobs, delivering newspapers in the morning and washing cars at a used-car lot in the afternoon, so with this new job I would be earning over $10 a week — an incredible amount of money at the time. I had been at it long enough to be able to clean the Boys Club in an hour; the office building took another hour. So Robbie talked to Janet on the phone for two hours every night. I couldn't figure out how they could see each other at school every day and still find something to talk about for two hours each night. I suppose it beat cleaning the bathrooms.

This arrangement continued for several months. I then learned, by accident, that Robbie was being paid $15 a week for each concession. That meant he was paying me $5 a week while keeping $25. And I was doing all the work. That didn't seem right to me, so I screwed up my courage and confronted him. He calmly explained that it took a lot of knowledge and effort to get a concession; if he hadn't done that there would be no jobs for me and I would not be earning $5 a week. He then used a phrase I'll never forget: "I'm management and you're labor, and management always gets paid more." I was still troubled, but I couldn't think of any rejoinder, so I left and continued the arrangement. But I recall thinking, When I grow up I want to be management, like Robbie.

Robbie was more than a brother to me. Although close in age we had an adult-child relationship. He got his first real job at the age of six. By the time he was in high school, besides the janitorial services, he had developed and was operating a golf driving range. He also bought a cotton candy machine and promoted entertainment and sporting events in Maine. He hired me and Ron Stevens to run the cotton candy machine. He rented a pickup truck and carted the two of us and the machine to several of the fairs that blanket rural Maine in the summer. He would drop us off in the morning at a space he had rented at whatever fair was taking place that week. We spent the day making and selling cotton candy, lots of it. Each night he picked us up, took the cash proceeds of the day, and paid us each $2. Once, after a particularly busy and productive day, Ron asked for more than $2. Robbie patiently explained that he had to pay for the cotton candy machine, for the pickup truck, for the gas, for the booth at the fair. He concluded by saying, "Now that I think about it, I may have to cut you guys back to one dollar a day." It had the predictable effect. He then gave Ron his management-labor speech. After Robbie left I said to Ron, "You've got to admit, he's a really smart guy." Ron agreed. We left, each to go home to bed, elated to be $2 richer but exhausted from a long hot day at the cotton candy machine.

Among the many events Robbie promoted, two stand out in my memory. He brought Emmett Kelly, a nationally known circus clown, for a performance at the field house at Colby College. It was well attended, though not sold out. As always, Robbie griped about the expenses, especially the $5 he paid Ron and me for our assistance in organizing and running the event. In the spring, after the basketball season was over for the colleges and high schools, Robbie hired well-known college players to barnstorm across Maine, playing against local semiprofessional or pickup teams. (Johnny, the real basketball star of the family, had done that the preceding two years.) The most notable player Robbie got to play was Walter Dukes, then a star at Seton Hall University, later a professional in the National Basketball Association. Dukes, an African American, was seven feet two inches tall. He was scheduled to take the train from New York to Portland, where Robbie and I were to pick him up and drive him to Waterville for the first game. I was with Robbie when he telephoned Dukes the day before the event to confirm the schedule. Dukes was concerned that we would have trouble finding him when he got off the train in Portland, so Robbie told him to wear a red rose in his lapel. After Robbie hung up I told him that we'd have no trouble recognizing Dukes and that the red rose was unnecessary. "I know," he replied, "but he's never been to Maine and is probably thinking about a big crowded station like New York City. He wants reassurance, and we should give it to him." The next day, when the biggest man I had ever seen stepped off the train in Portland, he was wearing a bright red rose in the lapel of his blue suit. On the drive to Waterville I sat in the backseat and listened in awe as Robbie and Dukes swapped basketball stories as though they were old friends.

THE TRIP TO BRISTOL

By the time the sun crept up over the eastern horizon we were well on our way. By car it's only about fifty miles from Waterville to Bristol, much less as the crow flies. Since my parents didn't own a car then, we rarely traveled. When we did we hitchhiked, as Robbie and I were doing that day in the summer of 1944.

I had never been to the town of Bristol and I was geographically bewildered by the fact that to get there from Waterville we had to travel country roads through towns with names like East Vassalboro, South China, and North Waldoboro. I had once been to Vassalboro, but the others were a mystery to me; that added to the sense of adventure. There weren't many cars on the most narrow of the roads, so Robbie insisted on an early start to make sure we got there before dark. He said he didn't want to keep Mr. Moran waiting.

I stood by the side of the road in the damp darkness, with my right thumb stuck out. Robbie crouched nearby, a few feet off the road. He liked having me out there because I was smaller and more fragile looking than he; he thought I'd have a better chance of getting a ride. I didn't know where we were going, or why, but Robbie said it would be a good adventure. I was pleased, even honored, that he'd asked me to come with him. As it turned out, we made it well before dark, which pleased Robbie and Mr. Moran.

The farmhouse was small, old, and rundown. Some of the window screens were torn, the front door didn't fully close, and a lot of junk — an old washing machine, a broken lawn mower, a table with two broken legs — marked a sort of path from the house to the barn. Inside the barn was more junk, including what looked like the carriage part of a horseless horse and buggy.

The Morans were old and stooped, like their house. They were kind and obviously pleased to see Robbie. We were quickly ushered into their kitchen for dinner. It wasn't very tasty, but it was hot and we were very hungry, so eating didn't take long. Robbie took me out to the barn, and we climbed up into the back of the carriage.

Two tattered blankets had been spread out and we slept on them. I asked Robbie again what we were going to do in the morning; he again said only that it would be a good adventure. I asked him how he knew the Morans; he didn't answer. I couldn't tell if he was really sleeping or just pretending to. It didn't make any difference; I was very tired and sleepy, so I rolled over and quickly fell asleep.

The next morning, after a breakfast that was even quicker and more quiet than the previous evening's dinner, Robbie led me out the back door and across a wide field to a dirt trail that led into the woods. The trail was rough, poorly maintained, and just wide enough for a vehicle to scrape through, although in some spots shrubs and tall grass intruded to narrow it even more. It was a cloudy and cool morning, good for walking, but an intermittent drizzle turned the trail into a series of puddles separated by patches of mud.

Several attempts to get Robbie to tell me where we were going and why failed, so we lapsed into silence. I trusted him totally, so I accepted his repeated assertion that this would be a good adventure.

We kept a steady pace for two or three hours. Then, without any warning, we walked into a small clearing. There, in front of us, was the rusty broken-down hulk of what had been a tank.

An army tank.

A German Army tank!

My surprise and astonishment were total and obvious. World War II had been raging for years. My father followed the news closely, and we were well aware of the major battles and had been surprised by reports of German spies in Maine. As we circled the tank and I reached out to touch it, Robbie asked if I'd like to see the inside. We jumped on the track that was closest to the ground, climbed up to the turret, and descended. The outside had been rusting and broken, but the inside was worse, a filthy shambles. There was little room, little light, and virtually nothing had been left to see. But of course none of that mattered, because we were able to imagine what it looked like and how it felt in combat. We fought several imaginary battles before climbing out and heading back home.

My questions now came firing out like bullets from the tank's machine guns. "What's a German Army tank doing in the woods near a small town in Maine?"

"They moved it from Dow Air Force Base."

"That's in Bangor."

"Right."

"Well, what was a German Army tank doing at an American Air Force base in Bangor?"

"To confuse them."

"Who's 'them'?"

"The spies."

"The spies? What spies?"

"The German spies. They're all over."

"They are?"

"Of course. Don't you remember the two that got caught after they were dropped off by a submarine near Bar Harbor?"

"Oh yeah."

"Well, they got those two, but there's lots others."

As we walked on I scanned the woods around us for spies. Nervously I stepped up the pace. If we ran into any it would be better to do so on the highway. After a long silence I resumed the questioning. "Robbie, I still can't figure it out. Why would the spies be confused by an old rusted tank in the woods?"

"*You're* confused, aren't you?"

"Well, yes, but I'm not a spy. And besides, how would they ever know about it?"

"Word gets around."

"What does that mean?"

"We make sure it gets around."

"You mean we tell the spies about the tank?"

"We don't tell them. We just make sure they know."

"What's the difference?"

"You'll figure it out."

"When?"

"Soon enough."

After another long silence, he said, "You're just a kid, I know, but can't you see that if the German spies are trying to figure out what the tank is doing here, they won't have time to do what they came here to do?"

I thought about that for a few minutes. "Robbie, you're a genius."

He repeated himself. "You'll figure it out."

We never actually went to Bristol. All of this was a tale Robbie told me as we lay in our beds, in the bedroom we shared one hot, sleepless night in the summer of 1944, one of many of his tall tales. His vivid imagination and the way he told the story had an indelible effect on me. I will never know if there really was a German Army tank hidden in the Maine woods. Many years later, as a candidate in search of votes, I went to Bristol for the first time. As I was driving into town, and later on the way out, I carefully scanned each house we passed to see if I could find one that fit Robbie's description of the Moran farmhouse.

Although I am close with all my brothers and my sister, it was Robbie with whom I grew up and spent the most time together. From my earliest conscious moment until his death, I loved him intensely. After graduating from college and serving in the U.S. Marine Corps, he entered the banking business, first as an examiner for the Federal Deposit Insurance Corporation, then as the president of small banks in Maine and Massachusetts. He retired at sixty, having been diagnosed with leukemia. Five years later, after a long and very difficult day at the peace talks in Northern Ireland, I got to bed after midnight, physically and emotionally exhausted. As I turned off the light, I hoped for a fresh start and a better day tomorrow.

The telephone rang. Slowly, drowsily, I picked it up.

"Hello."

"George, this is Janet."

"Janet! What's the matter?"

"Robbie's in very bad shape."

She put him on the phone and we spoke briefly. His voice was faint and weak. "George, I love you." "I love you, Robbie." We said a few more words. I fought back the tears until we hung up. Then I lay back down and cried.

Heather had been with me in Belfast until security officials urged her to leave because of the potential of violence. So she spent much of that summer in London, and I joined her there on weekends. I flew to London, the next morning. There, we spent a long and sad weekend. It was hard to focus, hard to talk, hard to do anything but wait with dread for the phone to ring. The call came, finally, on Saturday. He died that morning.

I've had the burden of delivering many eulogies; Robbie's was the only one I could not finish. After a slow and halting start I faltered and, unable to continue, ended by whispering, "Goodbye, Robbie. I love you."

He meant so much to all of us and he remains alive in our hearts and minds. When we get together as a family, there always are lots of Robbie stories. As he did in his life, he makes us smile and laugh today. It's as though he just left the room for a moment to go to the kitchen to get a glass of water.

■ ■ ■ ■

MAINE

■ ■ ■ ■

MAINE

They came from deep in Asia fifteen thousand years ago, in one of the great migrations in human history, across the bridge of land that has since disappeared into the Bering Sea, between Siberia and Alaska. They settled the continents now known as North America and South America, and they became Incas and Aztecs, Navajo and Sioux, Seminole and, in the Northeast, Algonquin.

Many tribes made up the Algonquin family. Those who settled in what is now Maine came to be known as Abenaki. The word is an English-language version of *Wabanaki,* which means "living at the sunrise." To the early Indians, this area was Dawnland, the place where the sun first rises.

We do not know how many there were or precisely how long they lived here. As happened throughout the Americas, they were displaced by whites. But they left their names to mark forever their presence. Madawaska is a town at the northern tip of Maine. At the southern border is the Piscataqua River. The highest point of land is Mount Katahdin. The three largest rivers are the Penobscot, the Kennebec, and the Androscoggin. The largest county in land area is Aroostook. Today only about three thousand Indians remain, mostly Penobscot and Passamaquoddy on reservations in central and eastern Maine and a few Maliseet and Micmac in the north.

For the Indians moving east across the continent, the Atlantic coast was as far as they could go. For the white men who came west across the ocean, it was the first place they came to. Several of the discoverers, some of them well-known, touched at or near Maine: Cabot in 1497, Verrazzano in 1524, John Walker in 1580. The earliest efforts at settlement failed: the French in 1604 at the mouth of the Saint Croix River in eastern Maine, the British in 1608 near the mouth of the Kennebec River in southern Maine. Over the next century more white settlements were established along the coast and up the rivers. Most of these failed too, victims of the continuing conflict between the British and the French. The Abenaki for the most part sided with the French, who used them to conduct raids on British settlers. This slowed the white settlement of Maine, even reversing it in some areas. But in the early eighteenth century, when the British and French had a quarter-century interlude of peace, the settling renewed and then accelerated.

Under the Treaty of Utrecht, signed in 1713, the British gained undisputed control of what was then known as Acadia, now the Canadian province of Nova Scotia. This eventually led to the departure of the French settlers, a noteworthy event in Maine history, and ultimately to the settlement of the northernmost part of Maine by French immigrants from Acadia. That area is now known simply as "The Valley," a shorthand description of the Saint John River Valley. The Saint John forms the boundary between the United States and Canada along much of northern Maine. In its fertile valley on both sides of the river the French settlers endured and prospered. Today it is a vibrant, friendly, distinct part of Maine where French is still commonly spoken.

White settlement continued to increase in Maine, even though fighting between the British and French was renewed. The final victory over the French in the Battle of

Quebec in 1759 consolidated British control over eastern North America. The distraction of a common foe having been removed, many British settlers began to question the motherland's economic policies, which seemed unfair to the colonies. Maine, by then a district of Massachusetts, had been largely settled from the coast inward. Its economy was based on its ports and the sea; thus hostility was intense to British policies that adversely affected coastal trade. When the colonists in Massachusetts revolted, they had much support in Maine.

Although statehood for Maine had been discussed earlier, it didn't gather momentum until after the War of 1812. Just as people in Massachusetts had protested British economic policies, people in Maine began to protest Massachusetts's economic policies. Maine tax dollars were being allocated disproportionately for the benefit of Massachusetts proper. The only way for the residents of Maine to take care of themselves was to govern themselves. In 1819 Maine voters in referendum approved separation from Massachusetts, and on March 3, 1820, Maine became a state. But it almost didn't happen.

The 1819 referendum provided that Maine would become a state if Congress approved within nine months, or by March 4, 1820. That was thought to be a mere formality that would be accomplished well within the required time. But in Congress Maine's application for statehood was considered along with Missouri's, and it became entangled in legislative efforts to end slavery there. For the first time decisions on statehood applications were linked to the question of slavery. From then until the Civil War, that became the standard practice. Finally, on the day before Maine's deadline, the Missouri Compromise was reached and the two states were admitted, Missouri as a slavery state, Maine as a nonslavery state. Although no one could foresee it at the time, that later became a transforming issue in Maine, shaping the state's politics for a century.

There were no slaves in Maine and few free blacks, but the linking of Maine's statehood with Missouri's, and therefore with the issue of slavery, appears to have generated interest in the subject. Over the first thirty years of statehood, support grew gradually in Maine for abolition. It rose sharply after the publication in 1851 of *Uncle Tom's Cabin,* written by Harriet Beecher Stowe at her home in Brunswick, Maine. By the time the Civil War began,

Maine was a fervent anti-slavery state.

The issue split the Democratic Party and led to the swift rise and long dominance of the Republican Party. Democrats had dominated the state's politics from statehood to the Civil War, but in the ninety-four years from 1860 to 1954 no Democrat was elected to the U.S. Senate, only one was popularly elected governor (Louis Brann in 1936), and Democrats controlled both houses of the state legislature only once (in 1912–13). Maine became known as a rock-ribbed Republican state. At the general election in September during the post–Civil War period, Maine citizens always voted Republican for president, as did most of the rest of the country. This led to the saying "As Maine goes, so goes the nation." In 1936, after Franklin Roosevelt carried forty-six of the forty-eight states in his landslide victory, his close friend Jim Farley laughingly changed the saying to "As Maine goes, so goes Vermont."

Edmund Muskie broke the Republican dominance in Maine. He was elected governor in 1954, reelected in 1956, and then was elected to the U.S. Senate and reelected four times. Today the state is about evenly balanced and politically competitive: about a third of the voters are registered as

Democrats, about a third are Republican, and a third are unenrolled Independents. Currently one U.S. senator is a Republican, and the other is an Independent, and one member of the House of Representatives is a Democrat, the other a Republican.

In Maine, as in much of the country, the years between the Civil War and World War I can be summed up in two words: industrialization and immigration. The two were closely related. The textile industry — cotton and woolen mills — thrived wherever there was an ample supply of water and of labor; Maine had the water, and after the mills came, so did the labor. Dozens of textile mills sprang up on Maine's rivers, and thousands of immigrants came to work in them: Irish, Italian, German, Swedish, Russian. But by far the largest number came from Canada, almost all of them French Canadians from Quebec. They settled in the industrial cities where the textile mills were: Lewiston, Biddeford, Sanford, Waterville. Some of them went to smaller, newer cities, like Millinocket, Rumford, and Westbrook, where the paper mills were also going up.

Once it became feasible to industrially mass-produce paper out of wood, it was inevitable that Maine would become a center of paper-making. With over 90 percent of its land area forested, with large, fast-flowing rivers to generate electricity to power the mills and move the logs, and with a poor, rural economy desperately in need of steady jobs, Maine must have looked like heaven on earth to the makers of paper.

WATERVILLE

As the Kennebec River flows south to the Atlantic Ocean it drops sharply at several places. These natural falls, which create turbulence in the water, apparently were responsible for the river's name. It was written "Quinebequi" by Samuel de Champlain, the French colonizer of North America who explored and charted much of the Maine coast. This was the French spelling of an Indian word that meant *monsters,* or *dragons,* which were presumed to inhabit the river and cause the rough waters at the falls. One of the falls, located between the modern communities of Waterville and Winslow, came to be known as Ticonic Falls, after the Indian settlement that once existed there.

In 1754 a British military officer, John Winslow, established the first white settlement in the area. He built a fort at the juncture of the Sebasticook and Kennebec rivers and gave it a famous English name: Fort Halifax. The fort provided some measure of protection against Indian raids. Gradually more and more white settlers sank their roots into the fertile valleys on both sides of the Kennebec. In 1771 the town of Winslow was incorporated. The area on the west side of the river continued to be known as Ticonic until 1802, when it was separately incorporated as the town of Waterville. Until well into the nineteenth century Waterville was inhabited almost exclusively by Protestant Americans of English heritage. The first French immigrant came in 1827. Those who followed congregated at the southern end of the town, an area called "The Plains." The number of French immigrants increased sharply just before the turn of the century. By 1900, according to one account, fully 45 percent of the city's population was of French heritage. They, and smaller contingents of immigrants from other countries, transformed Waterville into a microcosm of the melting pot that America had become. One of those other groups, much smaller, numbering only a few hundred, huddled on the banks of the Kennebec River. They were known as the Syrians.

THE LEBANESE

Sometime in the late 1880s, probably in
1888, a young man named Abraham Joseph
left the village of Choueir in Lebanon and
came to the United States. He made his way
to Bangor, Maine, where he earned a living
as a peddler, selling clothing door to door.
He peddled his way south to Waterville,
where he stayed and opened a store, apparently the first Lebanese immigrant to settle
there. Soon relatives and others from his
native village, and nearby villages, followed.
By the time the first restrictive immigration
laws were enacted in the 1920s, there were
about three hundred Lebanese immigrants
and members of their families in Waterville.
They settled there because they could find
work.

Around the turn of the century Waterville
was the fastest-growing city in Maine, growing from a rural town to a small industrial
center. In 1876 the Lockwood-Duchess

cotton mill opened; in 1900 the Riverview (later Wyandotte) Worsted woolen mill; in 1892 the Hollingsworth and Whitney paper mill in Winslow. Waterville became a rail center as well, with the expansion of Maine Central Railroad's maintenance and repair shop. Immigrants from Lebanon streamed into the factories. Although the work in the textile mills was hard, hot, noisy, and low-paying, to most of the immigrants it provided a level of income previously unimaginable and, above all else, the chance to become an American. In addition to the two textile mills in Waterville, there were several others (as many as a dozen at the industry's peak) in the Central Maine area. It was common practice for workers to move from one mill to another as work at one slowed down and work at another picked up. My mother worked at most of the mills at one time or another. Today there are no textile mills in the area.

The three hundred immigrants from the Middle East and their families living in Waterville in the 1920s were known as Syrians. They did not describe themselves as Lebanese, nor did anyone else, until later, when the independent nation of Lebanon was created. Over time, as a Lebanese identity became established in the Middle

East, the name began to be used more frequently in this country and the name *Syrian* fell into disuse.

SEEING MAINE

In 1938, just before we moved from Head of Falls to Front Street, a major event occurred in our lives: my father bought a car. Although it was an old 1929 Chevrolet, for us it was an unbelievable luxury. He kept the car for just a few years, until gas rationing began during World War II, and then he had to sell it. Many years then passed before he bought another car. But for the few years he owned the old Chevy, a window opened for us. For the first time I traveled outside of Waterville.

I do not recall my parents ever taking a trip while I was growing up, what I would now call a vacation. They had time off, of course, but that was usually spent working on or around the house. Once in a while during the summer, however, in the few years that he owned the old Chevy, my father took us to visit other places in Maine. These were always day trips, never overnight, and my mother prepared and brought along all the food we would need.

I vividly recall three places my parents took me to see: Moosehead Lake, Bar Harbor, and the Maine coast in the Belfast area. Moosehead Lake is Maine's largest inland lake. It was then about a three-hour drive north from Waterville. What I remember about that trip is that I was car sick all the way, so it seemed to me to take about three days. From that day until very much later in life, I was unable to read in a moving automobile without getting dizzy, and I always thought of the trip to Moosehead Lake. Finally, after entering the Senate, out of necessity I forced myself to read in the car, at least briefly, but I still can't do so for more than a few minutes at a time.

The other two trips also made lasting impressions on me, but they were positive. Bar Harbor is located on Mount Desert Island, now about a two-hour drive from Waterville. My father wanted to show it to us, along with the adjacent Acadia National Park. It was my first view of the Island, which since has become an important part of my life.

Belfast is a small city on the Maine coast, about an hour's drive from Waterville. My father liked to visit it because there was an outdoor pool nearby where we kids could swim, and just to the south, along Route 1, was Lincolnville Beach, a local public beach right on the ocean (not a common thing on that part of the Maine coast, north of Portland). Just to the north is the small town of Stockton Springs. There, on the west bank of the mouth of the Penobscot River, is a place called Fort Point, where a lighthouse stands. As lighthouses go, it is not an especially impressive structure, being short and relatively squat. But when my father took me there it was the first lighthouse I'd ever seen. It made a powerful impression.

The first lighthouse in the United States was built in Boston Harbor in 1716. In all over 1,200 have been built in this country, along the Atlantic and Pacific Oceans, the Great Lakes, and the Gulf of Mexico. But Maine is the Lighthouse State — an unofficial title, self-proclaimed, but deserved nonetheless. More than sixty lighthouses guard our rugged coast, from Kittery to Calais. The people of Maine, myself included, have a powerful emotional attachment to lighthouses. We're not alone. For many people these structures serve chiefly as romantic reminders of a time past, a time before radar, sonar, and on-ship electronics

94

combined to diminish the need for sailors to use lighthouses to navigate safely.

But there was a time when lighthouses served an important role, when the building and operating of lighthouses as aids for rendering safe and easy navigation of any bay, inlet, harbor, or port in the United States was one of the principal activities of the federal government. One of the very first undertakings of the first Congress, which organized on April 6, 1789, was to officially launch America's lighthouse system. In July of that year Representative Elbridge Gerry of Massachusetts introduced legislation that called for the establishment and support of navigational aids. It was passed by the House on July 20, amended by the Senate on July 31, and signed into law by President Washington on August 7, 1789. The act created a federal role in the support, maintenance, and repair of all lighthouses, beacons, bridges, and public piers necessary for safe navigation; it also commissioned the first federal lighthouse. It was our nation's first public works law.

For most people the term *public works project* means highways, bridges, dams, and public buildings, but two hundred years ago they included — prominently — lighthouses. As the first secretary of the

Treasury, Alexander Hamilton was responsible for the care and superintendence of the lights. He took this responsibility seriously. Many orders and contracts concerning the lighthouse service were personally approved by Hamilton, George Washington and Thomas Jefferson.

The value of lighthouses to the development of maritime shipping and transportation in our country can never be measured. Countless ships have made safe passage off our shores and on our lakes because of the beams of light from the towers standing at land's end. The architectural beauty of these structures cannot be fully appreciated without recognition of the skill of the engineers and workers who built them in what were often hazardous places and against almost insurmountable odds. Nor do most of us comprehend and appreciate the sacrifices made by the lighthouse keepers and their families. They devoted — and in some cases jeopardized — their lives for the safety of others. Lighthouse duty was difficult: lonely, boring for long periods of time, and dangerous in times of crisis. For two centuries these impressive structures and the men and women who served at them have come to symbolize stoicism, heroism, duty, and faithfulness —

characteristics that Americans admire in themselves and in others.

In 1989 the Coast Guard completed the automation of lighthouses. One of the last to be automated was the Portland Head Light. Located in Cape Elizabeth, just south of Portland, it is one of the most beautiful and most photographed lighthouses in the country. Protecting mariners against the rock-bound coast of Maine, it is a superb example of the grace and beauty of lighthouses.

Unfortunately that beauty is endangered. As automation has progressed, more and more lighthouses have been left without keepers, easy targets for vandalism and damage caused by erosion and storms. That is why in 1988 I introduced legislation to establish a Bicentennial Lighthouse Fund. Timed for the two-hundredth anniversary of the federal government's establishment of a lighthouse construction and maintenance program, it provided limited federal funds that, when joined with state and privately donated funds, have been used to repair and preserve lighthouses throughout the nation. Many lighthouses were already listed in the National Register of Historic Places; the legislation authorized a survey of others, which resulted in several more being included in the Register. It was a modest bill, one of the least noted pieces of legislation I authored while serving in the Senate, but it was one that brought me great pleasure and is a warm memory.

When I was notified that the president had signed the bill into law, my mind returned to the summer day many years ago, when I stood with my father before the Fort Point Lighthouse. As he did with other subjects, he had read up on this one, and he described to me what lighthouses were, what they did, how the lights worked, and the history of this particular light. He loved knowledge for its own sake, and he loved sharing it with us for our sake. As I reflected about that day, I thought my father would have approved of my effort to preserve the lighthouses.

BOWDOIN

One of the luckiest days in my life was the day I first walked onto the campus of Bowdoin College. My parents knew the hard life of those who lacked learning, so their central goal in life was the education of their children. But in my senior year in high school, because of my father's unemployment, there was little talk of my going to college.

One day that spring my father told me that he had received a call from the man who ran the division at the utility where my father had previously worked. His name was Hervey Fogg; he had asked that I go to see him. Neither my father nor I knew what it was about, but I went because my father felt it would not be polite to decline. Although I did not know Mr. Fogg, it soon became clear that all he wanted was to help me. He told me that he had gone to Bowdoin College and he encouraged me to consider it. He assured me that it wasn't too late to be admitted that year. In fact, he said, he had already set up an appointment for me with the director of admissions.

A week later I set off for Brunswick. I was sixteen years old, had traveled little outside of Waterville, had never been on a train or a plane. My mother made several sandwiches, which I carried with me. My parents didn't own a car then, so I got up very early in the morning and walked to the outskirts of Waterville to hitchhike to Brunswick. Within minutes I got a ride, and the driver took me right to the campus. Since I was several hours early for my appointment, I walked back and forth across the grounds, memorizing the name and location of every building. Then I went to the Office of Admissions to meet the director, Bill Shaw. Although I was very nervous and felt out of place, he was kind and thoughtful. When I told him that my parents couldn't afford to pay my tuition, he was reassuring. "Don't worry," he said. "If you're willing to work, we'll figure something out." He ultimately admitted me and then helped me with several part-time jobs that enabled me to get through college.

Many others also helped me. One of them was Mal Morrell, the director of athletics.

Although I was not a very good basketball player, Mal treated me as though I were an All-American. I think he initially confused me with my brother Robbie, who really was an all-star. I'm sure Mal figured it out after he watched me play a few games. Still he encouraged me and he arranged a succession of jobs for me, one of which was driving a truck for the Morrell family business, still operating in Brunswick.

I had just gotten my driver's license, had only driven a car a few times, and had never driven a truck. On my very first morning of work, a foreman asked me if I could drive. When I said I could, he pointed to a large flatbed truck parked nearby and said, "Take that truck up to the cement plant in Thomaston, pick up a load of cement, and bring it back here." I looked at the truck, gulped, walked over to it, and climbed up into the cab. I had never been in a truck. I looked at the dashboard, the gear shift, and tried quickly to figure out how to operate it. It seemed like seconds to me, but the pause must have been longer because the foreman yelled, "Are you okay?" "Oh, yes," I assured him, as my heart raced and my hands got sweaty, "no problem." It took me quite a while to back the truck out of the yard and onto the street. It was a terrifying experience to drive that huge flatbed truck fifty miles up the Maine coast on U.S. Route 1, a very busy highway, to Thomaston. There the truck was loaded up with dozens of ninety-pound bags of cement, and I then drove it safely back down to Brunswick. One of my proudest accomplishments at Bowdoin was that I got through four years without wrecking any of Morrell's vehicles or equipment.

I had many other jobs that kept me busy and enabled me to earn enough money to get through. In my sophomore and junior years I was the steward of the Sigma Nu fraternity house, managing all of its operations; my compensation was free meals for those two years. In my senior year I moved from the fraternity house to a dormitory, where I served as a proctor; my compensation was a free room for that year. Most important, for three years I had the concession for the basketball program. At home games every person entering the gym was handed a free program. I sold advertising space in the program to local businesses and arranged for the printing and distribution of the programs. I did well in sales and in controlling costs, so the profit margin was high; that covered most of my tuition payments.

I also worked every summer and was able to save enough to cover the rest of my tuition. Most difficult was the summer of 1953, between my junior and senior years, when I worked two full-time jobs. From eleven in the evening until seven in the morning I worked as a night watchman at the paper mill located just across the river from our home. Then, from seven-thirty in the morning until three-thirty in the afternoon, I worked on construction on what was then the new Colby College campus. Colby was originally located near downtown Waterville, just a few hundred yards from our home on Front Street. In the late 1940s and early 1950s the college moved to its present location on Mayflower Hill, on the outskirts of town. My primary job that summer was to build a large terraced lawn in front of Foss Hall, a women's dormitory. I still feel a sense of pride in "my lawn" every time I drive past it on my way across the Colby campus. It was hard, hot, heavy work. I had been working from an early age, but this was much more difficult than anything I'd ever experienced. There was no baseball, no book reading that summer. I struggled to fall asleep in the late afternoons and early evenings, and then struggled to stay awake on the job at night.

If it were possible to love and admire my mother even more than I did, it happened that summer. I was a young, healthy boy, but I was exhausted after just two months working the night shift. She did it for her entire adult life, while raising five children! It was with relief, and an overwhelming desire to sleep at night, that I returned to Bowdoin that September.

Although I was unaware of it at the time, by then Bowdoin already had a long and distinguished history. Created by an act of the Massachusetts Legislature (then known as the General Court), it was the result of years of effort by the residents of the District of Maine to establish their own institution of higher learning. By proposing to name the college after the former governor of Massachusetts, James Bowdoin, the wily Mainers hoped to influence both the General Court and the Bowdoin family. They succeeded: the General Court prepared and Governor Samuel Adams signed the bill establishing the college on June 24, 1794. Then the family came through. The former governor's son, of the same name, contributed land and cash and much more. It is in his memory that "James Bowdoin Day" is recognized each year.

The college quickly developed a reputation for excellence, in part through the achievements of its graduates. Henry Wadsworth Longfellow and Nathaniel Hawthorne both graduated in 1825 and went on to become authors of enduring fame. Franklin Pierce graduated the year before them and later became president of the United States. William Pitt Fessenden graduated in 1823 and became the first of several Bowdoin alumni to serve in the U.S. Senate. Joshua Chamberlain, Class of 1852, was one of the heroes of the Civil War and then served as governor of Maine. Robert Peary, Class of 1877, discovered the North Pole. Without going further for fear of boring the reader and slighting family and admirers of others not mentioned, it is sufficient to say that by the fall of 1950 Bowdoin was a well-established, well-regarded liberal arts college with about eight hundred male students. (The college now has about twice as many students and is coeducational.) For most of the next four years it would be my second home.

I was uneasy at first, homesick for my family, for my friends in Waterville, and especially for my mother's cooking. It was hard getting used to college food; the bread was never quite as fresh as my mother's, the rest of the food not quite as tasty. And eating with a lot of strangers was, well, strange. I also was afraid that I wouldn't fit in and that I would fail scholastically.

I was assigned a corner room in a dormitory named Hyde Hall. Not until later did I become aware of the great man after whom the building was named. William DeWitt Hyde served as president of Bowdoin from 1885 until 1917. Athletic, energetic, intelligent, he left an indelible mark on the college and the thousands of young men who learned there during his tenure. It is out of date and it includes passages that today would be regarded as unacceptably sexist and religiously rigid, but I still enjoy reading President Hyde's inspiring description of what the college had to offer:

To be at home in all lands and all ages; to count Nature a familiar acquaintance, and Art an intimate friend; to gain a standard for the appreciation of other men's work and the criticism of one's own; to carry the keys of the world's library in one's pocket and feel its resources behind one in whatever task he undertakes; to make hosts of friends among the men of one's own age who are to be leaders in all walks of life; to lose oneself in generous enthusiasms and cooperate with others for common ends; to learn manners from students who are gentlemen; and form character under professors who are Christians — this is the offer of the college for the best four years of one's life.

When I entered Bowdoin in September 1950, I had never heard of William DeWitt Hyde and the high sentiments of his "offer of the college" were way over my head. But as I look back with the perspective of time, I recognize that some — not all, by any means, as I shall shortly point out — of his words were relevant to my years at Bowdoin. They may not have been the best years of my life, but once I got over my early nervousness, the last three years there were the most fun.

Since graduating from Bowdoin in 1954 I have returned often to the campus. Each time I pass Hyde Hall I don't think of President Hyde. I think of Dan Gulezian. We shared a room there in our freshman year. Dan represented a lot of firsts for me: first roommate, first person from Massachusetts I got to know well, first person of Armenian extraction I'd ever met, first young person I'd known with a mustache. A freshman in college with a mustache! That alone made him seem mature and sophisticated. Dan was tall and easygoing and we got along well. But because we had pledged to different fraternities, our lives quickly diverged as more and more of our activities centered on fraternity life.

I became a member of Sigma Nu fraternity, described as the "jock house," a fraternity favored by athletes. To be considered enough of an athlete to be asked to join the jock house, even to try out for and play on the college basketball team — that was heady stuff for me. My brothers later deflated me by pointing out that the fact that I made the team at Bowdoin was more proof of the lack of emphasis on athletics there than of any ability on my part.

President Hyde's "offer of the college" is, as I have noted, somewhat out of date. In no respect was this more so than in his of-fer "to learn manners from students who are gentlemen." Gentlemen at Bowdoin in the early 1950s were few, and rather than learning manners, I learned the opposite, what I have come to call *unmanners.* I had been around athletes and locker rooms, had listened to my brothers and their friends, so swearing and gross behavior weren't new to me. But nothing I had seen or heard prepared me for the language or behavior of fraternity life at Bowdoin. There unmanners were raised to a high (or, depending on your perspective, low) level. In addition to the natural tendency of young people to exercise their liberty from family with exaggerated words and acts, the situation at Bowdoin was heightened by the presence of many veterans of the later years of World War II. Many of the men who graduated in the early 1950s had had their lives interrupted by military service. They were several years older than we freshmen, and their military service gave them a tougher, more hardened attitude. And a new language! I heard and learned more profanity in my first sixteen weeks at Bowdoin than I had heard in the previous sixteen years of my life. By the time I got into the army myself, five years later, I already knew almost every swear word in existence.

While much of fraternity life was good for me, some aspects were not. Although I didn't move into the fraternity house until my sophomore year, early in my freshman year I fell into the poor study habits of fraternity life. I lacked discipline and drive and was overwhelmed by my newly acquired independence. As a result I spent too much time fooling around, hanging around, and playing around — going to movies, joining in "bull sessions," playing sports of all kinds. I had a great time and I made many friends, but too little time was spent studying. It wasn't until I attended law school years later that I developed reasonable discipline in studying.

It was at Bowdoin that I finally came to terms with my lack of athletic ability. This revelation came back to me in a rush a half century later in South Florida. I sat behind a desk stacked high with copies of a book I'd written, signing them one at a time for the people in line; they had just listened to me speak about my experience in Northern Ireland and were now getting my signature on their copy of my book on that subject. An elderly couple were next in line. The man was short, stocky, and slightly stooped. As he shook my hand he said, "We've met before."

"Where?" I asked.

"Do you remember the name Bill Pappas?"

"Billy Pappas! Of course, University of New Hampshire. You were a great athlete, quarterback on the football team, high-scoring guard on the basketball team."

"We played against each other."

"I remember it as though it was yesterday. At the Bowdoin gymnasium. Great game.

You beat us by two points."

We laughed, he introduced me to his wife, and we had our picture taken. As they walked away, my mind drifted back many decades to a cold, wintry night on the Bowdoin campus. The New Hampshire Wildcats, led by their high-scoring guard, Billy Pappas, were heavy favorites to defeat a struggling Bowdoin team. It was my junior year. Although I was a starting guard, I had not yet lived up to expectations, mine or the coach's. But that night it all came together for me. Although he was clearly a much better player, I gave Pappas a battle.

I scored eighteen points, hitting on seven of eight shots from the field and four for four from the foul line. The game was close all the way and the lead changed several times. With just a few minutes to play and the score tied I committed a foul. I wasn't concerned because the game was nearly over and I had another foul to give before reaching the limit. To my surprise, the coach sent a substitute in for me. I watched the last few minutes from the bench, glum and bewildered.

I hardly slept that night, depressed by another close loss, and wondering why I was pulled in the last few minutes when I had played a near-perfect game, offensively and defensively, by far the best of my college career. The next day, unable to control myself, I did what for me would previously have been unimaginable: I went to see the coach. Edmund Coombs, known to all as Beezer, was one of the nicest men I've ever met. Friendly, honest, with impeccable integrity, every player loved him, even though he was not a great motivator. He didn't shout or threaten; he didn't give emotional pep talks. He treated us fairly and firmly, with a respect that we returned. Politely I asked why he had taken me out of the game in the last few minutes.

He was surprised. "I didn't take you out. You fouled out."

I was stunned. "What?"

"You fouled out."

"No, coach, I'm sorry, I had one more to give."

Now he was really surprised, but he remained calm, as I did.

"I don't think so, George, but here, I'll look and see."

He fished through a pile of papers on the desk in his tiny office and pulled out a scorecard. As he read it his face reddened. I knew what he was going to say as he put the scorecard down on the desk and looked up at me with the saddest eyes I've ever seen. "You're right, I thought you'd fouled out. I was wrong. I'm sorry," he said. "I'm really very sorry."

"Thanks, coach," I replied and got up to leave. I wanted to get out of the room before I said something I would later regret, so my back was to him when he again apologized.

I took a long walk around the campus. A man I looked up to and admired had made a mistake, a simple mistake; it was nothing more than that, I told myself over and over again. But, try as I might, I couldn't convince myself. I knew that my performance that night was an aberration, not the norm. Even then, on the best basketball night of my life, it had gone wrong. We had lost again, a very painful loss. I don't know exactly how or why, but that one good performance enabled me to step away from my obsession with basketball and from my inferiority complex. It's a game, I told myself, just a game. I've got to get out of my brothers' shadows; I've got to stop living my life on their terms. From now on basketball would not be my life; it would be just a small and declining part of it.

While attending Bowdoin I enrolled in the Reserve Officers Training Corps (ROTC), primarily because we were paid to participate and I needed the money. Early

113

in 1954, during my last year at Bowdoin, the ROTC members were notified that the army had a surplus of officers for the Transportation Corps, for which we had trained. We were asked to volunteer for another assignment. Many considered the Intelligence Service as an attractive alternative, but it had one huge drawback: instead of entering the army at an early definite time, those who chose the Intelligence Service were subject to an indefinite delay and had to commit to entering on two weeks' notice. That would make it impossible to get a permanent job, and there was no way of knowing how long the delay would be. As a result most declined.

I had been considering going to graduate school to get a master's degree (and possibly a doctorate) in European history, my major course of study at Bowdoin. I developed a lifelong love of reading history and greatly admired my professor, Dr. Ernst Helmreich, with whom I developed a close relationship. I imagined myself someday teaching at a small college like Bowdoin. But that was a vague dream, not a concrete plan. I didn't have a job lined up because I had assumed I'd be entering the army immediately after graduation. But Intelligence sounded more interesting than Transportation. So I volunteered.

The consequence became clear in June. After graduation I returned to my parents' home in Waterville with no job and nothing to do but wait to be called into the army. It could be a week, a month, or a year. To earn some money I looked for a temporary job. The only one I could find was on the grounds crew at Colby. For six months, until the army summoned me on December 26, I painted doors and window panes, mowed large lawns, dug ditches, and was an all-around handyman. I didn't especially enjoy the work, but I did enjoy going to and from work every day with my father, the janitor. He too loved it. Whenever anyone came within range, he would point to me working nearby and say, "You see that boy mowing the lawn over there? He just graduated from Bowdoin. Colby has reached such a level of excellence that to get a job on our grounds crew you need a Bowdoin degree!" He then laughed long and loud as the bewildered passersby wondered what was so funny. I loved hearing him laugh, even though it was at my expense.

Although I left Bowdoin in the spring of 1954, it has never left me. I am profoundly grateful to have had the chance to attend a college that took me in, nurtured me, taught me, and helped me get through the fog of uncertainty and insecurity that shrouded me for years. I established friendships there that would last for decades. I came to terms with the limits of my athletic ability. I looked forward to serving in the army with a degree of confidence that was unthinkable four years earlier.

A Brief Interlude

The months from June to December 1954
were long and slow. I turned twenty-one
that summer and was anxious to get into
the "real world," but I had to wait until the
army called me up. There was one small
benefit: for the first time in my life I had a
room to myself. But although I really
enjoyed the luxury, I missed Robbie. After
his graduation from the University of Rhode
Island he had entered the Marine Corps
and was now stationed at Camp Lejeune in
Jacksonville, North Carolina. I hadn't
missed him much while I was at Bowdoin
because I had lots to do and many friends;
indeed privacy was very hard to come by in
a college fraternity house. But now our
home in Waterville seemed empty, especially
after Barbara returned to the University of
Maine in September to resume her studies.

So I was pleasantly surprised to receive a
telephone call from Robbie in late

September. He and Janet had gotten married. While he was at Camp Lejeune, she was living in Waterville, teaching school. He had just received orders assigning him to a tour of duty on board a navy ship in the Mediterranean Sea. He asked me to come to Camp Lejeune to pick up his car and drive it to Maine so Janet could use it while he was overseas. I was excited about the possibility of a trip and asked him how I would get to North Carolina.

"The same way you've gone anywhere." It took me a few seconds to grasp his answer.

"You mean you want me to hitchhike to North Carolina?"

"Why not?"

"Because I've never hitchhiked anywhere but around Maine, and North Carolina's a long way from Maine." I knew exactly how far because the Bowdoin ROTC members had taken a bus to Fort Eustis, near Williamsburg, Virginia, for a two-week training session one summer.

"You're not scared, are you?"

"No, of course not," I insisted. But I was.

"I really need your help, and besides, this is mostly for Janet."

"Well, okay," I said, nervous and unenthusiastic.

The more I thought about it, the more

nervous I got. But I couldn't figure a way out, so a few days later I rose with the sun and walked across town to the same spot I'd started from four years earlier when I hitchhiked to Bowdoin for the first time. My mother had packed a bag for me with enough food for several days.

I was lucky again. Within a few minutes a nice elderly man stopped to pick me up. He asked me where I was going. When I answered, "North Carolina," he was surprised and in a loud voice repeated it. "North Carolina! You've got a long way to go, young man. I'll give you a good start and get you to Boston."

My luck continued for about a day. Most rides were short, a few quite long, but I waited no more than two hours between rides, and, as I made my way south, I developed a rhythm. I ate and went to the bathroom between rides and, as much as possible, slept during the rides. Every driver who picked me up was kind and generous and, after hearing my story, patiently let me sleep until we parted company. But my hitchhiking honeymoon came to an end in Petersburg, Virginia. The driver who dropped me there was an army sergeant returning to his home base just outside of Petersburg. He had warned me of what to expect, so when I got out of the car I was not surprised to see dozens of men in uniform, on both sides of the highway, hitchhiking. I walked south along the highway to find an empty spot. On and on I trudged, lugging my bag, but I found more and more soldiers. Finally, after walking what seemed like a few miles, I was on an open stretch of highway. I was exhausted and hungry and, although I didn't want to admit it, even to myself, I was worried. I walked into the woods a few feet from the highway, found some shade, and sat down. I ate one of my mother's sandwiches and rested for a while as I thought about my plight. I assumed that no one driving south who might be inclined to pick up a hitch-hiker would bypass the many soldiers on the road before they got to me. Even worse, as the soldiers now on the highway were picked up they would likely be replaced by others, so I might never get a ride. Fortunately I was wrong about that.

Eight very long hours later a young couple from Rocky Mount, North Carolina, picked me up and took me to their hometown. Although I had only a few dollars I desperately wanted to sleep in a bed, go to a real bathroom, and take a shower. When I explained my plight to them, they took me to an old hotel adjacent to the railroad station in Rocky Mount. There I was able to rent a room for just a few dollars. I immediately called Robbie.

"I'm really sorry," I began, "but I'm not able to get all the way to Jacksonville." I explained what had happened and where I was and braced myself for his reaction. He could not have been nicer. He said he understood, he was very grateful to me for making such an effort, and he would drive to Rocky Mount to pick me up the next morning. I realized then that he loved me as much as I loved him. I had two sandwiches left. I ate one and saved the other for the morning. There was no shower in the room, so I took a hot bath, went to bed, and had a long and deep sleep.

The next morning I sat in a rocking chair in the lobby and waited for him. When I saw his car pull up I ran outside and greeted him with a big hug. On the drive to Camp Lejeune I regaled him with a ride-by-ride account of my trip. He laughed, genuinely and hard, and expressed his gratitude several times. After we arrived at the camp we spent a long time loading the car, a small Chevrolet. Besides his clothes and other belongings there were several boxes and cans of food, so the trunk, the backseat, and the front passenger seat were packed full. There was just enough space on the driver's side for me to fit snugly. Doing his best to emulate our mother, Robbie prepared several sandwiches, which he placed on the front seat.

Early the next morning, well before sunrise, Robbie handed me enough cash to get me to Maine. I drove out of Camp Lejeune, turned toward Rocky Mount, and headed north. As I drove through Petersburg I regretted very much that I had no room in the car for the many uniformed men hitch-hiking. I ate while driving, stopping only for gasoline and bathroom breaks. The only incident occurred just outside of Boston. Traffic was dense and moving slowly in hurricane-like conditions of high winds and heavy rain. The car driving alongside me suddenly lurched into the side of Robbie's car, scraping it seriously. In the drenching rain the other driver and I got out of our cars and exchanged names and addresses. He apologized, saying that he had been blown into me by the high wind. Neither of us was in the mood for a long discussion, and in a few minutes I was back in the car, soaking wet but glad to be on the way home. I had driven slowly and continuously, and the roads then were not what they are now, so it was in the middle of the night when I pulled into the driveway alongside the house where Janet was staying. I was tired but proud; I had gotten Robbie's car and stuff home safely, with only a few deep scratches on the car. I then made one unbreakable promise to myself: I would never again hitchhike anywhere. From now on I would travel by bus, and I hoped, eventually by train and by plane. And who knew? Someday I might even get to take a taxi.

A few weeks later I received notice to report to the U.S. Army Intelligence School at Fort Holabird in Baltimore on December 26. I started very early, traveled by bus, and made it just before the close of business. For the next six months I attended what was, for all practical purposes, a graduate school. I studied history, languages, personal surveillance, report writing, the qualities of leadership, and much more, all with a heavy overlay of anticommunism. I loved the school and the army. I met and studied and worked with young men from all across America, and when we graduated we were sent to stations all around the world. It was an exhilarating experience. To my surprise and pleasure, I was selected to be the deputy commander of one of the student battalions. I took it seriously, did my job well, and graduated near the top of my class. I was thrilled to receive an assignment to serve in counterintelligence in Berlin and promptly read as many relevant books as I could get my hands on. After a brief visit to Waterville to say goodbye, I packed my bags and headed for Fort McGuire, New Jersey, for the flight to Germany.

THE ARMY

The Constellation seemed to shake as it lifted off the ground, and I shook with it. It was 1955; I was twenty-one years old, had just graduated from the U.S. Army Intelligence School at Fort Holabird, and was on my way to my first assignment. It was the first time I had ever been in an airplane.

The plane banked sharply to the right, and my heart and stomach banked with it. But within minutes my concerns seemed minor. Most of the passengers on the plane were children, some very young, dependents of U.S. military personnel based in Germany. Getting to cruising altitude required a very bumpy ride through bad weather that triggered an outburst of crying. The vomiting was not far behind. Trapped in a tight middle seat, surrounded by sick and frightened children, I felt sorry for myself but even sorrier for the mothers struggling to cope with and calm their children. By the time the plane landed in Frankfurt I had concluded that flying wasn't all it was cracked up to be. On deplaning I was relieved to learn that the next leg of the trip, to Berlin, would be by overnight train.

An army driver took me to the train station in Frankfort. There I met Bob King, a fellow second lieutenant (the lowest rank in the Officer Corps), who also had been assigned to Berlin. He was pleasant and open, and we had a friendly talk on the train. This was my first train ride and, like the flight, it was eye-opening, but in a good way. It was a sleeper, and I was pleasantly surprised to learn that I had a nice bed all to myself. The cold war was under way, and the train had to pass through Soviet-controlled East Germany to get to Berlin. It was exciting, though nerve-wracking, when the train stopped twice, on entering and on leaving East Germany. But there were no incidents and we arrived safely in Berlin early on a Sunday morning.

Another army driver took us to the headquarters of the U.S. Army Command in Berlin. It was a clear, sunny morning, and there was little traffic as we drove through the city. I strained to see reminders of the battle for Berlin that occurred a decade earlier in the final days of World War

II. *Battle* is not the right word since the Germans were unable to mount an effective resistance to the revenge-seeking Soviets who stormed and devastated Berlin. I had read many books on the great war and was eager to see the places where so much tragic history had been made.

The huge compound was virtually deserted. The sound of our heels clicking on the marble floors echoed as we were led down a long empty hallway to the office of the adjutant of the unit to which we were assigned. I got to the door first, pulled it open, and instinctively stepped aside and waved Bob into the room. He had taken a few steps and I had not yet pulled the door shut behind me when a young officer behind a desk pointed at Bob and barked, "You're the new supply officer!" There was no hello, no handshake, no "How are you?" or "Glad to meet you." We were both so startled that we stopped for a moment. "Come in, come in!" he yelled, his voice still with an edge of anger. As we gingerly approached his desk he pointed at me. "You," he said, "report to security downstairs right away." He then asked which of us was Mitchell and which was King. After we replied he completed some forms on his desk and sent us on our way. We later learned that the adjutant, a first lieutenant not much older than we were, was upset because having to receive us and give us our assignments meant that he missed his regular Sunday morning golf game. We eventually became friends with him and often laughed when we recalled our first meeting.

Beyond the laughter was a serious point: the significant role of chance in life. Had I been the first to step into the adjutant's office I would have spent the next two years as the supply officer, an important role in any army but not nearly as interesting, varied, and exciting as the work I was called on to perform.

Responding to the adjutant's order, I went directly to the Office of Security. I was informed that I would serve as part of a three-man protective detail, beginning that evening. That evening! I was stunned to learn that on the very day I arrived in Berlin I would be sent to a remote northern sector of the city, along the border with East Berlin, to protect a visiting dignitary.

I was instructed to take off my uniform and dress in civilian clothes. The next time I put on my uniform was on the day I left Berlin for good, eighteen months later. The dignitary turned out to be a prominent scientist who had worked on the German

rocket program in the late stages of the war. After Germany surrendered, several members of the scientific team were transported to the United States, where they continued their efforts on behalf of our country. The mother of one of them lived in West Berlin, directly adjacent to the border with East Berlin. She was in failing health, and her son was coming to visit her. The city was then a hotbed of espionage and cold war conflict, and kidnappings were common. So that evening three young Americans drove to the apartment building in which she lived and deployed to prevent a communist kidnapping. The leader of our group, Charlie McKelvey, stayed in the car, parked a discreet distance away and across the street. The other member of our team went inside the building, to a landing on the floor just above the apartment we were guarding. I was sent to the rear of the building, where, crouched in shrubbery, I watched and protected the back entrance. I was very nervous and regularly checked the revolver that I had strapped into a shoulder holster. Although I had trouble staying awake when I worked as a night watchman at the paper mill two years earlier, I was wide awake this night, as every sound raised an alarm in my mind. Fortunately nothing

happened, and when we were relieved by another detail the next morning I felt a sense of accomplishment and self-assurance. I'd gotten through the first night without shooting myself in the foot and I could now unpack and settle in. I was part of the team.

The rest of the week passed without incident, and the scientist returned safely to the United States. For the next few months I performed a series of tasks. I had the sense of being tested and knew I had passed when I finally received a permanent assignment.

Berlin in 1955–56 was an exciting city, and I came to love the place and the people. Divided by the cold war into four sectors — Russian in the east, French in the north, British in the center, and American in the south — it remained surprisingly open. The infamous Wall was a few years in the future, and people could travel with relative ease throughout the city. Indeed it was that very freedom that ultimately led to the erection of the Wall. Chafing under the constraints of communist rule, East Germans and other Eastern Europeans were pouring into West Berlin at a rising rate. To accommodate them in some orderly fashion the U.S. and West German governments constructed a refugee center in West Berlin. It was located along the border in the working-class district

of Marienfelde, from which it took its name. There teams of Americans and Germans worked side by side, receiving, screening, and assisting those fleeing communism, most of whom eventually settled in West Germany. One part of their processing involved being interrogated by a team whose specific task was to detect, intercept, and arrest those who might be entering for the purpose of becoming "sleeper spies" in the West and to identify and recruit those who might be willing to return to the East as spies for us. A delicate task, requiring a high level of personal skill and judgment, it was performed by a dedicated group of Germans, many of whom had served in the German Army in the war, and Americans, most of whom were career enlisted men who had served in the U.S. Army during the war and had stayed on after the fighting ended. All of the German veterans who worked with us said they had fought against the Soviets on the Eastern Front. We often joked with them, expressing amazement that it took Eisenhower so long to get to the Rhine River when there were no Germans fighting on the Western Front.

I was promoted to first lieutenant and assigned to that team. I reported to a captain who in turn reported to the colonel who was the commander of our unit. I was twenty-two, much younger than most of those I was working with. I had received limited language training and although I worked hard to improve my German I was far from fluent. Neither proved to be a fatal handicap, and the next year was one of the most interesting and exciting of my life.

Our unit maintained several safe houses in the American sector of West Berlin, ostensibly private residences that were in fact used to temporarily house refugees for extended interrogation or for their protection. I visited the houses regularly, often to make decisions for which I at first felt hopelessly unprepared. One visit took place soon after I started. I received a report that the screening process had produced strong suspicions about one refugee from a small town in East Germany. Two screeners, one American and one German, thought that he had been sent west by the East German government and should be arrested. He was accompanied by his wife and two small children. The screeners wanted me to come to the safe house to decide how to handle the situation. I drove to the house, which was located on a quiet, tree-lined street in a residential section of the city.

When I arrived the two screeners briefed

me in what had been the living room of the private house. The suspect was in an adjacent room, the wife and children in an upstairs bedroom. They were brought down first. The children were young, a four-year-old boy and a six-year-old girl; the wife was in her thirties. They were postcard-perfect Teutons: blond, blue-eyed, bright rosy cheeks, a hint of chubbiness. She was in tears and emotional; the children were frightened and silent. She didn't know why they had been detained, but she knew she had a problem. She pleaded for her husband's release and asked that they be permitted to go on to West Germany. After a brief discussion they were taken back upstairs and I was led by the screeners into the adjacent room to meet and talk with the suspect. As we entered the room we were shocked. He had committed suicide! There had been no indication that he might be suicidal, so his belt had not been taken from him. Somehow he had looped it over part of a protruding window frame and hanged himself, his body dangling against the wall by the window.

When we rushed over to him, we discovered that he was still alive, although barely conscious, the tips of his toes just touching the floor. He was a stocky, heavy man who weighed well over two hundred pounds. The three of us struggled awkwardly to lift him up high enough to enable us to unloop the tangled belt and let him down. As we did so he slipped out of our grasp and fell heavily to the floor, striking his head on the edge of a nearby desk. That sliced open a deep gash along one of his eyebrows from which blood spurted. I ordered the German screener to call one of the doctors who worked with us, while the American screener and I propped the suspect up into a sitting position, his back against the desk, his head elevated, as we tried to stanch the flow of blood by pressing a towel against the wound. Within a half hour he was conscious and sitting in a chair. I began to question him.

As the screeners had reported, he was emotional and inconsistent and contradicted himself frequently. It didn't take too much interrogation to get him to admit that he had faked the suicide attempt to gain attention and sympathy. Then, after what seemed like a long silence, he took the towel from his face, looked at me, and, in a voice drained of emotion, said, "Whatever you do with me, she and the children know nothing. Let them go." After thinking about it for the rest of the day, that's what I did. In accordance with our procedures he was turned over to the West German police; she and the children were returned to East Germany. I worried so much about what would happen to the woman and her children that I sought out two respected senior enlisted men in our unit, Felix Finn and Max Baer, to discuss my feelings. Both were old enough to be my father. "It's good you're concerned," Felix said, "but in this job you're going to have to make a lot of decisions tougher than this one. You'd better get used to it." He was right. There were lots of decisions, many of them much more difficult. I tried hard to get used to it, but I never did. I sought and welcomed the responsibility, but I was deeply uncomfortable about the fact that I, an inexperienced twenty-two-year-old, was making life-or-death decisions about people's lives. This discomfort has never left me. Later, as a U.S. attorney for Maine and then as a federal judge, I forced myself to act in a timely and decisive way, but both before and after each decision, I thought long and hard about the people whose lives would be irrevocably changed by my decisions, about my duties and responsibilities, and about my own fallibility and weaknesses. Some decision makers reportedly are able to quickly put each decision behind them. I have never been able to do so. I have made many mistakes and spent many sleepless nights reflecting on the morality and consequences of my decisions. Those two children in Berlin have been my companions for life.

While in Berlin I took a major step toward adulthood. For the first time I voted in a presidential election.* The curriculum at the Army Intelligence School was understandably focused on the threat of communism, its insidious nature, and the need for constant vigilance against those who would undermine American values.† In addition I loved the army and admired General Dwight Eisenhower for his service in World War II. I also admired Governor Adlai Stevenson, but to me the choice was clear and my decision simple. I voted for Eisenhower and was pleased that he was reelected. (I have felt ever since that he was underrated as a president.) But beyond that

* The legal voting age was then twenty-one.
† I later wrote a book on the contest between democracy and communism: George J. Mitchell, *Not for America Alone: The Triumph of Democracy and the Fall of Communism* (New York: Kodansha America, 1997).

I had little interest in politics. I was focused on my future. My term of service would soon expire. What should I do?

The cold war was at a peak of intensity: the United States versus Russia, NATO versus the Warsaw Pact, East versus West, communism versus democracy. And, especially in Berlin, spies versus counterspies. The Berlin airlift of 1948 was fresh in the memories of Berliners and Americans were welcomed and appreciated. The work we were doing was interesting and, we felt, meaningful. Berlin, one of the great cities of the world, was an exciting place of history, culture, and adventure. I enjoyed my time in the army so much that I seriously considered extending my tenure in Berlin and making the army my career. But I was pulled in other directions as well.

Charlie McKelvey had been born and raised in Pennsylvania. Following college, he attended and graduated from the Georgetown University Law Center in Washington, after which he was called into the army. He later had a successful career in the law in Williamsport, Pennsylvania. In Berlin we became close friends, along with a third colleague, George Padgett, who was from New Jersey. He later became the general counsel of the Lionel Corporation.

In long discussions over many pleasant evenings we and other friends talked about our lives and our futures. I was trying to decide whether to stay in the army or go to graduate school for an advanced degree in European history or go to law school. As always, money was a factor; I didn't know if I could afford either graduate or law school. McKelvey urged me to go to Georgetown. It had an evening program that would permit me to work full time. Padgett had already applied for and been accepted at Georgetown; he too urged me to go there and suggested that we could room together in Washington. Those were important factors for me. I applied for and was admitted to Georgetown for the semester beginning in January 1957.

It was a bittersweet decision. I looked forward to law school, especially since I would be living with someone I liked and trusted. But I was sad to leave Berlin and especially to leave the army. Those who don't serve in the military miss one of life's great experiences, although some who do serve would not agree. But my experience could not have been better. I was a boy when I entered. When I left I was, if not a man, at least well on the way. The army taught or reinforced for me the value of patriotism, discipline, loyalty, and how to work with others. During my lifetime I've been privileged to receive many honors and awards; none means more to me than the George Catlett Marshall Award "for selfless service to the United States of America" that I received in 2002 from the Association of the U.S. Army.

A LIGHT FOR INGRID BERGMAN

Before I entered the Army I had never been on a plane or a train, had never left the United States, indeed had traveled little within the country. So it was an unforgettable experience for me to travel with friends and see some of the great cities of Europe. Berlin was a wonderful and enjoyable city to live in. An extra benefit was the chance to visit London, Amsterdam, Paris, and Vienna. My visit to London coincided with the official celebration of the queen's birthday, which was colorful and crowded. Amsterdam and Vienna were fascinating. Paris, then as now, was special. There we did what young visitors have done for centuries: walked the cobbled streets, gaped at Versailles, the Louvre, and the Eiffel Tower, watched the passersby as we sat in the outdoor cafes, and lingered over conversation in inexpensive restaurants. Late one night, as we walked across one of the bridges over the river Seine toward our low-cost hotel, we saw bright lights and a small knot of people at the far end. Curious, we walked toward them and discovered that a scene was being shot for a movie. The film, later released as *Anastasia,* featured Ingrid Bergman, the beautiful and then famous Swedish actress. There were only a few members of the crew and spectators there, so we were able to stand right next to a camera on a large dolly and watch Bergman walk from the bridge down concrete steps toward the river. Then, suddenly, there was a pause in the filming, and there was Ingrid Bergman moving toward us. At first I thought it must be my imagination, but she was in fact looking right at me and then walking toward me. Although dressed in a long shabby coat with a kerchief over her head, with little or no makeup, she was as beautiful in person as she had been on the screen. She walked right up to me, pulled out a cigarette, and said, "Do you have a light?" My first thought was "This is what movies are made of. In the middle of the night, on a bridge over the river Seine, a famous forty-year-old actress asking an unknown twenty-two-year-old boy for a light!" I've never smoked, so I knew I didn't have a lighter or any matches. Nevertheless,

I went through the motions of going through all my pockets before I was forced to confess that I didn't. But, hoping to prolong the moment, I pointed to a member of the crew standing a few feet away and said, "I'll go ask him."

"That's okay," she replied as she walked toward the man, "I'll ask him." She did, he had a lighter, and he lit her cigarette. I watched in silent dismay as they then engaged in conversation for several minutes until the filming resumed. When we left to return to our hotel we all laughed as my friends made fun of me, and I spent the night wondering what might have happened if I'd had the chance to talk with her. What a missed opportunity! For several years thereafter I made it a point to carry matches whenever I went out just in case I ran into Ingrid Bergman again. But, of course, I never did.

I returned from Berlin in time to spend the Christmas holiday with my family in Maine. I hadn't seen them for eighteen months, so we had a great reunion. My sister had graduated from the University of Maine a few months earlier, so my parents had realized their dream: each of their five children had graduated from college. Paul had gone on to get a graduate degree from Columbia, and I was headed to law school, in part because of his influence. As the oldest child, Paul was treated with special respect, and I looked up to him for advice.

The intelligence unit to which I was assigned in Berlin worked with the Central Intelligence Agency, and I had somehow come to the attention of some of the agency's employees there; they urged me to join. I submitted an application to the headquarters in Washington; I thought it would be interesting to continue in intelligence while I attended law school. The money I earned there, combined with the GI Bill benefits to which I was now entitled, would be enough to cover the cost of law school and my living expenses.

I arrived in Washington with high hopes and with $100 in my pocket. I found a room for a few dollars a night in an inexpensive hotel not far from the agency's headquarters. Early the next morning I headed for my interview. I had done well in Berlin and had the endorsement of some of the agency's employees, so I was brimming with confidence. I told the official conducting the interview about my work in Berlin and about my plans for law school. In response he made it painfully clear that there were many well-qualified applicants for what were relatively few openings; the process was lengthy and competitive and would take months; if I were fortunate enough to be offered a position it would be full time, and to the CIA full time meant just that. Employment at the agency would preclude going to law school, by day or night. I was totally deflated.

Although my hotel was just a few blocks away, when I left the interview I walked the streets of downtown Washington trying to figure out what to do. I was in a precarious position. Foolishly I had assumed I would be hired by the CIA. I was scheduled to start law school in a week, and I had barely enough money to get through that week. After two hours of walking I was tired, discouraged, and hungry. But I knew I had to find a job, so I bought a morning paper and stopped in a small coffee shop to get a sandwich and read the want ads. One caught my attention. It sought applicants for the position of insurance adjustor for the Travelers Insurance Company. I quickly finished my sandwich, found a pay telephone, and called the number. The kind woman who answered set up an appointment for me for that afternoon, and when I explained that this was my first day in Washington, she gave me precise directions to their office on Fourteenth Street. It wasn't far from where I was standing, so I went immediately, arriving early to give myself plenty of time to complete the application form. I handed it in and was asked to wait. I used the time to read the rest of the want ads, circling a few for follow-up if that became necessary. I had been overconfident with the CIA; I wouldn't repeat that mistake.

Almost everyone in the large office worked out in the open, at desks in neat rows. In one corner a small office was separated by a glass-topped partition. There I was introduced to the office manager, a man named Rupert Morrill. I was immediately struck by the name; the Morrell family in Maine had been so helpful to me, perhaps this Morrill would also, even though the spelling was different. He was kind and considerate, and after a brief and friendly chat, he hired me on the spot, subject to verification of my record and checking with my references. I began a training program the next morning and spent the next four and a half years working as an insurance adjustor while attending law school five evenings a week from 5:30 to 7:30. It was both physically and mentally demanding, but it was good for me because it forced me to apply the discipline I had learned in the army and had so sorely lacked in high school and college.

I cannot say that I enjoyed either the working days or the evenings at law school. I found both occasionally difficult, sometimes unpleasant, often boring. They were far removed from the exciting and challenging work I'd done in Berlin, but I was thankful for both, and I knew I had to and could get through them. I also found it hard to adjust to the heat of summer in

Washington. Padgett was not due to arrive until later that year, so I shared an apartment in Virginia with a friend from Maine. It was not air-conditioned, which made it intolerable in July and August. When Padge arrived, we rented a townhouse in Washington, close to the Capitol building. Although tiny, it was air-conditioned and made me feel as though I had made a leap into luxury. Padge attended school full time during the day while I worked days and went to school at night, but we still spent a great deal of time together. Our friendship deepened and we never had a disagreement of any kind. Such a good relationship eased the difficulties of work and school.

Just around the corner from our townhouse was a Catholic church where I attended Mass every Sunday morning. For weeks, as I walked back to our townhouse afterward, I noticed a tall, slender, attractive woman walking just ahead of or behind me, to a townhouse just two doors away. I very much wanted to meet her but couldn't figure out an appropriate opening line. "I wish Robbie were here," I thought. "He'd know what to say." Thankfully, on the fourth week, as we walked down the church steps, she turned and spoke first. "Hello neighbor," she said. It wasn't much, but it was enough. Her name was Sally Heath. She was from Concord, New Hampshire, and she worked as a secretary for one of the U.S. senators from that state, Styles Bridges. Before that she had worked in the office of the governor of New Hampshire. We had a cup of coffee that morning, dinner a few nights later, and before long we were seeing each other regularly.

As an insurance adjustor I investigated, evaluated, and settled claims made against companies or individuals insured by the Travelers. My work included investigating automobile accidents, interviewing people who slipped and fell in grocery stores, evaluating disability claimants, and other similar activities. Washington is divided into four quadrants, centered on the Capitol building, and an adjustor was assigned to cover each of them. My first assignment was the Northwest, the largest of the four quadrants in land area and population. For two years I learned every street, block, and alley. Many years later, as Senate majority leader, I was assigned a car and driver. Willie was a cheerful and pleasant companion. While he generally knew his way around Washington, he didn't know every street as I did. More often than I should have, I gave him driving directions:

"Take a left here"; "No, don't go that way, go this way." One day, as he was about to drop me off at the Capitol, he suggested that I take up a certain bill on the Senate agenda. Surprised, I looked at him and asked, "What did you say?" With a huge smile on his face he replied, "Well, you're always telling me how to do my job, so I thought just this once I'd tell you how to do yours." We both laughed hard and loud. It was a good lesson. If you want people to work hard and succeed, there are times when you've got to let them find their own way. Overmanaging is a constant danger. I never again gave Willie driving directions.

After two years in Northwest Washington I was assigned to southern Maryland, a much larger geographic area but with fewer people. It was a promotion of sorts because I was also granted more autonomy in how I handled my time and in processing and set-tling claims.

I entered law school in the middle of the first year and had great difficulty adapting. The classes were much larger, the institu-tion less personal, the relationships more transient than they had been at Bowdoin. Many of the students were older, with families, so there was little or no time to get to know my classmates. The case method of study was unfamiliar, and I was a full semester behind in adjusting to it. But gradually my performance and my grades improved, and when I graduated I was near the top of my class. I had matured, acquiring some discipline in studying and writing, and had decided where I would live and work.

I wanted to practice law in Maine. My years in Berlin and Washington were exciting and interesting, but, far more than I had anticipated, I missed Maine and my family. As much as I had enjoyed new and different experiences, I found myself being pulled back by the old and familiar. My hopes fit in well with Sally's. She too wanted to leave Washington, and Maine was close to her family in Concord. In the early summer of 1959 we went on vacation together to Cape Cod. We had been together for nearly a year and a half, and it seemed inevitable to both of us that we would marry. It was only a long weekend, but we had plenty of time to share our hopes and dreams about the future. Living in Portland, less than two hours' drive from both families, where I could practice law and we could raise a family, seemed ideal. So she was not surprised when I asked her to marry me, and I was not surprised when she said yes. She expressed only one concern. Her years of working in political offices had bred in her an intense dislike of politics. She had left the Senate for a position in a nonpolitical department of the Federal Aviation Agency. Although she was not specific about the reasons, she made it clear she didn't want to have anything more to do with what she referred to as "that business." That was not a problem for me. While I had a general interest in public affairs I had no desire to become personally involved in any way. The first time I met a senator, governor, or other major elected official was when I shook hands with Styles Bridges at our wedding in Concord in August 1959.

As law school graduation neared I sent letters of application to fifteen law firms in Maine, most in the Portland area. I was uneasy when only three responded to my request for an interview but heartened by the fact that all three were well-known firms. Two of the three told me they weren't interested after the first interview. The third asked me to return for another meeting, but the result was the same; they offered the position to another applicant. Disappointed but still determined, I asked the Travelers to transfer me to their Portland office. I was confident that if I could just get to Maine I could find a position with a law firm. The Travelers may have discerned my motive because without explanation my request was declined. I began to research the possibilities of employment with a law firm in Washington or some other city, but it was halfhearted, not something I was interested in or enthusiastic about.

Just as my disappointment deepened I received a letter from the U.S. Department of Justice. It informed me that under the Department's Honors Law Graduate Program I was eligible for a position there. I had never met or spoken with anyone at the Department and had never heard of the Honors Program. My first thought was, "My father was right. It does pay to study and work hard." Without hesitation I accepted. In September 1960 I joined the Department as a trial attorney in the Anti-Trust Division. The people with whom I worked were first-rate and the work was interesting. With our combined incomes Sally and I could now begin to plan for a family, although buying a house was still beyond our reach. And I still had Maine on my mind.

Two months after I began working at Justice, John F. Kennedy was elected president. Sally and I had voted for him and were impressed by the new, young leader. On two occasions I was one of a large number of young Justice lawyers who met with the new attorney general, Robert Kennedy. It was an exciting time to be in Washington, in government, but I had no thought of elected office. My goal was unchanged. I wanted to move back to Maine to enter the private practice of law. I would work hard and do well at Justice until that opportunity came. It did so, again unexpectedly, in January 1962.

I received a telephone call from a man who identified himself as Don Nicoll, the administrative assistant to U.S. Senator Edmund Muskie of Maine. Muskie had a vacancy on his staff and was looking for someone from Maine with a background in law. Muskie's wife, Jane, was from Waterville, and he had lived and practiced law there. He knew my older brothers, but didn't know me. Would I come to his Senate office to meet him and discuss the position on his staff? I asked if I could have a day or two to think about it, and he readily agreed. I had competing concerns: this might give me the chance to meet and interact with many people in Maine, including and especially lawyers and law firms, but what would Sally think? Although she was wary about my getting involved in political office, she wanted to move home as much as I did, so she agreed that I should talk to Senator Muskie.

I liked and was impressed by both Muskie and Nicoll. Don was short, precise, and methodical. Muskie was tall, lanky, more expressive. Both were generous and kind to me in that first meeting and thereafter. I didn't want to mislead Muskie in any way, so I was frank about my goals. He said he understood. He asked me to draft and submit a memorandum on a legal issue then pending in the Senate. It was obviously a test, and I treated it that way. I worked hard to make my writing clear, responsive, and concise. Soon thereafter Don called again, this time to offer me the position of executive assistant to the senator. They understood and accepted my intentions; they asked, however, that I commit to remaining on the senator's staff through his next election, in November 1964. They offered a substantial increase in pay over what I was getting at Justice, and I accepted. My life was about to change, much more quickly than I could imagine.

Just seven days after I joined Muskie's staff, a tall man with dark hair and horn-rimmed glasses walked up to my desk and asked, "What are you doing here?" He was Albert Abrahamson, professor of economics at Bowdoin College. Without thinking I replied, "What are you doing here?" "I've known the senator for a long time," he replied. "I visit whenever I'm in Washington. Come on, let's have cup of coffee and a chat." Abrahamson had taught at Bowdoin for many years. I hadn't known that he had also been involved in politics in Maine and had gotten to know many prominent persons in both parties. When I told him about my hopes he said immediately, "Mert Henry's law firm in Portland is looking for someone." "Who's Mert Henry?" I asked. I then listened in amazement as he told me. Mert was born and raised in Maine, graduated from Bowdoin, then attended law school in the evening at George Washington University. While there he joined the staff of U.S. Senator Fred Payne of Maine, a Republican, who had been governor of the state. After one term Payne was defeated, in 1958, by the Democratic candidate, Edmund Muskie. Mert had then returned to Portland and joined the small law firm of Jensen and Baird. That firm, with five lawyers, was looking for a sixth. Abrahamson offered to call Mert to set up an interview for me. But I told him, "I made a commitment to Senator Muskie. I can't go anywhere until 1965." "It can't do you any harm to talk with them," he assured me, and I agreed.

The coincidences mounted. Mert called me and we had a pleasant talk. He asked me to send him my résumé. By chance one of the founders of the firm, Ken Baird, was coming to Washington the following week; would I meet with him? When I met Baird he was direct and energetic and offered me the position, and when I explained why I couldn't accept it, even though it was what I had hoped for and dreamed of for years, he said he understood. He suggested that we keep in touch, without any commitment on either side. I agreed.

I had a hard time getting over the irony of my situation. After trying and failing for years to get an offer from a Maine law firm, I received one just days after I had committed to serve for the next two and a half years in Washington in another position! In the end it worked out. I maintained my interest, they kept the position open, and in early 1965 Sally and I moved to Portland and I joined the firm. But the young lawyer who began the private practice of law in 1965 was not the same person he had been in

1962. I had changed. I had gotten a taste of politics, and I liked it.

MUSKIE

Ed Muskie was a towering figure in person, in Maine history, and in my life. I worked for him, traveled with him, celebrated victory with him, and tasted defeat with him. I admired and loved him. He was my employer, mentor, hero, and friend. His definition of public service became mine. His standard of integrity became mine. His political principles became mine. And finally his Senate seat became mine.

Muskie changed Maine politics, breaking nearly a century of Republican domination. He changed the lives of all Americans by writing and passing our nation's landmark environmental laws, the Clean Air and Clean Water acts. He had a brilliant, inquiring mind, a natural talent for legislating, and he could readily deploy patience or impatience, as the situation demanded. His impatience was frequently accompanied and amplified by a severe temper. He was human and had his faults, not the least of which was his inability to control himself when he got mad. Late in his life he told an interviewer that it was tactical, turned on and off as necessary to achieve his objective. It may have been tactical, but it was real. I can testify that those who were on the receiving end of one of his tirades — as I was on occasion — never forgot it. But though he could not control his temper, he could and did control the aftermath. As quickly as it came the storm passed and to a remarkable degree he forgot it and moved on. He disagreed with you, he let you know it, and then it was forgotten. He never carried a grudge.

His father was a tailor, born and raised in Poland. His mother was raised in this country by Polish immigrants. Muskie was in every sense a self-made man who rose to national prominence on his talent, intelligence, and drive. Growing up in Rumford, Maine, a paper mill town, he was aware from an early age of the effects of uncontrolled pollution on the everyday lives of ordinary Americans. This led directly to his becoming the greatest environmental legislator in our nation's history. His successes were many: two-term governor, four-term senator, secretary of state, author of the nation's basic environmental laws and of much other important legislation. His losses were fewer, but they cut deep, most prominently his failure to win the Democratic nomination for president in 1972, a race he entered as a favorite based on his superb performance as his party's nominee for vice president in the 1968 campaign.

I have been helped by many people in my life, but none more often or more meaningfully than Ed Muskie. When I left his staff in 1965 I realized what had for years been a strong desire to return to Maine to live and to practice law. But it was with a deeply ambivalent feeling that I left the man I most admired and learned so much from.

BACK TO MAINE

Back in Maine I started a new life and a
new job. Most important of all, our daughter
Andrea was born in Portland on May 14,
1965, just a few months after we arrived.
We bought our first home, a small one-story
in Falmouth, just outside of Portland. For a
time all went well. I worked very hard and
did well, becoming a partner in our small
firm within a year. But there was a growing
problem in our lives: as I became more
involved in politics, Sally's unhappiness with
my involvement increased. During my years
on Muskie's staff I had traveled across
Maine with him, meeting and working with
people at all levels of government and
politics, and I thoroughly enjoyed it. So in
early 1966, when I received calls from
several members of the Maine Democratic
State Committee urging me to run for the
position of chairman of the Maine
Democratic Party, their pleas found ready

acceptance. I had been back in Maine for less than a year and I was already plunging into the very politics I had had no interest in six years earlier, when Sally had been straightforward about her feelings and I had been sincere in my response. But, as is inevitable in human affairs, I had changed. Without ever having intended or planned it, I found myself involved in, enjoying, and succeeding in politics. I asked for her understanding. She wanted to accommodate me and did her best to do so. But it was obviously very hard for her, especially when my political activities took me away from her and our infant daughter.

As happens to almost all working parents, there began for me a lifelong struggle to find the right balance between work and family. Self-doubt has been my constant companion. The struggle continues to this day, when, at the age of eighty-one, with two teenage children, I maintain a full schedule of work and travel.

I served as chairman of the Maine Democratic Party for two years and then for eight years served on the Democratic National Committee. This led to many interesting assignments. At the 1968 Democratic National Convention in Chicago, Senator Hubert Humphrey of

Minnesota had accepted nomination as the party's candidate for president. He chose his friend and fellow senator, Ed Muskie of Maine, as his running mate. As chairman of the Maine Democratic Party I attended the convention as a delegate. There I was chosen to be one of Maine's two members to the Democratic National Committee. Shortly after he learned of Humphrey's decision, Muskie asked me to take a leave of absence from my law firm in Portland so that I could serve as his deputy campaign manager. When I agreed he asked me to go immediately to Washington to set up a campaign organization. Because of the late date of the convention, we found ourselves in a campaign before we had an organization. I began immediately and spent a week in a round-the-clock effort to build that organization from scratch.

As I plowed through the hundreds of messages, telegrams, and letters addressed to Muskie, many of them from volunteers, I stopped when I saw one from Ed Stern. Although he didn't fit the stereotype, Ed was a successful trial lawyer. He had a high-pitched voice and his presentations included occasional rambles, but they merely disguised his high intelligence and engaging personality. He had a great sense of humor, and the permanent sparkle in his eyes suggested that, no matter how serious the subject, another joke was on the tip of his tongue. Ed's legal skills were well-known locally. He had gained national attention four years earlier, in the general election of 1964. Bangor, where Ed lived and worked, was then solidly Republican, as was the county in which it is located. For years the struggling local Democratic Party sought candidates to fill the ticket so that no office would go uncontested, although the chances of winning were slim. As a loyal Democrat, and a close friend of Muskie, Ed for years had consented to be nominated for a variety of offices; he never campaigned and, predictably, he never won. Then came Lyndon Johnson's landslide victory over Barry Goldwater in the presidential election. As usual Ed had not campaigned. On election night, while the more traditional candidates gathered with the party faithful in a local hotel, Ed was in Los Angeles on a business trip. As the tidal wave rolled across the country, it became clear that many candidates whose prospects were considered nonexistent were in fact going to win. Ed was one of them. When he received the telephone call informing him that he had been elected to the Maine senate, Ed was so surprised that he blurted out in response, "I demand a recount!" That made news around the country and elevated Ed to folk-hero status at home. He ultimately served in the state senate and then as a distinguished trial judge on the Superior Court of Maine.

His message to Muskie was brief and direct. His son, Marshall, who had taken over Ed's law practice, wanted to be part of Muskie's campaign team. I knew that Muskie would not turn Ed down, so I called Marshall and brought him on board, literally. I assigned him to Muskie's campaign plane, where he worked tirelessly and effectively. We became very close friends.

Harold Pachios did not seek a position on Muskie's staff; I sought him out. He had worked at the White House in the Johnson administration under his friend Bill Moyers. He may not have been well known elsewhere, but every political junkie in Maine knew that, in the 1964 campaign, while serving as President Johnson's advance man, he had organized a crowd of seventy-five thousand people to greet LBJ on a campaign visit to Portland. It was by far the largest crowd ever for a political event in Maine. Harold was from Maine and a top-notch advance man. I wanted him to run Muskie's advance operations. But there was a problem: he had been advance man for a president, and I was asking him to do the same job for a candidate for vice president. And now he was an assistant secretary of transportation in the U.S. government. As I expected, when I reached him by phone, he turned down my request. His logic was impeccable: I was asking him to take a step backward, to a job he'd done years earlier at a much higher level. But I had prepared carefully for our conversation. "Harold, what do you want to do over the next few years?" I asked him.

"Just what I'm doing, serving as an assistant secretary of transportation."

"That's a political appointment, isn't it?"

"Yes, it is."

"So, if Nixon wins you're out. Isn't that right?"

"Yes, that's right."

"So the only chance you've got to stay there is if Humphrey wins, right?"

"That's right."

"Well, I'm sure you realize that if you say no to Muskie, and Humphrey wins, you'll be out, the same as if Nixon wins."

There was a pause. "Well, yeah, I guess I realize that," he agreed, but his voice betrayed uncertainty.

"Will you think about it and call me back?"

"Yeah, I'll call you back." I was confident that reality had sunk in.

He finally accepted the offer and did an outstanding job for Muskie. But, of course, Nixon won. Harold left the Department of Transportation and returned to Portland to practice law. Back in Portland myself, I helped him find a job with one of the firms that three years earlier had turned me down. He ultimately ascended to managing partner of what became one of Maine's largest law firms, and we became and remain very close friends.

After the raucous national convention in Chicago in 1968, the party established a national commission to examine the manner in which delegates to the convention were chosen. I was an active member of the commission, which was chaired by Senator George McGovern. I got to know the senator very well and we became friendly. But when he and Senator Muskie both sought the party's nomination for president in 1972 my loyalty and effort were with Muskie. I took a lengthy leave of absence from my law practice to work on his campaign, just as I had done in 1968, when he was the nominee for vice president. Late in 1972, after Mc-

Govern was defeated by Richard Nixon, I was one of three candidates for chairman of the Democratic National Committee; I came in second to Bob Strauss, an experienced and able Texas lawyer who had previously served as the party's national treasurer.

A year later, with the support of several prominent members of the Maine Legislature, I announced my candidacy for governor of Maine. I couldn't afford to stop working, so for a full year I tried unsuccessfully to balance the three-way demands of family, work, and campaign. In June 1974 I won the nomination after a hard-fought primary election campaign with four other candidates, all of whom were friends. Joe Brennan, the district attorney from Cumberland County, the state's largest, came in second. A few years earlier I had worked for Joe as an assistant district attorney. I knew him well and admired him. Running against him was difficult for me to begin with, and it got more difficult as the campaign intensified; the more I saw and heard Joe speak, the more I respected him. The candidates appeared together frequently. There were very few differences among us on issues, so organization — identifying and getting out the voters — proved decisive. Sally was not happy with my decision to run for governor, but she loyally supported me and gamely participated in a few events that I knew she would have preferred not to attend.

In the general election I faced two opponents, both of whom were at the outset better known than I was. Jim Erwin, the Republican nominee, was the attorney general of Maine. He had run and lost in the gubernatorial campaign four years earlier, so he had high name recognition and was a trusted public figure. James Longley, an insurance salesman, was an Independent candidate. He was a precursor to Ross Perot, a charismatic businessman who was proudly "not a career politician." His campaign was greatly aided by the fact that earlier, at the request of the incumbent Democratic governor, he had chaired a commission to identify waste and fraud in state government. That commission's report served as the basis for his campaign. Intense, with a strong personality, Longley was an effective campaigner. It was the year of Watergate, so there was then, as now, a deep disgust with politicians, from which he benefited. Political campaigns in Maine then were relatively mild, with few bare-knuckle attack ads on television. The early focus was on the major party candidates. In that contest I was doing well. But, ignored by Erwin and me, Longley steadily gained.

A few weeks before the election the three of us sat together in a Bangor television studio for a joint interview. Longley astutely got there early and took the middle seat, leaving Erwin and me on either side of him. At one point, as Longley was speaking, Erwin reached behind him and passed me a note: "How long are you going to let this guy get away with this stuff?" There were some inconsistencies and unrealistic claims in Longley's speeches and proposals, but nobody was challenging him. Erwin wanted me to do so, but we were both well aware of the hard reality that if I attacked Longley the beneficiary would be Erwin, and vice versa. After the interview Erwin and I talked about our common dilemma. We had known each other for years and our relationship was very good, considering the circumstances. While I disagreed with him on many issues I liked him as a person. I argued that his campaign was being hurt by Longley more than mine was and that he needed to go on the attack more than I did. He of course took the opposite position. We parted with a friendly handshake and a smile, both heading amiably for defeat. I knew it was coming despite polls that predicted I would win. Although it didn't do me any good, I had been right about Erwin. His candidacy collapsed in the final days of the campaign as Republicans in large numbers shifted to Longley. In the end Erwin received only 23 percent of the vote, and Longley edged past me by about ten thousand votes, or less than 3 percent. There were two obvious and painful lessons I never forgot: you can't let untrue statements or inconsistent claims go unchallenged, and if something needs doing, don't rely on others, do it yourself.

I was prepared for the defeat and returned to my law office to resume my practice early on the morning after the election. But I was not prepared for the intensity of the postelection commentary in which I was described as too stiff, too lawyerly, lacking in appeal and charisma. I read and listened to so much of this analysis that I eventually accepted it as true. I increasingly focused on a future in law and tried to rationalize away the pain of defeat. I enjoyed politics and public affairs and would continue to participate, but not in elected office; much as I would have enjoyed serving, I doubted my ability to ever win an election.

U.S. ATTORNEY AND FEDERAL JUDGE

After Jimmy Carter was elected president in 1976, Senator Muskie announced that he was forming a committee to advise him on appointments to federal offices in Maine, one of which was U.S. attorney. As the chief federal law enforcement officer in the state, the U.S. attorney is responsible for the prosecution of all violations of law on federal property (e.g., federal offices, military bases, American Indian reservations) and all violations of federal statutes anywhere in Maine (e.g., bank robbery, drug smuggling, crimes involving interstate commerce). In the later years of my private practice and in my service as assistant district attorney, I had become involved in litigation representing a diverse group of parties in both civil and criminal trials. As U.S. attorney I could continue and expand on that interest, while also engaging in public service. I submitted my application to the committee and was one of three persons they recommended to Muskie. He in turn recommended me to the president, whose nomination of me moved quickly through the Senate. In 1977 I became the U.S. attorney. It meant a cut in pay, but that was more than offset by the enormous satisfaction of public service. I assembled an excellent staff and spent most of the next two and a half years trying a wide range of cases in court. The only U.S. District Court judge in Maine was Edward Gignoux, a distinguished Portland lawyer and an outstanding judge. I appeared before him regularly and interacted with him often. Although unaware that I would soon join him on the bench, I watched and learned how a great judge conducted himself.

Every trial lawyer I know loves to tell and listen to war stories. Over the years in which I was engaged in the private practice of law, and then as U.S. Attorney, I heard and enjoyed many such stories, some true, some exaggerated, some obviously not true. One of them I like especially and hope it's true because it illustrates common sense in rural Maine. The defendant had moved to Maine from a large city. He was charged with knowingly failing to file federal income tax returns for two years. The defendant and his attorney offered several possible alternative explanations. One was based on the fact that he lived on a farm on which he kept many animals. On his front porch was a small stand on which he placed his outgoing mail and the rural carrier left the incoming mail. It was possible, he suggested, that the goats chewed up his returns; it was well known that goats will eat just about anything. After the closing arguments were made and the judge read his instructions, the jury retired to deliberate. A few hours later they returned a verdict of guilty.

The next day, the court employee whose responsibility was to care for the jurors during their service asked the Assistant U.S. Attorney who tried the case, "Would you like to know what happened?" He explained that "the door to the jury room kinda didn't close tight, so I kinda heard some of what they said." He then told this story.

"Well, you know, the jury foreman is a farmer; he's got animals too. He doesn't talk much but he's got a good way about him, and the other jurors liked him. After they went over the judge's instructions and the evidence, the foreman asked each of them to give an opinion. It was wide open and they had a long discussion. Then one of them said to him, 'You asked us for our opinions, but you haven't said a word. I'd like to know what you think.' There was some quiet, then he says, 'Well, the thing I can't figure out is how them goats knew it was April 15 two years in a row.' So they voted, then he says to them, 'Okay let's go tell the judge, then we can go home to supper.' You know, it's interesting, in all that time he only said three things: What do you think? Then about the goats. Then let's go home to supper."

In the transition from the private practice of law to the Office of the U.S. Attorney, and then federal judge, I had to make adjustments in my personal relationships with other lawyers. It is one thing to try a civil case against a friend; I had done that often. It was more complex and difficult in criminal cases, especially after I became a judge. But difficulty often is accompanied by humor.

My friend Marshall Stern specialized in criminal law. That led to some awkward moments. Short, a little overweight, occasionally flamboyant, Marshall was, like his father, an outstanding trial lawyer. A good and fast talker, he too had a perpetual twinkle in his eye and a quip on his tongue. To Marshall no one and no subject were above humor; he had a joke, usually an insulting one, to fit every occasion and deflate every ego. When we were together I was one of his favorite targets.

One of the many cases in which we clashed involved a shipload of illegal drugs that was intercepted by federal agents just off the Maine coast. Thirty-two persons were arrested and charged with crimes. As required by federal law they were promptly brought before an independent magistrate who would determine whether they would be held in jail or released on bail pending trial. The hearing began late in the evening in the federal courthouse in Portland. I represented the government. Marshall represented the defendants. I began by asking the magistrate to set bail at $50,000 cash per defendant. I pointed out that the defendants had been caught red-handed by federal agents (they claimed they were going fishing, but none had any fishing gear); that all were from out of state (most were from Brooklyn, New York); and several had extensive criminal records. The risk of flight was high, I argued, so the bail should be high.

Marshall began his response by correctly pointing out that the defendants had not been convicted of any crime. Unless and until they were, which he assured the magistrate would not happen, it was unjust and un-American to deprive them of their liberty. But, perhaps recognizing that the facts were such that release without bail was unlikely, he focused on the amount of bail that should be required. He ridiculed my request, and me, as harsh and punitive, even outrageous. Then, with rising emotion and intensity, he said, "Your Honor, these are just a bunch of poor boys from Brooklyn who came to Maine to go fishing. They're all from poor families. Just this evening I called their homes. I talked with their fathers and mothers, their aunts and uncles, I even talked with some of their neighbors. The absolute most they can raise for bail is five thousand dollars per defendant. Not one cent more. If you set bail at one cent more than that you're condemning to prison thirty-two people who are innocent and haven't been convicted of anything." After hours of further wrangling the magistrate set bail at $15,000 per defendant. It was long after midnight when we left the courthouse, with Marshall complaining, even though the magistrate had split the difference in his favor. But just a few hours later, as the sun rose and the office of the clerk of the court opened, a shabbily dressed man appeared with a green garbage bag filled with $480,000 in cash. "I guess you missed a couple of aunts and uncles," I laughingly told Marshall when we spoke later that day. "But," I said, "you did put on an unforgettable performance." Ultimately, in the face of overwhelming evidence of their guilt, the defendants pleaded guilty.

In 1978 Congress enacted and the president signed legislation creating several new judgeships to meet the growing demands on the federal courts. In its more than 150 years of history Maine had had only eleven federal district court judges, one at a time. Now there was to be a twelfth, and the court would have two judges. I accepted the reality that if appointed I would be finished with electoral politics. A federal judgeship would be a tremendous honor and opportunity. Because of the importance of the position Muskie formed another independent committee. I submitted my application. My experience as U.S. attorney gave me a decisive advantage and I was again one of those recommended. Once again Muskie recommended me to the president. My nomination sailed through the Senate and in November 1979 I was sworn into office. I was forty-six years old and felt that I had reached the pinnacle of my career. It was a wonderfully exciting and challenging task. Every day brought new questions, new issues, new opportunities to learn. And occasional humor.

I presided at the federal court in Bangor, which served the northern part of Maine. The caseload there was lighter than in Portland; there was no full-time magistrate, so I handled a wide range of assignments. On the court calendar one wintry day was a bail hearing for a young man from South Carolina, charged with the interstate transportation of stolen goods and represented by none other than Marshall Stern. I brought the courtroom to order and called on the assistant U.S. attorney who was prosecuting the case. I had hired him a few years earlier; he was from Bangor and he and Marshall had known each other all their lives. The prosecutor laid out the basics of the case and, citing the substantial evidence of guilt, the fact that the defendant had a criminal record, and was from another state, argued that the risk of flight was high enough to justify cash bail of $15,000. When Marshall began his response it seemed vaguely familiar. Then he stopped pacing, turned toward me, and said earnestly, "Your Honor, this is just a poor boy from South Carolina who came to Maine to go fishing. He's from a poor family. Just this morning I called his home. I talked with his father and mother, his aunt and uncle, I even talked with some of his neighbors. The absolute most that he can raise for bail is five thousand dollars. Not one cent more. If you set bail at one cent more than that you're condemning to prison a man who is innocent and hasn't been convicted of anything." The prosecutor saw no need to respond, so I set bail at $10,000 cash, adjourned the hearing, and returned to my chamber. As I walked past her I said to my secretary, "In about two minutes Marshall's going to come steaming in here, asking to see me. Call the assistant U.S. attorney and ask him to come over. As soon as they're both here, send them in."

The prosecutor was smiling and Marshall was scowling as they entered. "How can you do this?" he shouted. "He doesn't have any money. You've put an innocent man in jail. How can you live with yourself?"

"Calm down," I said. "Marshall, do you remember that big, late-night arraignment in Portland a year ago? I told you that you'd made an unforgettable statement. Well, it was unforgettable. I recalled it, word for word, as you spoke today."

He paused, thought a moment, then replied, "Jesus, I forgot about that."

We all burst out laughing.

"Listen," I said, "you're practicing law in a state where there are only two federal judges. You've got to vary your routine."

He acknowledged the point, then again pressed the case for his client. I turned to the prosecutor. "He's got the money," he said to Marshall. "You've just got to figure out how to get him to put it up."

"That's it," I said. "Go talk with him and then get back to me."

Late that afternoon my secretary informed me that Marshall and the prosecutor were back. Marshall was uncharacteristically subdued, so I knew what he was going to say before he said it. "You won't believe it. He had more than ten grand in cash."

"What do you mean we won't believe it?" the prosecutor asked with a laugh. "I told you so." The defendant ultimately pleaded guilty.

Fifteen years later the man with whom I shared so much laughter was dead, killed in a horrific automobile accident. His beloved son, Jason, an outstanding student and athlete, had taken a year off after his first year at law school. With friends he traveled around the world and made his first trip to Israel. There Jason discovered his heritage and, indulging his recently developed talent for photography, took hundreds of pictures. On his arrival back in Bangor he excitedly telephoned his father, eager to see him and to show him his photographs. Marshall was about to leave his office to drive to a town about fifty miles away to file some legal papers in a local court, just prior to a deadline. They decided that Jason would accompany Marshall on the drive. On their return to Bangor, when they were just a few miles from their home, their car was struck head-on by a pickup truck that had crossed into their lane. Marshall was killed instantly and Jason was severely injured. Also killed were the driver of the other vehicle, a recent high school graduate who was a volunteer social service worker, and his passenger, an eleven-year-old boy who was being driven to his new foster home.

Just a few years earlier I had delivered the eulogy at Ed Stern's funeral. Now, with a very heavy heart, I found myself delivering the eulogy for his son, Marshall, one of my closest friends. As best I could I tried to celebrate Marshall's life by describing some of the great moments we had enjoyed together. Before and after the service Marshall's many friends swapped stories about his antics and jokes, describing how he had lit up their lives. Marshall's lovely wife, Donna, had suffered terribly. But for her the worst was yet to come.

Five years later, wracked by guilt over his being the only survivor of that crash, Jason committed suicide on Mount Desert Island, just a few hundred yards from the place where my home now stands. It is impossible to adequately describe the sadness and sense of loss that enveloped Jason's funeral as I delivered yet another eulogy. There was no humor, no sense of a life lived fully. To the contrary, we all had a profound sense of the loss of a life that was full of promise cut short. A shining star had been snuffed out suddenly and far too early.

Within the space of ten years I had publicly mourned the loss of three generations of men from one family, all of whom I had known intimately and one of whom was like a brother to me. I remember, as though it were yesterday, sitting with Donna just before Jason's funeral service, trying unsuccessfully to find the words to convey my feelings and those of so many others. In the end I just hugged her, admiring her strength and fortitude.

During our summers in Maine I occasionally see Marshall's brother, Deane. Like his father and brother, Deane has a lively personality and a great sense of humor. In addition to the pleasure of his company, our visits keep alive for me the memory of my friend Marshall.

When I left Berlin I feared that I would never again find work as interesting and stimulating. I felt the same way when I was U.S. attorney. I was wrong both times. For me, being a federal district court judge, especially in Maine, was as good as it gets in life. I especially enjoyed those occasions when I presided over naturalization ceremonies. A group of people who had come from all over the world and who had gone through all of the required procedures gathered before me in a federal courtroom in Maine. There I administered to them the oath of allegiance to the United States, and by the power vested in me under our Constitution and law, I made them Americans. These ceremonies were always very emotional for me because my mother was an immigrant, my father the orphan son of immigrants. I made it a point to speak personally with each new American, individually or in their family group. I asked them how and why they came. I asked about their hopes and dreams, about their fears. Their answers were inspiring. Most of us are Americans by an accident of birth. Most of them are Americans by an act of free will, often at great risk to themselves and their families. Although their answers were as different as their countries of origin, there were common themes, best summarized by a young Asian man who told me in slow and halting English, "I came because here in America everybody has a chance."

Think about the fact that a young man who'd been an American for just a few minutes, who could barely speak English, was able to sum up the meaning of America in a single sentence.

■ ■ ■ ■

THE SENATE YEARS

■ ■ ■ ■

APPOINTMENT TO THE SENATE

April 29, 1980, was a routine day at the federal court house. I was at my desk, absorbed in a legal brief. Suddenly, without knocking, my secretary rushed into my office. Just as I looked up she shouted, "Muskie's going to be secretary of state. He's leaving the Senate." I was startled, as were most Mainers. Well into his fourth term, Muskie had recovered from his loss in the presidential campaign of 1972 to win reelection in 1976 and regain his influence in the Senate. The later years of Jimmy Carter's presidency were dominated by the Iranian hostage crisis. Over the objections of his secretary of state, Cyrus Vance, the president had ordered a military rescue mission, which failed. In protest, and for other reasons, Vance resigned. It was easy to understand why President Carter would want Muskie to replace Vance. It was more difficult to understand why Muskie would accept, since the election, in which Carter faced a difficult contest, was just six months away.

In the few days between the announcement of Muskie's departure and the appointment of his successor, the subject dominated the news in Maine. The decision was to be made by the governor, Joe Brennan. He had recovered from his primary election loss in 1974 to win both the nomination and the general election in 1978. There was a great deal of speculation about the many potential candidates. Two men led the list of prospects: Ken Curtis had served two terms as governor, then as chairman of the Democratic National Committee and as ambassador to Canada; Bill Hathaway had served in the House of Representatives and then one term in the U.S. Senate. Ken and I were especially close. I was chairman of the Maine Democratic Party when he was elected governor in 1966, and I was actively involved in his campaign and helped draft his inaugural address. Four years later I was involved in his campaign for reelection; Jim Erwin was the Republican candidate, and it was an extremely tight race, which had to be decided in a recount, for which I was one of the lawyers who represented Curtis.

There were several other qualified candidates to fill the vacancy left by Muskie. My name was rarely mentioned. Just six months earlier I had been appointed to the federal court, a lifetime position. Everyone, including me, assumed that I would serve in that position for the rest of my working life. By early May, just a few days after Muskie's announcement, word seeped from the governor's office that he was nearing a decision, and the expectation grew that he would make an announcement early the following week.

That weekend I was at my home in South Portland when the phone rang. "George, it's Shep Lee."

Ed Muskie had broken the Republican dominance in Maine, but he hadn't done it alone. A small group of young men and women had worked with him to organize and execute what was a political upheaval. Frank Coffin, then the chairman of the Maine Democratic Party, was Muskie's principal accomplice. He went on to serve in the U.S. House of Representatives, as director of the U.S. Agency for International Development, and as chief justice of the U.S. Court of Appeals for the First Circuit. One of Coffin's close friends was Shepard Lee, a political activist and brilliant businessman who built what became the largest automobile dealership in Maine. Much later in life Shep achieved the rare distinction of serving simultaneously as a director of the National Association of Automobile Dealers and of the American Civil Liberties Union. I met him shortly after I joined Muskie's staff in 1962. We became and remained good friends until his death in 2011.

"Hi, Shep. What's up?"

"I'm calling about the Senate seat."

"What about it? Have you already got the inside scoop?" Shep knew everybody in Maine Democratic politics. I guessed that he had somehow found out who the governor was going to name and was calling to tell me. I was surprised by his answer.

"No. Joe hasn't made up his mind yet. He wants to know if you've thought about it."

I sat upright. "You talked to him?"

He dodged the question. "I'm telling you he wants to know if you've thought about it."

I had thought about it, of course. But I had quickly dismissed it for the obvious reasons: I'd been appointed a federal judge just six months earlier and I was widely considered to be a political loser. "Well, yes, I have thought about it."

"Are you interested?"

"Well, I don't know, I'm not sure. I just assumed that he'd appoint Ken."

"I don't think so. I don't know all the background, but I've heard it's not going to be Ken."

"What do you think I should do?"

"You should do it, George. You know the Senate, you know the issues, you can handle it."

"I don't know. I'm not sure." I repeated myself, fumbling for time, trying to think of what to say or do. It wasn't the last time I would find myself in this position. I wanted it, but I wasn't sure if I should try for it. I loved being a federal judge. It was a safe, secure, meaningful position, and I knew I could do it well. But the Senate! And Ed Muskie's seat! What an honor. What a challenge. I'd have to talk to Sally. She certainly would have concerns and most likely would prefer that I not accept, though, despite reservations, she had gone along with my earlier political efforts. I also feared another failure. I was vaguely aware of the dismal record of appointed senators. Most didn't seek election to a full term or were defeated if they did; very few went on to successful careers in the Senate. Both of Maine's members of the House of Representatives were popular Republicans; either would be heavily favored to beat me in the next election. I had lost once in a statewide election. What reason was there to believe that I wouldn't lose again? My mind raced with uncertainty.

"Why don't you think about it, George, then call me back? But there's not much time. He's going to make a decision soon and announce it next week. I think you should do this. Let me tell him that you're interested."

When Sally returned home later that afternoon, I told her about the call. As I had anticipated, she preferred that I not consider the Senate. Although there were other stresses in our marriage, unrelated to politics, we had a life that overall was good and comfortable. But, as had happened before, she said she'd go along with it if that's what I wanted. She was insistent, however, that no matter what happened, she would not move to Washington. She had been there once, and she didn't like it. In addition Andrea was about to turn fifteen and was in her first year of high school. So we agreed that if I was appointed they would stay in South Portland and I would commute to Washington.

That evening I called Shep. I wasn't sure

this was a serious inquiry. I didn't know (and never will) who, if anyone, in the governor's office Shep had talked to, or whether this was his own initiative. But in the end, all of the uncertainty and all of the obstacles were outweighed by the opportunity. In life risk is unavoidable. I told Shep to let the governor know I was interested.

Word spread quickly. Within twenty-four hours I received calls from two friends who urged me not to get involved. One thought he was being considered and said candidly that he'd have a better chance if I was out of the picture. Our discussion was friendly, with a lot of good-natured banter. The other caller said he'd heard I was going to be chosen because Muskie had "forced" me on Brennan. I told him that anyone who believed that didn't know the governor. I knew Joe Brennan well, and of one thing I was absolutely certain: he would make up his own mind. While he would seek and listen to advice, in the end it would be his choice, for his reasons.

Then the governor called. I had known him for nearly twenty years. I had worked for him in the District Attorney's Office, and we had run against each other in a primary election. The conversation was brief and cordial. He wanted to talk to me about the Senate. We agreed to meet and did so soon afterward. He was direct and to the point. He said he would appoint me to the Senate for one reason, and one reason only: "I think you can do the best job for the people of Maine." He passed on to me the request from Muskie that I keep on as many members of his staff as possible. He then paused, looked me straight in the eye, and said, "I have only one request of you." I braced myself. I had no idea what he might want from me. "What is it?" He replied, speaking slowly to give emphasis to his words. "I ask only that you do the best you can for the people of Maine and the nation based on your conscience and your best judgment. I will never ask you for anything else." And he never did. Not once, ever, did he ask or suggest or hint that I vote a certain way, act a certain way, or speak a certain way. I left that meeting confirmed in my belief in his integrity. My conscience and my best judgment! I was impressed by what he asked for and relieved that he hadn't asked for anything else. I also left with a deep determination to succeed, for him as well as for myself. I was keenly aware that he was taking an enormous political risk in appointing me. The governor would be up for reelection in two years and right there at the top of the ticket with him would be his appointee to the Senate, seeking election to a full term in his own right. The governor's own reelection could be affected by my performance. I was determined not to let him down.

It was widely reported, and even more widely assumed, that Senator Muskie had urged Governor Brennan to appoint me to the Senate. There were obvious reasons for that. I had served on Muskie's Senate staff and had taken leaves of absence from my law firm to work on his campaigns for vice president and president. He had helped me to become U.S. attorney and then U.S. District Court judge. We had a very close and warm relationship. But the reports and the assumptions were wrong. Muskie had urged Brennan to appoint Ken Curtis, and he would have been justified in feeling that he had done more than enough for me. But he had other reasons, consistent with his lifelong practice of always trying to do the right thing. I was a federal judge. Curtis was not then holding any public office. By any reasonable standard Curtis appeared to be a much stronger candidate than I. And on the most important issue of all, Curtis had served as governor for eight years and before that as secretary of state of Maine; he could be expected to more quickly adjust to the demands of the Senate than I and more effectively represent the people of Maine. Muskie genuinely and rationally believed that Curtis was the best choice for the position. Had Brennan agreed, his decision would have been widely accepted and applauded. But while deeply respectful of Muskie, Brennan, as always, made his own decision. Unlike Muskie, who knew me only as a member of his staff, Brennan had seen me close up as a candidate in a political campaign. As a result he saw something that few others did: the possibility that the widespread view of me as a political loser might not be correct, that I might be able to do a good job as a senator and be an effective candidate for election to a full term.

ELIZABETH TAYLOR'S HUSBAND

When I entered the Senate in May 1980 it had been in session for five months. Although I had worked there as an aide to Senator Muskie, nearly two decades earlier, I had never personally experienced a filibuster. Not long after I arrived one occurred. Curious, I went to the Senate chamber at the appointed hour and took my seat. I was surprised to see that I was the only senator there. After several minutes another senator entered. He stood, was recognized by the presiding officer, and began to speak. He then spoke for a long time. He was followed by another senator who did the same thing, and then another. I spent several hours in my seat, listening. I eventually realized that I wasn't learning anything, so it was well after midnight when I walked over to a Senate aide standing by the door to the chamber.

"Excuse me," I said, "I'm new here."

Before I could go on he said, "Senator, that's obvious to everyone." Undaunted, I asked him where all the other senators were. "Where did they go? What do they do during a filibuster?" I asked.

"They're doing the sensible thing. They're sleeping," he said. "Come on, I'll show you." With that, as I followed, he walked out the door, took a few steps, and entered a large darkened room. There, to my astonishment, I saw, spread out, many canvas folding cots of the type I associated with emergency shelters. On the cots were United States senators: all male, all sleeping, mostly elderly and snoring. "There," the clerk said, pointing, "There's an empty cot in the middle. You'd better grab it." There were no aisles, so to get to the empty cot I had to climb over other senators. The first was Ted Kennedy. He was a big man, and at that moment he looked to me like Mount Everest. But, slowly and carefully, I got over him without waking him up. I finally made it to the empty cot and as I lay down I began to have second thoughts about having given up a federal judgeship for the Senate. I had been a dignified person in a black robe; now, here I was, lying on a narrow, uncomfortable cot in my suit with a bunch of old men in suits, while a few senators spent the whole night on the Senate floor talking but saying little. I began to feel a sense of regret, even self-pity, when I rolled over on the cot and looked, on the next cot, directly into the sleeping face of Senator John Warner of Virginia. He then was married to Elizabeth Taylor. After a few minutes of wallowing in self-pity I thought, "Who am I to feel sorry for myself? There, just a few inches away from me is a man who could be home, legally in bed with Elizabeth Taylor, but who instead is spending the night with me." At that moment I recalled what we all know to be true: No matter how bad off you may think you are, somebody is worse off. You can waste your time in self-pity, or you can do something about whatever problems you face. Then and there, I decided that's what I would do. I haven't felt any self-pity since, thanks to John Warner, who I hadn't then met but who was a very capable senator and later became a good and valued friend.

ELECTION TO THE SENATE

My appointment to the Senate in 1980 and my election to a full Senate term in 1982 represented peaks of success, but there was a long and very deep valley between them. It was a time of testing and near despair. My problems burst into full public view almost exactly a year after I was appointed. In early May 1981 most of Maine's newspapers ran prominent articles on a public opinion poll commissioned by Congressman David Emery, which showed that in an election to the Senate he would defeat me by 36 percentage points (61 to 25). One not very subtle headline said of me, "He has no chance to win." Emery had been elected to the House of Representatives in 1974, when he was in his twenties, following two terms in the Maine Legislature. He had never lost an election. Maine's other representative in Congress, Olympia Snowe, also had served in the Maine Legislature before her election in 1978 to the House. She too had never lost an election. She immediately responded to Emery by announcing her interest in the Republican nomination for the Senate, and she released a poll she had commissioned: it showed her defeating me by 31 percentage points. In the matchup with me, Snowe's poll was as disturbing as Emery's. But her poll went further; to emphasize the extent of my political weakness it included a matchup of Curtis and me. While the margin was less, the result was even more negative: among Democrats in a primary election Curtis would beat me by 22 points (57 to 35). In what the press labeled the battle of the polls, Emery fired back two days later with more information from his poll. Not surprisingly it affirmed that he would be a very strong candidate, heavily favored to trounce me in the general election. The battle of the polls triggered a series of newspaper articles and other political commentaries about me and my political prospects, almost all of which were heavily negative.[1]

The other members of Maine's delegation to Congress — Emery, Snowe, and Senator Bill Cohen — were Republicans, but in our work there were few partisan differences. We were a small delegation from a small state, so we knew we had to concentrate on Maine issues of common interest and work together. As a result, on a personal level, I developed a good relationship with each of them. There were of course some disagreements and misunderstandings, but none was significant enough, individually or collectively, to adversely affect our overall relationships. Obviously, because we served in the Senate, I saw and worked with Cohen more often; we got along so well that a few years later we wrote a book together.[2] But my relationship with Emery and Snowe was good enough that I knew it would complicate the upcoming campaign.

In June I got a slight reprieve when Snowe announced that she would not seek the Republication nomination to the Senate. Emery had argued successfully that it was "his turn" because he had entered the House before Snowe. The view that either Snowe or Emery would easily defeat me gained wide acceptance. One reporter who covered Washington for Maine newspapers asked to see me for personal reasons. He was somber but kind as he expressed what amounted to his condolences. It took me a few minutes to realize that he was speaking about me in the past tense: "You have nothing to be ashamed of, you've done your best, and I'm sure there's still a good future for you somewhere in Maine." I tried to lift the gloom by saying, "In a sense I feel privileged because not many people get to hear the eulogies at their funeral." We both laughed, but after he left the gloom stayed with me.

Although I didn't realize it at the time I hit rock bottom in September, when Ken Curtis announced that he had established an exploratory committee for his candidacy for the Senate. His argument was simple and direct: I was such a weak candidate, certain to lose, that Democrats needed to replace me with a candidate who had a chance to win. He had twice been elected governor; I had run for governor and lost. To emphasize his point he released yet another poll; it confirmed Snowe's poll that in a Democratic primary election he would beat me easily.

I had been discouraged by the Emery and Snowe polls, but I was devastated by Curtis's announcement. A fellow Democrat, a truly close friend I liked and admired and with whom I had worked for twenty years, he gave public expression to the doubts and fears of many Maine Democrats, and his poll was itself more evidence of my political weakness. The doubts and fears increased.

But so did my determination. On September 30, Curtis's committee distributed to all Democratic members of the legislature and all members of the Democratic State Committee a memorandum making the case for his candidacy. It cited the poll numbers that had previously been made public, then added other supportive information. I braced for a rush away from me and toward Curtis. To my surprise it didn't happen. A few expressed their support for him, but most held their fire, at least publicly. It may have been faint, but I still had a political pulse.

I had been working hard, but to deal with my many problems I could think of nothing other than to work harder. When the Senate was in session I attended and participated in every committee meeting, studied every bill, met every constituent. My time in Maine, on weekends and during congressional recesses, became a whirlwind of school and factory visits, service club luncheons, church bean suppers, and private and political meetings of every kind.

I had been shocked by the findings of the polls, and several newspaper reports, that a large number of voters didn't know who I was. They weren't unfavorable; they simply had no impression or opinion of me. In desperation I tried to connect favorably with as many as I could. I announced that I would meet personally with any Maine citizen who requested a meeting. I began the process of traveling to my field offices around the state on weekends and during congressional recesses. There I spent hours meeting one-on-one (with one staffer present to take notes) with anyone who asked. A few were cranky, a few came just for the pleasure of telling me what a jerk I was (there were other even more unfavorable and unprintable phrases). A few brought up pending legislation. But the overwhelming majority were serious and sincere, intensely personal, often hurting and aggrieved by some adversity. Many had lost their jobs. As I listened to their stories, my mind returned to my father's year of unemployment; my heart ached for him, and for them. It was a sobering experience for me. After every round of meetings I thought, "And I think I've got problems!" I was forced to stop thinking about myself, to stop feeling sorry for myself. My resolve and determination to win increased, in part to be able to do what I could for the people who poured out their problems and their hearts to me.

When I started this process it was not especially demanding because not that many people were interested in meeting with me. But, as time passed and I got better known, the number of requests steadily increased. Then, after I was elected majority leader, they shot up exponentially. As a result, those seeking a meeting had longer waits, as the list grew ever longer and the number of days on which I could hold meetings declined. Despite the difficulties, I was determined to maintain the effort, and did so, to the very end of my tenure in the Senate.

Another practice I adopted was to have my staff select each day several of the most negative letters I'd received from Maine. I read each letter carefully, then from my office in the evening I telephoned each of the letter writers. Almost everyone I reached was surprised and many doubted that it really was their senator calling. Once I was able to convince them that the call was genuine, I told them that I had read their letter, that while we disagreed I welcomed their views and appreciated that they had taken the time to write to me. With a few exceptions the conversations were polite and civil. Later, while travelling in Maine, I was approached by many people who had received such calls and wanted to meet me in person. Unfortunately, I was not able to continue this practice after I became majority leader. The burden of managing the Senate, which then met often in the evening, was too great. I still tried to read the negative letters from Maine but couldn't make the calls. To my surprise, I missed them.

My father had told me that hard work could solve any problem. I was now putting his words to the test. All of that activity came at the expense of time with my family, of course, and created for Sally an inner tension. She resented the description of me as a loser and very much wanted me to win. But she despised politics and what I had to do if I were to have any chance to win. We did our best to accommodate each other, but there was no mistaking the increase in stress.

Working hard was not a problem for me, but fundraising was. I found it difficult and demeaning and, as a result, was not very good at it. As the cascade of bad news continued, even accelerated, fundraising became even more difficult. Two events forced me to change my approach; they were far apart in geography and context but similar in result. One was a modest event, held on a Sunday afternoon at a farm in rural northern Maine. I didn't expect a large crowd at the farm of the friendly, supportive young couple, and my expectations were met. Fewer than ten people attended, and the only contributors were the hosts. I shrugged it off. In campaigns some things work and some don't. The other event was to be a Sunday brunch in Beverly Hills. Soon I would be in sunny California, the land of big bucks.

When Senator Muskie ran for president in 1972 one of his strong supporters was Paul Ziffren, a prominent and politically active lawyer in Los Angeles. I did not have a close relationship with Ziffren but hoped that the Muskie connection would help. However, when I called and asked him to host a fundraising event for me, he declined, pointing out, quite logically, that he didn't know me well and that there already were too many events scheduled that fall. In desperation I asked Muskie to call Ziffren and urge him to reconsider. With obvious reluctance, Ziffren agreed, and a Sunday brunch in October was scheduled. I flew to Los Angeles on Saturday evening. The brunch was scheduled for eleven in the morning, and Paul was to pick me up at my hotel at quarter to eleven. The phone rang a few minutes before then. He was calling from the lobby. I said I'd be right down. No, he said, stay in your room and I'll be right up, I want to talk to you. I knew something was wrong. He came in, we sat down, and there was no small talk. "I'm sorry to have to tell you that there won't be a brunch today."

I said nothing and tried to hide my growing anxiety as he continued. "I sent out one hundred forty-five invitations and no one accepted. Not one." I felt very bad, for him and for me. He was obviously embarrassed and tried to be positive. "Scoop is having a brunch in Beverly Hills at noon. That's one of the reasons we got no response. But I talked to him this morning and he's willing to let you come to his function and introduce him. That way you can meet a few contributors and maybe, if you're lucky, you can come back next year and try again."

"Scoop" was Senator Henry Jackson of Washington state, a well-known and highly regarded member of the Senate. He had run unsuccessfully for president in 1972. He and Muskie had fought a committee turf battle earlier and were not close. Jackson was relieved when Muskie left the Senate, and he treated me very well, in part, I assumed, because I wasn't Muskie. Although Ziffren was trying to be helpful in a difficult situation I didn't see the offer as significant. To spend two days flying to the West Coast and back just to speak at another senator's fundraiser, at a time when I was desperate for campaign funds, didn't strike me as good use of my time. As I looked at Ziffren I saw the face of my high school basketball coach telling me that I didn't make the tournament team. I choked back my hurt, my anger, my welling feeling of despair and said simply, "Thanks, Paul. I appreciate your effort." I did appreciate it, even though I knew that very few political fundraising events succeed if all that's done is to mail invitations. The reality of course was that Paul hardly knew me and had agreed to host the event only to accommodate the senator he genuinely and strongly cared about.

Ziffren got up and walked across the room. Just as he reached the door he turned and said to me, slowly and sadly, "I do have two checks, from me and my wife. They'll pay for your airfare." I smiled weakly, took the checks, shook his hand, and thanked him again. It really wasn't his fault. I had put him in this awkward position. I would still need others to help me, but I had to do more, lots more, on my own.

It was another in a series of painful lessons. If I really wanted to be elected to the Senate I had to shed my reluctance about fundraising. Right or wrong, it was how the system worked. I had wanted the honor of the Senate without having to do all of the unpleasant but necessary work to get there. I now knew I could not have the one without the other. If I was going to raise enough money to make this a competitive race I would have to ask others, including complete strangers, for money, directly and aggressively. That's what I did. And gradually the money started coming in.

Larry Benoit turned the campaign around. He had earlier worked for a member of the House of Representatives, then for Senator Muskie. When I replaced Muskie I inherited Larry and the rest of Muskie's staff. Now he was on leave from my staff and running my campaign. Larry had run several campaigns and knew Maine politics well. I liked and trusted him. Alarmed by the parlous state of affairs he proposed a simple but striking strategy: we would have to start a television advertising campaign one year before the election. In the round-the-calendar campaigns of the twenty-first century, early advertising is not new or daring, but in 1981 it was not widespread. The conventional wisdom then was that voters didn't focus on political campaigns until after Labor Day of the election year; any advertising before that was wasted. Besides

213

the conventional wisdom was the harsh reality that we hadn't raised much money, so even if we went ahead with a television buy it wouldn't be large, and when it ended, our campaign coffers would be empty. Larry argued, insistently and persuasively, that these objections were irrelevant when measured against the near certainty of defeat if we continued the course we were on. "We can't make up thirty-six points between Labor Day and the election. We need a year for that." The hope was that a brief, early television campaign would attract enough attention and money to repeat and expand it in January or February, and so on, to victory in the election.

The first ad was broadcast more than a year before the election. The effect was instantaneous. It may be a sad commentary, but it is a fact that many people equate political campaigns with television advertising. If you're on the air, you're campaigning; if you're not on the air, you're nowhere. Just days after the first ad appeared, several people I encountered commented on it. Especially to active Democrats it was a statement that I was going to put up a fight, no matter how slim my chances appeared to be. Then several events occurred that collectively reversed the trajectory of the campaign. Fundraising picked up, just as Larry had predicted, the result of the appearance of a real campaign and a more personal and aggressive effort by me. In November Curtis suffered a mild heart attack and a month later quietly abandoned his effort. He had been disappointed, and I had been heartened, by the absence of a rush to his side. I regretted his health problem but was delighted by his decision. The prospect of running against him in a primary was extremely unpleasant. He had been an effective and courageous governor. We were close friends and had worked together for many years. The differences between us on the issues were minor, which meant that a campaign would have turned on personal matters. Fortunately our friendship endured and continues to this day.

As 1981 came to a close, I felt surprisingly good for a candidate who was still far behind in the polls. I had survived a half year of setbacks and bad news. The field on both sides had been cleared. The general election campaign would begin several months earlier than anyone had anticipated. The press and public now had nearly a year to focus on two men: David Emery and me.

In January we ran another round of television ads. Although it was a modest buy, it produced another good result. I didn't want to delude myself, but I sensed and believed that we were starting to close the gap. Once it became clear that Emery and I would be the candidates, we were deluged with invitations to appear jointly before groups and organizations in Maine. I accepted every one I could, consistent with the Senate schedule. They weren't exactly the Lincoln-Douglas debates, but we offered our contrasting views and answered questions. Many of these joint appearances went well for me. Even before heavily Republican audiences I held my own. With each successful event my confidence grew, so I wasn't surprised when Emery began to decline more and more of the invitations for joint appearances, opting to campaign on his own. Much earlier he had challenged me to several formal broadcast debates. The first, held in June, went well for me, as did the rest of them.

But there were surprises. One came in late June, when I had a good feeling about the way the campaign was going. I had just finished speaking to a small crowd in a coastal town when a gray-haired man stood up and asked, in a loud and belligerent voice, "Why are you against veterans?" I was startled by the question. "What are you talking about?" I asked back. "I'm not against veterans." "Yes you are," he shouted. "I've got proof right here," and he waved a document in the air. He walked to the front of the room and handed it to me. It was titled "Special Report to Maine Veterans," mailed by Emery's Senate campaign to every Maine veteran of military service. Right at the top of the front page, just below his name and directly across from his photograph, a box enclosed the message "DAVE EMERY/ GEORGE MITCHELL check the ratings, there is a difference! Veterans of Foreign Wars EMERY 92% MITCHELL 0%."

"It just can't be," I protested. I was a veteran; Emery was not. I served on the Veterans Affairs Committee; Emery did not. I had spent my two years in the Senate working diligently on measures to improve health care for veterans (a cause I continued to work on through my entire tenure in the Senate). I was baffled, angry, fearful. I couldn't understand how it could be true. But what if it was? Surely Emery would not have said it if it weren't true. I had no idea how the VFW rated members of Congress. I took a few more questions but ended the meeting as soon as I could. I called Larry Benoit, told him what had happened, and asked him to look into it immediately. He was as surprised as I was. "That can't be right," he said, as he pledged to get an answer as soon as possible.

I've always had trouble getting to sleep. I still do. On that night I couldn't get to sleep at all. My mind was a jumble of conflicting thoughts as I tried to remember votes I had cast on issues important to veterans. Try as I might I couldn't recall a single vote, a single statement, a single action of any kind that would be condemned by any veterans organization. And yet there it was, in black and white: 92 percent for Emery, zero for me.

It was early the next afternoon when Larry called me back. I was somewhat relieved by the fact that he began by saying, with a chuckle, "You're not going to believe this." The Political Action Committee of the VFW had published a pamphlet evaluating the voting record of every member in the 95th and 96th Congress. The votes they selected occurred between January 1977 and June 1980: before I entered the Senate! As the report itself made clear, I wasn't even in the Senate when the votes were cast.

There are lots of exaggerations and misrepresentations in political campaigns. But this was different. This was a serious allegation that was totally false. I liked Emery and found it hard to believe that he knew about it, although it also was hard to believe that a candidate would not have seen a document that his campaign had mailed to tens of thousands of households all over the state. Whatever the case was with Emery, I knew that for my own sake I had to reach everyone who had received and read the document. If his allegation went unchallenged, I really would have no chance to win.

I did not have a mailing list of veterans, so Larry and my staff drafted a statement, which was released publicly, pointing out and criticizing the error and asking Emery to correct it in another mailing. Although almost all of Maine's daily newspapers then leaned Republican, they were for the most part fair and reasonable, and they quickly published editorials critical of Emery, which we in turn distributed widely. Emery blamed the error on his staff, and they at first tried to minimize it, calling it an honest mistake. But after much criticism from the press and public he said he would make a correction in another mailing. As it turned out he didn't produce another mailing until just before the election, and in it he didn't correct the earlier false statement. But by then it didn't make any difference. Although there were many more charges and countercharges, dueling TV ads, and some uneasy moments, the tide turned decisively in my favor. On election day I received 61 percent of the vote.

I was in a car with Sally, being driven to Lewiston for an election eve party, when the polls closed at eight o'clock. On the car radio we listened to the audio of the local NBC television affiliate and heard Tom Brokaw proclaim me the winner. I was happy for Sally as well as for myself. Despite her genuine and often stated distaste for politics, she badly wanted me to win and had even participated in a few campaign events. I felt as though a huge weight had been lifted off my shoulders. I made a brief appearance in Lewiston, then we returned to Portland to attend a similar event there. The crowd was large and boisterous and there were so many people on the stage I had a hard time climbing up and squeezing in behind the lectern, which was packed with microphones. Just as I got there my brother Johnny grabbed and hugged me. He was one of the greatest and best-known athletes in Maine history; famous for his high-arcing shots that dropped through the net with a swishing sound, he was universally known as the Swisher. The cameras clicked and whirred. The next day the *Portland Evening Express* carried the picture of me and my "unidentified supporter." Since then, whenever I'm asked to describe the most enjoyable event of my political life, I refer to that picture: I'm in the spotlight, and the Swisher is an unidentified supporter. Gone were my high school basketball coach, those Portland law firms that wouldn't even talk to me, the pollster who said I had no chance to win, the Beverly Hills noncrowd. Now, in a role reversal I could never have imagined, the Swisher was cheering me on. On the many occasions on which I remind Johnny of that evening we both laugh with pleasure.

A CHRISTMAS DECISION

Christmas 1982 was a time for celebration and reflection. My next birthday would be my fiftieth. In the previous month I had won election to a full term in the Senate, despite having trailed in the polls and having been counted out by many people. I looked forward to the next six years with enthusiasm and was certain that I could have a productive and long career in the Senate. Yet even as I planned for the future, I wondered if serving in the Senate for the rest of my life was really what I wanted. As I talked about it with Sally during a few long and quiet evenings at home over Christmas, my doubts grew. Her unhappiness with public life was part of my concern, but that wasn't new. My own doubts were.

Having worked in the Senate for Ed Muskie for three years and served as a senator for nearly that long, I had seen the institution close up. There's much, with which most people are familiar, to commend it. Not as well known, at least then, is how totally the Senate consumes its members. For two and a half years I had worked long hours, seven days a week. Getting elected to a full term became the overwhelming focus of my life. Fundraising took more and more of my time. During the 1982 campaign I had become more aggressive and adept at asking for money. But the better I got, the more I disliked it. And I was dismayed to learn that it required a permanent, ongoing effort. Six-year terms for senators didn't provide relief from the money chase; it meant just the opposite: six years of fundraising! I was too busy attending fundraising events and making fundraising calls to even read books, instead spending what little reading time I had on an unending stream of briefing papers.

When I returned to Washington in January 1983, I felt that I should not try to spend the rest of my working life in the Senate. I didn't know exactly when, but I knew that at some point I would term-limit myself. I would leave while the people of Maine wanted me to stay rather than wait until they asked me to leave.

IRAN-CONTRA

Oliver North sat at the witness table, erect in his Marine colonel's uniform, his chest gleaming with ribbons and medals. He was appearing before a Select Committee of Congress, a joint Senate-House body established to investigate the controversy over the provision of missiles to Iran and aid to the so-called contras in Nicaragua by some members of the Reagan administration. Beside him sat his skillful and combative lawyer, Brendan Sullivan, who had spent the past week lecturing any member of the Committee who dared to challenge his hero-client. In a single week that strategy had transformed North from the potential fall guy in a national security fiasco to a television star and national icon, praised effusively by his many supporters for standing up to communists and congressmen. He was a man of action against men of words, and it was no contest.

Or was it?

While most viewers saw the medals on North's chest, few noted that as he raised his right hand to be sworn in as a witness, the Committee's chairman, Senator Daniel Inouye, raised his left arm as he administered the oath. His right arm had been buried in the hills of central Italy, where he lost it while serving as an infantryman in World War II. Yet North's fervent supporters glorified him as a hero and pilloried Inouye. Few then could know that North's testimony, which so dominated the news and captivated the public, included many false statements. In a bold move he not only admitted that he lied; he boasted about it. He had to lie, he said, to save lives. But that too was a lie.[3]

By the time it was my turn to question him he was a national sensation. Acting on advice from my good friend Harold Pachios, a skillful Maine lawyer, I decided not to engage North on his false statements but to concentrate on an important principle. As Harold put it, "North said today that you guys should vote aid for the Contras for the love of God and country. That's outrageous. It's insulting. You can take that and turn it around. Not only can you do it, you have to do it." That's what I did. Other than my announcement eleven years later that a peace agreement had been reached in Northern Ireland, it was perhaps the most widely watched and publicized statement I ever made.

You have talked here often eloquently about the need for a democratic outcome in Nicaragua. There's no disagreement on that. There is disagreement over how best to achieve that objective. Many Americans agree with the President's policy; many do not. Many patriotic Americans, strongly anti-communist, believe there's a better way to contain the Sandinistas, to bring about a democratic outcome in Nicaragua and to bring peace to Central America.

Many patriotic Americans are concerned that in the pursuit of democracy abroad we not compromise it in any way here at home. You and others have urged consistency in our policies, you have said repeatedly that if we are not consistent our allies and other nations will question our reliability. That is a real concern. But if it's bad to change policies, it's worse to have two different policies at the same time; one public policy and an opposite policy in private. It's difficult to conceive of a greater inconsistency than that. It's hard to imagine anything that would give our allies more cause to consider us unreliable than that we say one thing in public and secretly do the opposite. And that's exactly what was done when arms were sold to Iran and arms were swapped for hostages.

Now, you have talked a lot about patriotism and the love of our country. Most nations derive from a single tribe, a single race; they practice a single religion. Common racial, ethnic, and religious heritages are the glue of nationhood for many. The United States is different; we have all races, all religions, we have a limited common heritage. The glue of nationhood for us is the American ideal of individual liberty and equal justice. The rule of law is critical in our society. It's the great equalizer, because in America everybody is equal before the law. We must never allow the end to justify the means where the law is concerned. However important and noble an objective, and surely democracy abroad is important and is noble, it cannot be achieved at the expense of the rule of law of our country. . . .

Now, you have addressed several pleas to this committee, very eloquently. None more eloquent than last Friday when in response to a question by Representative Cheney you asked that Congress not cut off aid to the contras for the love of God and for the love of country. I now address a plea to you. Of all the qualities which the American people find compelling about you, none is more impressive than your obvious deep devotion to this country. Please remember that others share that devotion and recognize that it is possible for an American to disagree with you on aid to the contras and still love God and still love this country just as much as you do.

Although He's regularly asked to do so, God does not take sides in American politics. And in America, disagreement with the policies of the government is not evidence of lack of patriotism.

I want to repeat that: In America, disagreement with the policies of the government is not evidence of lack of patriotism.

Indeed, it is the very fact that Americans can criticize their government openly and without fear of reprisal that is the essence of our freedom, and that will keep us free.

I have one final plea. Debate this issue forcefully and vigorously as you have and as you surely will, but, please, do it in a way that respects the patriotism and the motives of those who disagree with you, as you would have them respect yours.[4]

The response was immediate and overwhelming. Before I finished speaking, every line in every one of my offices was busy. By the thousands they came in, first the telephone calls, then the telegrams, then the letters. Most were favorable. The unfavorable, although few in number, were intense in their hostility.

I felt at ease. I don't think I dented Ollie North's image one bit. I'm sure the supportive comments to him far outnumbered those I received. But at least I got across a different point of view, one worth restating: although He is regularly asked to do so, God does not take sides in American politics, and in America disagreement with the policies of the government is not evidence of lack of patriotism.

Lawrence Walsh, a former federal judge, was appointed independent counsel to investigate the Iran-Contra affair to determine whether any criminal action had occurred. Ultimately he brought criminal charges against fourteen participants.[5] Eleven were convicted, either after trial or on pleas of guilty.[6] On December 24, 1992, five years after the Committee had concluded its hearings, George H. W. Bush, now president, granted pardons to six defendants; four of them had previously been convicted,[7] while two more were awaiting trial.[8] In defense of these six pardons, Bush stated, "[The] common denominator of their motivation — whether their actions were right or wrong — was patriotism." He criticized the years-long investigation run by Walsh as reflective of "what I believe is a profoundly troubling development in the political and legal climate of our country: the criminalization of policy differences."[9]

Walsh released a response: "[The] pardon[s] . . . undermine the principle that no man is above the law. It demonstrates that powerful people with powerful allies can commit serious crimes in high office — deliberately abusing the public trust without consequence." He concluded, "The Iran-Contra cover-up, which has continued for more than six years, has now been completed."[10]

Although Democrats were in the majority in both the Senate and the House, the Select Committee inquiry was conducted in a largely nonpartisan manner. Inouye insisted that the ranking Republican senator on the Committee, Warren Rudman of New Hampshire, be named and function as vice chairman instead of simply ranking minority member. This had significant implications: in Inouye's absence, Rudman, not the Democratic senator next in seniority to Inouye, would chair the Committee. Senator Inouye and Representative Lee Hamilton, an Indiana Democrat who was the House chairman of the Committee, treated the Office of the President, and President Reagan personally, with careful consideration, even deference.[11]

On March 4, 1987, in a nationally televised address, President Reagan said, "A few months ago I told the American people I did not trade arms for hostages. My heart and my best intentions still tell me that's true, but the facts and the evidence tell me it is not."[12] In the immediate aftermath of the Iran-Contra disclosures his approval rating fell sharply, from 67 to 46 percent. However, by the time he left office two years later, his rating had recovered to 64 percent.

The Iran-Contra affair was complex and involved several strands, each in its own way dramatic, especially, in light of current events, the secret sale of missiles to Iran by the Reagan administration. Even as the president was saying publicly that he would not negotiate with terrorists to obtain the release of hostages, his aides were doing precisely that, in the end secretly sending missiles to Iran.

But looking back twenty-five years later, my dominant impression of the affair is how thoroughly the process was permeated by false testimony. As a former U.S. attorney and federal district court judge, I am sadly familiar with the reality that the oath to tell the truth is not always honored. But the massive scale of false testimony in the Iran-Contra hearings exceeded anything of which I was previously aware. To his credit, Oliver North at least admitted that he lied. Many of the other participants made statements that in retrospect can only be described as deliberately false and misleading. There were many victims of Iran-Contra, but none more so than the Truth.

DIVORCE AND REMARRIAGE

In March 1987 Sally and I were divorced. It was uncontested, by mutual agreement. During the seven years of my service in the Senate we had drifted further and further apart. In a sense, as I became more public she became more private, increasingly reluctant to participate in public events. We also had other differences that had nothing to do with politics. The concern we shared about the effect of divorce on Andrea no longer seemed relevant, as she was on the verge of graduating from college. Following the divorce Sally and I remained friendly and in regular communication. For several years thereafter we spent the Thanksgiving and Christmas holidays together with Andrea, and I regularly visited her when in Maine. Her health gradually declined, and she passed away in October 2003.

In July 1993 I received a telephone call from Andy Garcia Jr., an uncle of the prominent actor of the same name. We had met twenty years earlier in Key Biscayne, a beautiful island just outside of Miami. Andy was born in Tampa to immigrants from Cuba. When he was still a boy his family returned to Cuba, where he lived for several years before coming back to Florida for good. He became a lawyer and a professional tennis player. After he retired from active competition he became a tennis coach and teacher on Key Biscayne, and he ran a family produce business that operated throughout southern and central Florida. We met when I visited my sister and her husband, Eddie Atkins, at the home they bought on Key Biscayne in the early 1970s. I was in my forties and had just taken up tennis. Andy taught me the game and encouraged me to continue. I've been playing ever since.

On the day he called I was at my desk in the majority leader's office. After brief pleasantries he got to the point of his call: he asked that I meet with a delegation of Romanian officials, led by Ion Tiriac, a former professional tennis player, now a successful businessman in Bucharest. Tiriac had been trying for some time to get an appointment with me. Frustrated, he had called his friend Andy because he heard that

Andy and I were friends. I asked why Tiriac wanted to see me. Andy wasn't sure. "But," he said, "Ion's a good guy. I'm sure it's important, so please give him a few minutes." I agreed, and within a few days Tiriac brought a delegation of Romanian businessmen and officials to my office.

After the death of the dictator Nicolae Ceausescu and the overthrow of his communist government, the people of Romania were trying to create democratic institutions. Their economy, which had functioned poorly under Ceausescu, had declined further in the turbulence of revolutionary change. They wanted and needed better relations and increased trade with the United States and other Western countries. The first critical step was to gain Most Favored Nation trading status with us. The designation, which suggests preference, is a misnomer. As a member of the Soviet bloc Romania had been subject to trade restrictions. Most Favored Nation status meant only the removal of those restrictions and the establishment of normal commercial relations with the United States. But to achieve that status legislation had to be enacted by Congress and signed into law by the president. The Romanians told me that the president and the State Department supported the legislation, but it was tied up in the Senate, for reasons they could not determine. Could I help to move the legislation forward? I asked a member of my staff who had attended the meeting to look into the matter and report to me. She did so the next day. There was no problem with the legislation; it was supported by the administration and was unopposed in the Senate. It had been delayed simply because the Foreign Relations Committee staff was overloaded with this and other matters and had not yet had a chance to schedule and act on it. In view of my staff member's inquiry the committee would move the bill; it wouldn't take much time or effort.

A few days later the bill was included in a long list of routine and noncontroversial matters that was approved by the Senate late in the evening, after most senators had gone home. Typically the majority and minority leaders (or occasionally their designees) stand in the well of the Senate and go through the approval process for such matters, all of which have been cleared by every member of the Senate. Then the leaders shut down the Senate and go home. It was very late when I left the Capitol building and stepped into a muggy Washington night. As I reached for the door handle of my waiting car I heard someone say my name. Surprised, I turned to see a group of the Romanians walking toward me. They had waited outside the Capitol to thank me. I was touched by the gesture and told them candidly that I really hadn't done much, that it eventually would have been approved anyway. They didn't believe me, or at least they pretended not to believe me, and the expressions of gratitude grew longer, louder, and more fulsome. Finally I told them I really had to go to bed, jumped into the backseat of the car, and sped off.

The next day I received a phone call from Tiriac in which he again thanked me. He then said that Andy had told him that I played tennis. He offered to set up a match for me with Ilie Nastase, who was going to be in Washington the next week. Those who follow tennis know Nastase as a former professional tennis player from Romania, a colorful figure who was one of the most talented men ever to play the game. A doubles match was set up, and we played late in the evening, under lights. For a beginner like me it was a lot of fun to play with Nastase and others whose talents were far superior to mine. Ilie and I subsequently became friends. Afterward Tiriac, who watched but didn't play in the match, asked if I would be interested in tickets to the U.S. Open tournament, which was scheduled to start in New York in a few weeks. I thanked him but declined his offer. He then gave me the phone number for the U.S. office of his company, which was based in Europe. The company served as a manager and business agent for professional players and also owned and operated tournaments in Europe.

I had already arranged to go to the semifinals and finals of the Open and a few weeks later did so with a group of friends, one of whom was my brother Paul. After the semifinals on Saturday, as we were having dinner, one of my friends said that he'd gotten a phone call from an associate of his who, along with a companion, was in New York for the weekend and would like to go to the finals the next day. Did I know how they could get tickets? I told him I didn't, this was my first Open and I didn't know anyone here. The conversation moved on to other subjects. We were staying at different hotels, and as we parted after dinner, we agreed to meet the next morning for breakfast at my hotel.

On the way down to breakfast I suddenly remembered my conversation with Tiriac. I had written the number he gave me in a small notebook I carried with me. I told my friend about it at breakfast. We agreed that the chances of getting tickets were slim since it was nine o'clock on a Sunday morning and the final match was just a few hours away, but he asked me to try anyway.

I went back to my room and dialed the number. A woman answered. I explained why I was calling, and she said simply that she would see what could be done. Thirty minutes later there was a knock on the door, and a hotel clerk handed me an envelope with my name on it; inside were two tickets to that day's final match. Attached to the tickets was the business card of Heather MacLachlan. I was amazed and impressed. My friend picked up the tickets and gave them to his friends. I never met them; to this day I don't know who used those tickets. We then headed to the tournament to root for Pete Sampras, the young American who was playing in the finals.

We arrived early at the stadium, where we met and had a pleasant chat with Nastase. He invited us to join him for lunch at one of the many private lounges that operate at major tennis tournaments. As we entered the lounge and walked toward a table, we encountered a tall, very attractive woman with long black hair. Ilie spoke to her in

French, then turned to me and said, "This is Heather MacLachlan." For the second time that day I was amazed and impressed. As we shook hands I thanked her for the speed and efficiency with which she'd arranged delivery of the tickets. She modestly said it was nothing, she was glad to be helpful. The lunch was pleasant, and Sampras easily defeated Cedric Pioline to win the Open for the second time. On the trip back to Washington my thoughts were not of Pete Sampras or tennis, or of the next day's business at the Senate. I made a few phone calls and learned that Heather is a Canadian whose ancestors had emigrated from Scotland to Montreal. She was in her midthirties and had worked in professional tennis for several years, most of them in Paris and London. Now she was in New York, running the U.S. office of a European company. She was highly regarded, having been the first woman to represent a male professional player, and she directed several tournaments in Europe. The next day I sent her a thank-you note. We had dinner a week later. Within a month we were seeing each other regularly. A year and a half later we were married. We now have two teenage children. All thanks to Andy Garcia, Ion Tiriac, and Ilie Nastase, a Cuban American and two Romanians who introduced an American of Lebanese and Irish heritage to a Canadian of Scottish heritage. Life is both a mystery and a surprise. So much that we do, or don't do, is the result of chance, the fickle dictator who rules and roils our lives.

Frank Sinatra's Throat

Shortly after the election of 1984, Senator Robert C. Byrd of West Virginia, the majority leader, appointed me to serve as chairman of the Democratic Senatorial Campaign Committee. I served for two years, through the midterm elections of 1986. The purpose of the committee (both parties have such committees in both houses of Congress) is to help members of their party to get elected. Over my two years of service I recruited candidates, raised money for them, and campaigned across the country in their behalf. One of my earliest and best decisions was to appoint Nancy Pelosi of San Francisco as chair of our fundraising efforts, a task at which she excelled. She was so impressive that I urged her to consider a run for governor of California. She decided to run for the House of Representatives instead and eventually became the first female speaker of the House. Despite President Reagan's popularity, the election went well for us. Eleven new Democratic senators were elected and we regained the majority. In gratitude Byrd appointed me to serve as deputy president pro tempore of the Senate, an entirely honorary position.

It was in that capacity that I served on the welcoming committee that greeted the president when he came to the Capitol to deliver his State of the Union address the following January. In a pleasant but nonsubstantive role, several members of the House and Senate gather to formally welcome the president on that occasion each year. After the president enters the Capitol building he and the members of the welcoming committee are taken to a room just off the House chamber as they wait for the chamber to fill. On this evening I asked the president if there was anything we could get for him. Yes, he replied, he'd like a cup of very hot water, as hot as we could get it. I asked one of the House clerks standing by the door to get it and he did so, returning within a few minutes. As Reagan gingerly sipped from the steaming mug he explained that for years he'd sipped on very hot water before major appearances because it relaxed his throat and lowered his voice a couple of octaves. "Frank Sinatra told me about it. He swore that it helped him get through many long performances. Well, I thought, if it's good enough for Frank Sinatra's throat, it's good enough for me. So I've been doing it ever since and I'm telling you, it works."

"Well," I responded, "if it's good enough for Frank Sinatra and Ronald Reagan, then I'm sure it'll be good for me, so I'm going to try it."

I've been drinking hot water before every major speech ever since, including, ironically, the occasions on which I delivered the Democratic response to some of President Reagan's nationally televised addresses. I don't know whether it works in a physical sense or just psychologically, but it does seem to relax my throat and put me at ease.

REELECTION IN 1988

Just before the debate began I reached out and shook hands with my opponent. Jasper Wyman is tall and erect, handsome and articulate. An ordained minister, he had served for two terms in the state legislature. Now he was running for the U.S. Senate, trying to unseat me. Under other circumstances he would have been a formidable candidate, but his campaign had been slow to gain traction. His principal problem was that while he was now the Republican candidate, he had been a Democrat during his tenure in the legislature. One of the reasons I knew him so well was that in one of his earlier campaigns I had traveled to his hometown to appear with him and campaign in his behalf. I had urged the residents of Pittsfield to vote for him because his character, intelligence, and ability would serve them well. And he did serve them well in the legislature. During that time, however, the role of the Christian Right in American politics grew. The Moral Majority, led by Jerry Falwell, gained adherents and influence. Jack (as Wyman was known) became the director of the Christian Civic League of Maine and increasingly focused on the policies and politics of abortion. He then left the Democratic Party and became a Republican. Unfortunately for him, in his candidacy for the Senate he now had the worst of both worlds: Democrats disliked him for his departure, and many Republicans didn't fully trust him. Despite his ability, his sincerity, and his effort he was unable to raise much money or garner much public support, and he never seriously threatened me.

That had not been obvious a few months earlier. On paper, at least, he seemed to be capable of mounting a serious challenge. So I worked hard to conduct an effective campaign. I visited every part of the state, defending my record against his criticism. It helped that in Washington I was in a highly publicized race for Senate majority leader; the prospect of a Maine senator leading the Senate was attractive to many Mainers.* It

* *Mainers* is the name for those who choose to live

246

also helped that I was able to outspend him in advertising by a wide margin. As a result what had been a comfortable margin in the summer grew as the election approached. My goal in the televised debates was not to make a major mistake. I didn't, and the debates passed with little attention or effect. On election day I received 81.3 percent of the votes cast to Wyman's 18.7 percent, the largest margin in a contested Senate election in Maine's history.

Within days I returned to Washington for more campaigning. Democrats had retained a majority in the Senate. The incumbent majority leader, Senator Byrd, had announced that he would not seek reelection to that position. I was one of the three candidates from which the fifty-five Democratic senators would choose the man who would lead the Senate for the next two years. The election was scheduled for late November, just after Thanksgiving, and, unlike the Maine Senate race, this outcome was very much in doubt.

---

in Maine, whether born there or elsewhere. *Mainiacs* is the name for those who are born in Maine but choose to live elsewhere. At least that's my understanding of the terms.

My Friend Bill Cohen

When Ed Muskie left the Senate Bill Cohen became Maine's senior senator at the age of thirty-eight. An attractive, moderate Republican, he had risen rapidly in Maine politics. After a few years in the private practice of law he served on the City Council and then as mayor of Bangor. Elected to the House of Representatives in 1972, he distinguished himself in the Watergate hearings. In 1978 he unseated the Democratic incumbent in the Senate, Bill Hathaway. Just two years later he was the senior senator.

Our early contacts in the Senate were limited, due in large measure to the circumstances in which we found ourselves. Trailing badly in the polls, I had to campaign early and often. Cohen supported my opponent, sending two of his most trusted aides to Maine to take charge of David Emery's campaign. Inevitably our relationship was somewhat strained. But once I won election in 1982 to a full term, the tension dissolved. As we increasingly worked together on issues important to our state, our friendship blossomed. Although in future races I supported his opponents and he supported mine, we were both careful not to criticize each other, not to make it personal.

Our friendship deepened in 1987 when we served on the Select Committee on the Iran-Contra affair. The Senate Democrats on the Committee were appointed by Majority Leader Byrd, the Republicans by their leader, Bob Dole. When the appointees were announced, the only state with two senators on the Committee was Maine. After the investigation was over and the Committee's report was published, Cohen approached me with a proposal: Would I join him in coauthoring a book on the hearings? His agent thought a book written by two senators from the same state but of different political parties would have considerable appeal. I had never written a book; he had written and published several. When I expressed concern about my literary inexperience he was reassuring. "Don't worry," he said. "I can help you on that." And he did. With his agent he devised a chronology with suggested chapter headings and subjects, and he proposed that we divide the writing roughly in half. I then agreed enthusiastically and immediately began the process of research and organization that preceded actual writing. Over the next few months we worked together, at times like teacher and student, to produce what turned out to be a reasonably successful book, *Men of Zeal: A Candid Inside Story of the Iran-Contra Hearings.*

When I retired from the Senate I told Bill that one of the things I would miss most was working with him on issues important to Maine and the nation. So I was delighted when, after several years of only occasional contact, we found ourselves working together again. After leaving the Senate Cohen served as secretary of defense in the Clinton administration. When he left that position he established the Cohen Group, a business consulting firm. The law firm in which I now serve, DLA Piper,* works

* When I retired from the Senate in 1995 I joined the Washington law firm of Verner, Liipfert, Bernhard, McPherson and Hand. I did so primarily because I had long-standing friendships with two of the principals: Berl Bernhard and Harry McPherson. It proved to be one of the best deci-

closely with the Cohen Group on international business issues, and as a result Cohen and I regularly appear together at conferences. There, with his consent, even encouragement, I like to tell the story, some

---

sions I ever made. I admired and respected them and learned a great deal from both. Verner, Liipfert subsequently went through a series of mergers, culminating in the creation in 2005 of what is now DLA Piper, the world's largest law firm in number of lawyers, 4,200, operating in seventy-nine cities in thirty-three countries. I served as chairman of the firm from 2003 until I reentered government service as U.S. special envoy for Middle East peace in 2009. When I left that position in 2011 I returned to DLA Piper as chairman emeritus; I am very fortunate to still be with the firm, working full time. Its founding leaders — Frank Burch in Baltimore, Lee Miller in Chicago, Terry O'Malley in San Diego, and Nigel Knowles in London — along with current leaders Roger Meltzer in New York, Jay Rains in San Diego, and Tony Angel, who joined Nigel in London, have been extraordinarily helpful to me. They have taught me, each in his own way, so much about the practice and the business of law. A firm of 4,200 lawyers operating worldwide is of course much different from a six-lawyer firm in Portland, Maine.

of which is true, of how Senator Cohen was responsible for my becoming majority leader of the U.S. Senate.

How could a Republican senator get a Democratic senator elected majority leader? When I was appointed to the Senate I was, of course, the junior senator. Whenever we appeared jointly, which was often, Bill, as the senior senator, spoke first, usually at great length. He always finished by saying he had to go to an important meeting; then he would hand me the microphone and leave. Since he had talked so long the audience was invariably smaller and exhausted by the time I started speaking. I became more and more frustrated but couldn't figure out how to change the situation.

Then one day I was visited by the president of the Bath Iron Works, the largest employer in Maine, a shipyard that builds cruisers and destroyers for the U.S. Navy. Back then there were celebrations a couple of times a year when one of their ships was launched. If the launching was in the summer, tens of thousands of people attended. Senator Cohen invariably was the keynote speaker, and the beneficiary, because these are great events for politicians. Although the crowds were much smaller in the winter, because the launchings are of course outdoor events, it's still a plus for a politician to appear and speak. So I asked the president of Bath Iron Works how come he always invited Senator Cohen but never me to speak at the launchings. He looked at me as though I was crazy, paused, then replied, "Well, I like you, but you're the junior senator, not very well known, with no clout. He's the senior senator, a member of the Armed Services Committee, and the chairman of the Seapower Subcommittee. If you were me, who would you invite?" I replied, "You've got a point there." There was a long and embarrassing silence. Then, obviously feeling sorry for me, he said, "Look, we've got a small launching coming up in February. It'll be cold, there probably won't be too much of a crowd, how about if you come up and speak at that launching? I don't think Bill will mind too much." I thanked him profusely and immediately began planning for my first-ever keynote speech at a ship launching.

It was a cold and windy day in February as I took my seat in the front row on the platform, nestled up against the large ship. I had prepared a short but, I hoped, effective speech and looked forward to giving it. The launchings at Bath were choreographed to the second because the ship had to hit the waters of the Kennebec River at precisely high tide. At the designated moment a loud whistle would sound and the ship would start its slide down the ways. On this day the designated moment was 1:15 P.M. As I took my seat next to the president, who was scheduled to introduce me, I glanced across the platform. To my astonishment, there, seated at the other end of the front row, was Senator Cohen. "What's he doing here?" I asked.

Shrinking in his seat from the cold and the embarrassment, the president spread his hands, palms up, and asked, "What could I do? He just showed up. He's the chairman of the Seapower Subcommittee. What could I do?"

"Well, at least he's not speaking," I said, trying to sound emphatic.

He didn't say anything, but his look, like a puppy who's just made a mistake on the living-room rug, was answer enough.

"He's speaking?" I asked. "How could you do this to me?"

Again he said, "What could I do?" After a pause he went on, "But he promised me he'd keep it short."

"Short?" I yelled. "You've heard him speak. What's short for him is a lifetime for the rest of us."

Despite the circumstances I admired Senator Cohen's speech. Without notes, speaking confidently and with obvious knowledge and authority, his presentation was perfect, right down to the timing. Just seconds before the deadline, he thanked the crowd and basked in their applause. Then the champagne bottle cracked against the hull, the whistle blew, the band started playing, the crowd cheered as the massive ship slid slowly into the cold gray water, and the crowd began to disperse. My name had not been mentioned. I hadn't said a word.

After the ceremony we returned to Washington, he by navy jet, I in commercial coach. As I sat in that cold and crowded cabin, gloomily pondering a career of playing second fiddle, a thought struck me. If I were the majority leader of the Senate I would outrank Senator Cohen! I could be introduced first, speak first, and then leave just as he was being introduced. I could be invited to a shipyard launching in the summer and bask in the applause of tens of thousands of grateful constituents! So, thank you, Bill Cohen. It was because of you that I ran for and was elected Senate majority leader.

I love to tell that story, Bill enjoys hearing it, and the audience usually gets a kick out of it. But what really happened when I ran for majority leader was not funny.

MAJORITY LEADER

On the morning of November 29, 1988, fifty-five Democratic senators entered the Old Senate Chamber to meet in caucus to elect a new leader. I was outwardly calm but inwardly nervous, hopeful but worried. I thought I had the votes needed to win. Twenty-seven senators had personally told me they would vote for me on the first ballot; my vote would make it twenty-eight, precisely the majority needed. But I couldn't stop thinking about Mo Udall.

A congressman from Arizona, Udall thought he had the votes to win when he ran for leadership positions in the House of Representatives in 1969 and 1970. But it turned out that he didn't have the votes and lost. Later he wryly commented, "The difference between a caucus and a cactus is that on a cactus the pricks are on the outside." Commitments were not to be believed; promises were not kept.

The U.S. Capitol building has undergone construction, destruction, and reconstruction almost from the very beginning. Its foundation stone was laid in 1793; its north wing required reconstruction by 1806, and it was barely twenty years old when it was burned to the ground in the War of 1812. The Old Senate Chamber likewise has seen its share of demolition and renovation. It was the third chamber used by the Senate, from 1819 to 1859, when it housed just sixty-four senators representing the thirty-two states which then existed. When it was abandoned for the current Senate chamber in 1859, it was taken over by the Supreme Court, for which it served as the principal courtroom for seventy-five years, until the Supreme Court building was constructed in 1935.

In this chamber occurred the great debates over slavery, states' rights, the nullification of federal laws, and the admission of new states. Washington society gathered in the two balconies of this room and in the fenced-off visitors' section on the floor of the chamber itself to see and hear the political life of the growing nation. Debate could be heated, and there was occasional violence. In 1856 the Radical Republican, Senator Charles Sumner of Massachusetts,

was severely beaten by Representative Preston Brooks of South Carolina, and it was three years before he was able to return to his Senate seat.

The Old Chamber was refurbished in anticipation of the nation's bicentennial in 1976. A Ladies Gallery that had been removed in the nineteenth century was reconstructed, new raised flooring was laid over the old masonry, the ceiling beams were fireproofed, and reproductions were made of the original Senate desks and the vice president's desk. The crimson-and-gold color scheme reproduces the opulent Victorian atmosphere suggested by the large chandelier and the ornate swagged canopy with its gold fringes that looms above the vice president's seat.

Standing at the dais, the outgoing majority leader, Senator Byrd, presided. With him were representatives of the three candidates: Senators Daniel Inouye of Hawaii, Bennett Johnston of Louisiana, and I. Our representatives would together count the ballots, small, blank pieces of paper on which each senator would write the name of his or her choice.

Over a year earlier, before he decided not to seek reelection as majority leader, Byrd had asked me to support him. I agreed, without hesitation. Although we had differences on some issues, I admired and respected Byrd. The word *unique* is overused, but surely it applied to him. Born into deep poverty, he was raised by an aunt and uncle in West Virginia. Through unremitting hard work, keen intelligence, and a natural sense of oratory and drama, he rose steadily to the peak of his ambition: majority leader of the U.S. Senate. Along the way he acquired a formal education — a high school diploma and a law degree — and an extraordinary passion for and commitment to the Senate. No one ever served longer in the Senate, cast as many votes, knew its rules better, understood its workings better, or more totally devoted his life to the institution. Some of his Senate records may be surpassed, but his love for and contribution to the Senate will forever remain unequaled.

Shortly after I became majority leader I continued the tradition of hosting a private dinner for all of the senators and their spouses. It was a purely social occasion, intended to welcome the new members and to give the returning members an opportunity to reengage after the Christmas break. I asked Senator Byrd to speak and suggested he talk about the Senate itself.

He did so in lengthy remarks that were riveting, inspiring, and at times melancholy.

With power and passion he described the origin and evolution of the Senate, what it meant to the country, and to him. The longer he talked, the more emotional and personal he became. He had devoted his life to the Senate, to the benefit of the institution and the nation, but at great cost in his personal and private life. He worked very long hours, and when he wasn't working he read extensively. He had read all of the works of Shakespeare seven times and all of the classics of Roman literature several times. He seemed to remember everything he'd ever read. And yet, along with pride and devotion, there was a clear sense of poignancy, even loss, at what he had missed and especially of the burden his career had placed on his beloved wife.

When I returned home that night I couldn't get his words out of my mind. Six years earlier, on Christmas Day 1982, shortly after I had unexpectedly won election to a full term in the Senate, I had decided that I would not try to make the Senate a career for life. In my short time there I had seen how the office consumed those who occupied it, and how it was starting to consume me, to the exclusion of every other interest in life. I was working long hours, seven days a week. The phone calls, the meetings, the issues, the problems seemed endless. I resolved to do my best while I was there, but I would leave on my terms and at a time of my choosing. Now, six years later, I had just been reelected to the Senate and then elected majority leader. After listening to Senator Byrd that evening I had two thoughts. I admired and respected him more than ever, and as an American I was grateful for his devotion. But I knew that I could not live as he had lived, and I reaffirmed my decision not to stay for the rest of my working life.

Not all Democratic senators shared my view of Byrd, and during 1987 internal speculation and discussion began about his future. Although it wasn't until April 1988 that he formally announced he would not seek another term as majority leader, it was evident that would be his decision long before then. So the campaign to succeed Byrd started early and was long. Unlike public campaigns for the Senate, the elections for the leadership tend to be private and intensely personal. There were, after all, only fifty-five eligible voters.

Inouye and Johnston made their candidacies known first. Both were well qualified.

Inouye was a decorated army veteran of World War II. He had served in the Territorial House and Senate in Hawaii and then for four years in the U.S. House of Representatives before his election to the Senate in 1962. He was pleasant, able, and universally liked by other senators, Democratic and Republican. Several press accounts described him as a natural successor to Byrd. Johnston was exceptionally intelligent, with well-honed debating skills. He had served in the Louisiana House of Representatives and Senate before being elected to the U.S. Senate in 1972. I had a good relationship with both of them. Inouye had chaired the Iran-Contra Committee; there I had worked closely with him. Johnston and I had become friends outside of the Senate. He was one of the best tennis players in the Senate, and I had shared the court with him many times. I would have had a hard time choosing between them.

Shortly after they began to campaign among their colleagues, on an otherwise unremarkable day, I got up to leave the Senate chamber following a vote. Senator Max Baucus, a Democrat from Montana, walked up to me and asked, "Have you got a minute? I'd like to talk to you." "Sure," I answered. Max and I served together on two committees, Finance and Environment and Public Works, and had collaborated on a lot of legislation. We found two empty seats in the rear of the chamber.

As we sat down Max got right to the point. "Have you thought about running for majority leader?"

I was aware that my name had been included in press speculation, but I had done nothing to prepare or advance my candidacy. My answer, "Well, not really," was unconvincing, even to me.

"Well, you should."

"You think I should run?"

"Yes."

"Are you serious, Max?"

"Yes, I'm serious."

There was a pause. "Well, I'll have to think about that."

"That's what I'm asking you to do. Think about it. Now. Will you?"

"Well, yes, I will."

"If you run, I'll support you and I think a lot of others will too."

At first I didn't tell anyone about our conversation, but for two days I thought about little else. The arguments against my running were strong. I had been in the Senate only seven years; in fact I was still in my first full elected term. Inouye and Johnston were far senior, far better known, far more experienced. The positive arguments seemed less strong. I had worked hard on legislation, with a modest but good record of success. I had done well in the Iran-Contra hearings and as chairman of the Democratic Senatorial Campaign Committee in the 1986 election. Several senators had been very complimentary about my comeback victory in 1982, but I took that to be routine political flattery. I'd worked well with colleagues on both sides of the aisle and was not aware of having made any enemies. But was that enough?

Two days later Bill Bradley came up to me on the Senate floor and bluntly urged me to run. A former professional basketball player, Bill was a well-known, highly regarded senator from New Jersey. I worked with him on the Finance Committee, where, with a few other senators, we had been deeply involved in major tax reform legislation in 1986. He said that he would vote for me and would actively work for me. "You can win. But you've got to get in and get to work."

Max had gotten me thinking hard. Bill focused my thoughts. I convened a meeting of a few members of my staff. I described my conversations with Baucus and Bradley and asked them for their reactions. They all urged me to run. That wasn't a surprise; it was as obvious to them as it was to me that I wanted to do it. But I didn't want to make a fool of myself. I didn't know (and still don't) whether Baucus and Bradley had acted independently. I had no way of knowing whether there was wider support, as they both had indicated. After considerable discussion I decided to talk with John Glenn.

I knew of no senator who didn't respect Glenn. A true American hero, who will be remembered long after all of his Senate colleagues, John was personally modest and politically moderate, a perfect bellwether from a bellwether state. It was difficult for me to even raise the subject of my running for the majority leader position, but my fears were unfounded. He was, as ever, gracious. He said he thought I would be a strong candidate and, if elected, an effective leader. I didn't directly ask for his support then, but I was encouraged enough to get into the race. Later, after I asked for and received his commitment, I went further and asked him to give the nominating speech for me at the caucus. He agreed and delivered graceful and low-key remarks that may not have changed any votes (every senator had made a commitment before the nominating speeches began) but provided reassurance to those who had committed to me.

The campaign continued for months. I met individually with every Democratic senator except Johnston and Inouye. A few committed to me in the first meeting; a few others told me they were committed to someone else. But most said they were undecided. So there followed several rounds of meetings. Many didn't decide until the weekend preceding the election. It was the Thanksgiving holiday and I spent the entire weekend packing for a move from my apartment in Northwest Washington to a small townhouse on Capitol Hill, just minutes from my Senate office. For the four days of that holiday, between opening, filling, and closing dozens of cardboard boxes, I made and received scores of calls from senators who were in the final stages of decision making. By Monday, the day before the election, I thought I had the votes to win.

But I was wary. Not long before, Senator Byrd had asked to see me. I sensed what was coming and steeled myself as I entered his large and impressive Appropriations Committee office in the Capitol building. He seated me in a soft cushioned chair and pulled up a small wooden chair on which he sat directly in front of and looking down at me, our knees almost touching. It was a bright sunny day and light poured into the room through the spacious windows behind him, creating a halo-like effect around his silver hair. Although I had guessed right about what he would say, it still hit me hard when I heard it. He began by reviewing my Senate career, our relationship, and all he had done for me. It was all true, as I acknowledged. He reminded me that much earlier I had committed to vote for him for majority leader. I acknowledged that as well. Then he pulled his chair up even closer, leaned in until his face was right next to mine, and in a low but intense voice asked me to honor that commitment by withdrawing from the race so that he could seek reelection. He said he thought I couldn't win because of my inexperience and lack of seniority, but he was confident that he could win if I dropped out and supported him.

I pointed out to him that he himself had changed the circumstances by not seeking reelection; it was not reasonable to now expect me to withdraw my candidacy, and I would not do so. He didn't like my answer, and we repeated the essence of the conversation several times before the meeting ended.

It was one of the most intense and difficult of my Senate tenure. He made it clear that he wouldn't vote for me, but my admiration for him was undimmed. He was a great man, strong and proud, and he was reluctant to cede power. In a perverse way I admired him more than ever.

Three seats in the first row of the Old Senate Chamber were reserved for the candidates. I sat on the aisle just a few feet from the dais. To my left was Johnston, and to his left was Inouye. As we each wrote our names on the ballot we joked about the fact that no one would be shut out in the balloting. Under the rules of the caucus, to be elected a candidate needed a majority of votes. If no candidate received twenty-eight or more votes on the first ballot, the candidate with the fewest votes was eliminated and the other two would compete in a run-off election.

As the ballots were passed up to the dais for counting I reviewed my situation. I thought I knew how every senator would vote. I expected to be elected on the first ballot with twenty-eight votes; Inouye would get fourteen and Johnston thirteen. In addition I had second-ballot commitments from six senators; they had promised to vote for one of my opponents on the first ballot but had assured me that they'd be with me on a second. But I couldn't be sure that all of my first-vote supporters would stay with me on a second ballot. And there was always the chance that Mo Udall had been right. I remained outwardly calm, but my heart was thumping hard when Byrd announced the result.

"Mitchell twenty-seven, Inouye fourteen, Johnston fourteen."

My first thought was that Mo Udall was wrong. In a secret ballot fifty-four out of fifty-five senators had voted as they said they would. A good record by any standard. But my thoughts shifted quickly. I was one vote short. One senator had not kept his commitment to me. Instantly the face and name of that senator came to my mind. I don't know how or why I knew who it was, but I did know, with absolute certainty. I started to turn to look at him, seated somewhere behind me. But I suppressed the urge. That could wait. For now I had to think clearly about how to proceed.

Before I could do anything, before any other word was spoken, Bennett Johnston rose and asked for recognition. "Mr. Chairman," he said, in a clear and strong voice, "I move that Senator Mitchell be elected majority leader by acclamation." Dan Inouye rose to second the motion, and instantly the other senators stood, applauding and shouting their consent. When the new Congress convened in January 1989 I would be the majority leader of the Senate. I shook hands with and thanked Johnston and Inouye. It may sound trite, but I really did like both men and regarded them, then and thereafter, as friends. I then thanked and accepted congratulations from Byrd and most of the other senators.

The rest of the day was a blur of press conferences, congratulatory calls, meetings and more meetings. It was after eleven o'clock that evening when I finally lay down in bed so physically and emotionally exhausted that I fell quickly into a deep sleep.

Through a haze I heard the telephone ringing, loudly, insistently. I had been sleeping so soundly that for an instant I didn't know where I was or what time it was. I picked up the phone.

"George?"

"Yes."

"It's ——." He said his name.

My mind snapped to full alert. "I know why you're calling."

There was a long pause. "You do?"

"Yes, I do."

"How do you know?"

"I can't explain it, but I know. I knew it the moment the vote was announced."

There was another, much longer pause. "Well, I want to apologize and to explain."

"Go ahead."

"I'm truly sorry. I did it. I shouldn't have, but I did."

He then explained what had happened and why. Although they didn't justify what he did, I understood his reasons. Politics, like life itself, can force painful choices.

"I accept your apology," I said. "You've shown a lot of guts in calling me. You had no way of knowing that I knew. As far as I'm concerned it's over. It's behind us. I've got to run the Senate now, and I'll need your help and the help of a lot of other senators. Let's concentrate on the future."

I assured him that I would never disclose his name to anyone. I never have. His name will go with me to my grave. He went on to an outstanding career in the Senate, and I served for six difficult but exciting years as majority leader.

The next day I called Bob Dole, the Senate minority leader, and asked to meet with him. I felt it important to establish a good relationship with the man I would have to work closely with for years to come. Bob had been in the Senate for twenty years; before that he had served eight years in the House. He had been chairman of the Finance Committee and majority leader and was the Republican nominee for vice president in 1976. He was nationally known; I was hardly known at all. My only real contact with him had been during our shared assignment to the Finance Committee. To the limited extent that we had interacted, our relationship was polite and cordial. I was aware that there had been occasional tensions between Dole and Byrd, and I wanted to avoid that in my relationship with Dole, if possible.

When I entered his office Dole again congratulated me on my election. I thanked him and then went directly to my reason for asking to see him. I said that while I was a relative newcomer in the Senate, I was aware that the leaders' jobs were extremely difficult, with a high potential for misunderstanding and mistrust. I told him that I wanted to have a good personal and working relationship with him. I had come to tell him what he could expect from me: "I will never surprise you. To the extent that it's humanly possible, I will always give you notice of my intentions, hopefully far enough in advance that you'll have time to consider your response. I will never attack or criticize you personally, in public or in private. I will always be available to you. We're going to disagree often. But I hope and intend that we'll do so in a way that's not personal and that permits us to continue to work together. Finally, I pledge to you that I will always honor and keep my commitments to you. I hope I can expect you to act the same way toward me." While I was talking I could tell by the look on his face that he was pleased. His response was positive, enthusiastic, and generous.

Among the reasons I admired Bob Dole was his moving personal history. From the small town of Russell, Kansas, he entered the army during World War II and soon found himself in the mountains of Italy. There, as a twenty-one-year-old platoon leader, he was grievously wounded. After years of rehabilitation he continued in public service, ending in his long Senate career. His war wounds resulted in the loss of the use of his right arm, so as I rose to leave the meeting I extended my left hand. We shook hands and I left, determined to keep my word and confident that he would keep his.

For the next six years we worked together in the Senate leadership, I as majority leader, he as minority leader. When the Senate was in session we met and talked several times a day. We occasionally had lunch or dinner together. We represented different parties with different political philosophies. We negotiated hundreds of agreements on Senate business and procedures. We discussed, debated, and voted on many hundreds of issues, some of them extremely contentious. We often disagreed. But not once did a harsh word ever pass between us, in public or in private. I kept my word to him and he kept his word to me. Over those six years our relationship grew close. It has mellowed in the nearly two decades since I left the Senate. We don't see each other as often as we once did, and the differences are now muted and often unspoken, but there remains between us an enduring bond. We share pride in the fact that we represented our country, our parties, and our constituents vigorously (and, we hope, effectively) but without rancor or hostility.

TALMADGE

Two days after the general election in early November 1988, I read in a newspaper that I had won all but one of Maine's 673 voting precincts. The only one I lost was in Talmadge, a small town in eastern Maine, not far from the Canadian border. Naturally this aroused my interest, so I asked my staff to obtain a list of voters in Talmadge. I then wrote to each of them, referring to the newspaper article and inviting them to attend a town meeting with me in Talmadge. I told them I wanted to find out what they thought I was doing wrong. The meeting was set for early December.

Route 1, one of the oldest and best known roads in America, runs from Fort Kent, at the northern tip of Maine, to Key West, at the southern edge of Florida. Unlike more modern highways, it rarely follows a straight line. To the contrary, like a retired couple heading south for the winter with lots of time on their hands, it meanders back and forth across the vast landscape of eastern America as if searching (but not too hard) for the warmth of the Florida sun. For its first two hundred miles it traverses just two Maine counties, Aroostook and Washington. Both have lots of land and few people. The landscape is varied and beautiful, the people hardy, resilient, and very independent. Just over halfway in that first stretch it passes by Talmadge. There, just a few miles from the Canadian border, in the election of 1988, I received twelve votes to Jasper Wyman's eighteen.

It was my first stop on my first trip to Maine after my election as Senate majority leader. It did not get me off to a good start with the good people of Talmadge that I appeared with a large contingent of national press in tow. For eight years I had traveled from one end of the state to the other, almost always with just one aide who did triple duty as advance man, driver, and note taker. Now here I was with a large, noisy, busy caravan, and I worried that the locals would think I'd gotten too big for my britches.

The only nonresidential structure in town was a small church where a crowd much larger than the thirty who had voted were gathered. Like most Mainers, the pastor who introduced me got right to the point: "Senator Mitchell, abortion was the issue here." But, also like most Mainers, while direct she was civil, respectful, and willing to listen. When I rose to speak I thanked her. It was not a formality; I was grateful for the manner in which she had set the tone for the meeting. I told the assembled crowd, which obviously included many people from other towns in the area, that I'd come to find out what they thought I was doing wrong, and they had answered my question. While I knew that many of them disagreed with me, I wanted them to hear my views and I wanted to listen to theirs. I explained my position as clearly and concisely as I could. I then said that I respected their views and hoped they would respect mine. I offered to stay as long as they wished, to hear them and to answer their questions. As I expected, while the first few comments were on abortion, many other subjects were raised, and the discussion went well, as several of my answers drew sustained applause. Just when it seemed that there were no more questions or comments and I thought it would be a good time to end the meeting, a husky man with close-cropped hair, who was standing in the rear of the church, spoke up in a loud voice. In a rapid-fire delivery, with an accent that made it clear he was not from Maine, he delivered a blistering attack on me and anyone else who did not oppose any and all abortions, no matter the circumstances. When I tried to respond to his comments he interrupted me and shouted me down. As he continued, his emotion and voice rose and his words grew louder and more insulting. I sensed that the crowd was becoming as uncomfortable as I was and searched for an opening that would give me a chance to interrupt him. It came when he bellowed that President Bush and I were acting like "pimps and prostitutes." (Unfortunately for the president, he was lumped in with me on the issue, although there were differences in our positions.) I raised my hand and interrupted. "Wait a minute, wait a minute," I yelled. "You've gone too far. I've stood here and taken all of your criticisms and insults, but you've gone too far. You've had your say, and I'm not taking any more from you." To my pleasant surprise, some in the crowd applauded, and the pastor brought the meeting to an end.

By prior arrangement I then went to the basement of the church, where a spread of sandwiches and cookies had been laid out. At first the reporters gathered around me in a way that made it difficult for me to talk with the local citizens. Then a small, elderly woman broke in, walked up to stand beside me, and, without looking at me, said loudly, drawing out her words in a strong Down East Maine accent, "He's from Nooow Yaaawk!" Without another word she walked away. To her that explained everything.

I broke away from the reporters and talked with several of the townspeople. Most were friendly and positive. Most disagreed with me on the issue of abortion, but they were grateful that I had come to their small town to explain my position directly to them and to hear their comments and concerns. As I was preparing to leave I spotted the New Yorker across the room and walked over to him. I extended my hand and he took it with a smile and a firm shake. "You've got a lot of guts to come here," he said, "and I admire that." We chatted briefly, and just before we parted he said, "There's something you should know. I was career army, an enlisted man, and I always wanted to get an officer. This was my chance and I took it."

I never ran for office again, but if I had I

like to think that I would have carried Talmadge.

CLEAN AIR

I woke up with a throbbing headache, a sore throat, and a very runny nose. On any other day I would have stayed in bed, but March 29, 1990, was not any other day. It was the day on which the Senate was scheduled to vote on an amendment to the Clean Air Act offered by Senator Robert Byrd. For nine years I had struggled to make progress on legislation to deal with the growing problem of air pollution. Now we were on the verge of success. But adoption of the Byrd amendment could mean the end of our effort. The outcome was uncertain; the vote would be very close. I had to be there to speak and to vote against the amendment, no matter how bad I felt. I knew that exhaustion and stress from two relentless, pressure-packed months of negotiating, debating, and voting were contributing factors. But I had to retain my focus, for today and for a few more days.

The early settlers had spread across a continent that seemed limitless, but the steady increase in population, rapid industrialization, the movement of people from farms to cities, and the invention of the motor vehicle irrevocably changed the lives of Americans. By the time Ed Muskie entered the Senate, 85 percent of our waterways were polluted, as was the air in most large urban areas. Muskie was the principal author of the landmark laws that reversed both trends. Today 85 percent of our waterways are clean and the level of air pollution has been substantially reduced despite increases in the numbers of people and motor vehicles. The assault on air pollution began with the emergence of clear and convincing evidence of its adverse effects on the health of millions of Americans. That led directly to passage of the Clean Air Act of 1970, which was aimed primarily at automobile emissions. The Act was amended in 1977 to extend some deadlines for compliance, and also to bring under its scope new industrial sites in those areas in which the law's air quality standards were not being met and to prevent the degradation of air quality in those areas in which the standards were being met.

I was appointed to the Senate just three

years after adoption of the 1977 amendments. It was already clear then that further changes were needed to meet new challenges. On July 31, 1981, I said, in a speech to the Senate:

> The issue of acid rain continues to grow as an environmental, international, and economic problem. . . . It has already been documented that approximately 50 percent of the high elevation lakes in the Adirondack Mountains no longer support fish life . . . as the acidity of these lakes has markedly increased. Maine lakes have undergone a similar change over the past 40 years; an eightfold increase in acidity has been measured.

For the next nine years I was among a small group of senators who worked hard to bring the issue to the attention of the public and to move legislation forward. Through a series of public hearings and statements on the Senate floor we made some progress in publicizing the problem, but we were wholly unsuccessful on the legislative front. There were many obstacles; among them were the president and the Senate majority leader.[13] President Reagan wanted to terminate the Clean Air and Clean Water acts, not improve them. He nearly succeeded on the Clean Water Act, but it survived because the Senate overrode two presidential vetoes. Although Reagan was not as aggressive in trying to end the Clean Air Act, he was adamantly opposed to expanding or improving it. Senator Byrd did not share Reagan's broad hostility to regulation but was concerned about and protective of West Virginia interests, in particular the jobs of coal miners. Clean air legislation was seen as a threat to those miners, especially any action on acid rain. The principal objective of the proponents of legislation, like me, was to reduce the amount of sulfur emitted from midwestern power plants, many of which burned high-sulfur coal from West Virginia. Over the decade of the 1980s evidence had accumulated that emissions from those plants were being deposited in the lakes and streams of the northeastern states and the provinces of eastern Canada. The Canadian government, alarmed by the acidification of its waters, actively urged a reduction in emissions. But the possibility of action remained remote. Then came the elections of 1988.

During my campaign for majority leader I made it clear to my Democratic colleagues that if elected I intended to vigorously pursue clean air legislation. I did not want anyone to feel misled. Of much greater significance was the decision by the newly elected president, George H. W. Bush, to support clean air legislation. Within a month of his inauguration, in a break with the policies of the Reagan administration, Bush announced that he would propose legislation for a new, more effective Clean Air Act, including action on acid rain. President Bush's courageous decision made action on clean air legislation possible. Suddenly, dramatically, the question shifted from "Will there be a clean air bill?" to "What will be in the clean air bill?" I was impressed and heartened by the president's statement. My colleagues on the Senate Committee on Environment and Public Works and I immediately began to prepare for what we knew would be a long and complicated process. But we greatly underestimated just how long and how difficult it would be.

To highlight the importance of the issue, in June President Bush used the East Room of the White House to outline his clean air proposal. The centerpiece was control of acid rain. Several factors led the president and his advisors to that decision:

(1) The subject had received the most political attention during the national clean-air debate and for years had been widely discussed on Capitol Hill, though consensus had proved elusive. (2) Resolution of the issue was especially important to Canadian prime minister Brian Mulroney, who had become a confidant of Bush. (3) The solution to the acid-rain conflict offered a market-oriented mechanism that appealed to the administration's free-market ideological principles. (4) In the end, the debate over acid-rain control became a numbers game that the Bush team knew could be settled with old-fashioned horse trading, at which members of Congress are especially adept.[14]

Making an announcement and drafting a bill in formal legislative language are two very different things. When the president sent his bill to Congress in late July its provisions did not fully match the rhetoric of his statement in June. But that did not detract from the importance of his action. We had a serious proposal to consider, and we began immediately. Within days a House subcommittee chaired by Representative Henry Waxman of California, a staunch advocate of strong clean air legislation, held the first congressional hearing on the president's bill. Waxman, a dynamo of intelligence, energy, and intensity, had been elected in 1974 and was involved in a wide range of legislation on health care, the environment, and women's rights.

The relevant committee in the House was the Energy and Commerce Committee, chaired by Representative John Dingell Jr. of Michigan. Like many immigrants, Dingell's father, of Polish descent, had changed the family's original name, Dzieglewicz; he was elected to Congress in 1933. When he died in 1955 his son won a special election to succeed him. John Jr. was the longest serving member of Congress in American history.

In the Energy and Commerce Committee the bill fell within the jurisdiction of the Health and Environment Subcommittee, chaired by Waxman. Dingell and Waxman are dissimilar in size, approach, and outlook on issues, but both will be judged by historians to be among the greatest and most influential legislators in the House in the late twentieth and early twenty-first century. Much attention has been paid to their differences, and less than is justified to their similarities. The fact is they both represented their constituencies with a high level of intelligence and energy. It just happened that their constituencies had different interests. Waxman's district, based in Beverly Hills, is one in which air pollution, and public concern about it, is high. Indeed concern is high in all of California, a fact recognized in the autonomy granted by federal law to that state in air pollution issues. The California Air Resources Board is widely recognized as one of the world's preeminent public bodies dealing with such issues. Dingell's district, based in the suburbs of Detroit, is home to automobile manufacturers and thousands of their workers.

For the previous decade, from my position on the Senate Committee on Environment and Public Works and especially when I served as chairman of the Environmental Protection Subcommittee, I worked with Dingell and Waxman on a wide range of issues. Despite their differences, despite the widespread view among some business and environmental groups that Dingell would oppose any meaningful clean air legislation, I believed that if we in the Senate could somehow pass a bill, Dingell and Waxman would resolve their differences and enact good and strong legislation.

The Senate does its business through committees; each senator serves on several. When a senator is elected majority leader he (and soon, hopefully, she) may continue to serve on committees and as chair of a subcommittee, but not as chair of a full committee. I therefore could have continued to serve as chair of the Environmental Protection Subcommittee, but I voluntarily relinquished the position, although I continued to serve on the committee. I gave it up because I wanted to concentrate fully on the position of leader and also because I liked and trusted Max Baucus, who replaced me as chair.

As Dingell and Waxman struggled to move a bill through their committee in the House, Max and I worked diligently to gain approval of a strong bill in the Senate committee. We were greatly aided by several of the other senators on the committee who were deeply committed to the passage of strong clean air legislation. Among them were Frank Lautenberg of New Jersey, a Democrat, and John Chafee of Rhode Island and David Durenberger of Minnesota, both Republicans. Chafee and Durenberger were following a long tradition, since abandoned, of Republican leadership on environmental issues. The previous Committee chairman, Republican senator Robert Stafford of Vermont, a soft-spoken and reserved man with a spine of steel, was a staunch protector of the environment and an advocate of clean air legislation; he had helped to keep the issue alive through the previous decade. We all knew that the Senate Committee bill would be the high-water mark for the legislation and that we would have to compromise it down with the White House, so the Committee approved the strongest possible bill in November.

There were substantial differences between the Committee bill and the administration's proposal. On every issue, including the major ones — acid rain, smog, toxic chemicals, fuel efficiency standards on motor vehicles to reduce emissions of carbon dioxide — the Committee bill generally required more and faster action than the administration's bill. The administration estimated that its bill would cost $20 billion a year and that the Committee bill would cost twice as much. We believed that the difference was not that great and that the estimated health costs of $40 billion to $50 billion a year should be considered in evaluating the costs and benefits of the two bills. There also was a significant difference in how the bills would be enforced. The Committee bill relied on the existing regulatory mechanism; it had been in place for years. The president proposed a new, untried, market-based system that he called cap-and-trade.

I had stated several times my intention to bring the bill to the Senate floor for consideration as soon as possible after Congress returned from its Christmas break. I did so on January 23, 1990, knowing that the technical complexity of the issues meant that we would not be able to move the bill rapidly. Senators, most of whom were not on the Committee that had drafted and reported the bill to the full Senate, needed time to review and digest its contents. I was optimistic and thought it might take two weeks. In fact it took ten intense and difficult weeks.

Just before I brought the bill up in the Senate, the president sent a letter to Senator Dole setting forth his opposition to several provisions in the Committee bill. For their part the environmental groups suggested ways the bill could be strengthened. I found myself in the middle, trying to find a way to satisfy several competing interests. Almost immediately the environmental organizations proposed and pushed for an all-or-nothing approach. They wanted me to force a vote by the full Senate on the bill as it was reported out of the Environment and Public Works Committee. But everyone knew that would trigger a filibuster; the bill was very complicated and several senators, Democrats and Republicans, would vote against it because they couldn't accept one or more of its provisions. After a decade of working on the issue I had a good sense of where each senator stood. Not only could we not get the sixty votes necessary to end a filibuster, we couldn't even get a simple majority of fifty-one. In addition I felt the president had made a good faith effort in advocating for clean air legislation; it would be wrong and unfair to start the process by forcing him into a position of opposition.

I talked through the situation with my staff, with my colleagues on the Senate Committee, and with Bob Dole. Dole had been through an intense primary battle with Bush for the Republican nomination for president in 1988. On one memorable occasion Vice President Bush was presiding over a Senate debate when Dole, angry about a Bush campaign ad that he felt misrepresented his record, walked up the few steps to the presiding officer's chair and said to Bush, "Stop lying about my record." I was standing just a few feet away and was startled, as was Bush. He denied the charge, Dole repeated it, and the incident ended. But it was clear that relations between them were strained. However, once Bush was elected they patched up their relationship, and now Dole was being a good soldier, working to protect the president's position on clean air. Dole also personally opposed the bill the Senate Committee had produced and made it clear to me that unless some changes were made he would work hard against it. He suggested that he and I meet with some of the key administration officials on this issue. Those involved in the drafting of the administration's bill included Roger Porter, the principal domestic policy advisor to the president; Boyden Gray, the White House counsel; Bill Reilly, the administrator of the Environmental Protection Agency; and Robert Grady of the Office of Management and Budget. Throughout the process that followed I talked with all of them and with others, including the president himself and his chief of staff, former New Hampshire governor John Sununu. Our first meeting was with Porter and Grady. Over the following weeks they served as the principal negotiators for the president. They proved to be effective and honorable negotiators. I developed, and retain, great respect and affection for both of them. We had many differences, but we were able to compromise them to a reasonable conclusion through a difficult but fair and responsible negotiation.

I knew that I and the other members of the Committee had to negotiate with and reach agreement with the White House, but I was determined that these negotiations not be exclusive. We had to get the interest and involvement of senators who were not on the Committee, including, perhaps especially, those who were opposed to one or more provisions in the Committee bill. So I invited all senators to join the discussion to enable them to ask questions, express concerns, and offer changes. Thus began an extraordinary process that took a full month and in which a large majority of senators personally participated. It grew much larger and took much longer than I had anticipated, but in the end it proved to be the right approach at the right time.

That was not obvious at the outset. I had two conference rooms, one on either side of my personal office in the majority leader's suite. To allow me to maximize my personal participation and to maintain a degree of control when I could not be there, I instructed that the negotiations take place in the larger of these rooms. The first few days of negotiations were essentially between the Committee and the administration. At the end of the long rectangular table closest to the door to my personal office I sat with Baucus, Chafee, and Durenberger. At the other end of the table, closest to the door that led out into the hallway alongside the Senate chamber, sat Porter and Grady; they were occasionally joined by other administration officials. Along both sides of the table sat other senators. They came and went, depending on the issue under discussion. John Breaux of Louisiana was a regular and helpful participant, as was Frank Lautenberg. In the first few days only a handful of senators participated. Gradually, as the process gained traction, more and more joined, as did their aides. Two rows of chairs were set up for the aides behind the senators at the table. Soon they were packed in, many of them standing, from morning until late at night. More participants meant more discussion, more debate, more controversy. The issues were many and technical. Few of the participants had a perfect understanding of every aspect of every issue. I was able to keep the process under control because I was assisted by a superb group of staff members with long experience and deep knowledge of the issues. They were led by Kate Kimball, a personable young woman who over the previous decade had mastered every detail of every aspect of the issue. The other key senators also were well-served by their staffs.

It soon became apparent that those of us who supported the Committee bill were fighting a four-front battle. Across the table was the Bush administration, which wanted a bill, but only their bill. Their goal was to persuade us to accept it. Our goal was just the opposite: to persuade them to accept the Committee bill. We all believed that somewhere in between a reasonable compromise could be found. But there were many outside the room who did not share that view. Two of those groups battled to influence the process. The environmental organizations, aided by many Democratic senators who shared their views, opposed any weakening of the Committee bill; they advocated an all-or-nothing strategy. But they greatly overestimated their influence in the Senate. The other outside group was the business organizations, aided by many Republican senators and a few Democrats as well. They regarded even the administration's bill as too strong and wanted no bill, or, if there had to be one, the weakest possible bill. They overestimated their influence in the House. Finally there was Senator Byrd. He had long opposed clean air legislation. His devotion to his constituents was total, his influence in the Senate high. He had been the Democratic leader for many years, and now he was in what was arguably an even more influential position, as chairman of the powerful Senate Appropriations Committee, through which every dollar of federal funding passes. As the *Washington Post* noted in reporting on Senator Byrd's effort to amend the Clean Air bill:

As chairman of the Senate Appropriations Committee, which he took over after stepping down as majority leader, Byrd holds the fate of every senator's pet project in his hands and, according to colleagues, he has not been shy in reminding them of that fact.

By Byrd's count, he has paid "house calls" to at least 25 senators in their offices. "He's been on the phone. He's been in their offices. He writes them letters. He's everywhere. I've never seen the likes of it," one senator said. "He reminds you of every project he helped you pass . . . he hasn't forgotten a one," another said.[15]

Byrd was not principally motivated by the concern over cost that drove the administration and some of its allies, or the dislike of regulation that motivated the business groups and their allies. His concern was more specific, more human: coal miners, their jobs, their families. It was a concern that resonated with many other senators.

The negotiations were not open to the press or the public, but much of what was said soon became public. Those senators who were close to the environmental organizations kept them informed; senators on the other side of the issues kept the business groups informed. As the negotiations intensified the environmental leaders stepped up their criticism of me and the other senators who supported and participated in the process. In an effort to persuade them that our approach was the only one that had any chance of succeeding, I met with several leaders of the environmental movement.

I was in the large conference room, engaged in negotiations with Porter and Grady. Max Baucus was to my left. To my right, just at the corner of the table, sat

Senator John Heinz, a Republican from Pennsylvania. He was not a regular participant, but the subject that day happened to be of interest to him. He was wealthy, moderate, handsome, and well-spoken, and many thought he would at some point be a candidate for president. When an aide informed me that the environmental leaders had gathered in my small conference room, I turned the gavel over to Max, excused myself, and crossed through my office to the other meeting.

I shook hands with each of the several leaders. They were good men, well-meaning, well-informed, who worked hard for a good cause in which they believed deeply. I liked and respected them, had worked with them for years. But on this day there were no smiles, no small talk. We sat down to a discussion that was serious and direct, even blunt. No one swore, no one yelled, but there was no mistaking the tension that filled the room. As the chairman of the Environmental Protection Subcommittee I had been the author and supporter of most of the environmental legislation enacted or considered for nearly a decade. During that time they trusted me. Now, I knew, they did not. They were so committed to gaining enactment of the strongest possible clean air bill that they had talked themselves and their allies in the Senate into believing that sixty or more senators would vote for the Senate Committee bill. That was the number necessary to overcome the filibuster that senators opposing the bill would mount. In their view the only remaining obstacle to a glorious victory was my unwillingness to bring the bill to the floor for a vote. Although no one directly called me a coward, that was the implication of their statements. I carefully explained to them, not for the first time, that I would gladly bring the Committee bill up for a vote if I thought there was any chance that we could pass it. But we couldn't pass it. We didn't have sixty votes. We didn't have even fifty votes. I had worked with and talked with these senators for years, on a wide range of issues, especially on those relating to the environment. I knew their views and their concerns. I was absolutely certain that we did not have sixty votes at this time. If I forced a vote now we would get about forty-five votes for it, and our weakness would be fully exposed, whatever negotiating leverage we had would vanish, and the bill would be lost, perhaps for another decade. I couldn't let that happen. I wouldn't let that happen. I would continue negotiating to find the strongest bill that could become law. If I couldn't get it done, if the best available bill was too weak to do the job of cleaning the air, I would stand up, say that publicly, and admit defeat. But I sure wasn't ready for that yet. I told them I thought they had become so accustomed to glorious defeat that they were too quick to proclaim and accept it. They were good at making statements; they should try harder to be good at making laws.

I was sensitive to and somewhat defensive about their constant criticism of me and the other leaders of the Committee. I felt reasonably secure in Maine; I wouldn't be on the ballot again until 2004. But Baucus would soon be up for reelection, and his opponent claimed that acid rain was a hoax; yet these groups were attacking Max. I criticized them for that. They didn't appreciate my comments, of course, and they responded vigorously to each of my arguments. Then they handed me a list they insisted was a hard and accurate head count on the Committee bill. It showed that sixty senators would vote for it. I slowly read down the list. I knew it wasn't accurate. "Are you telling me that you got all of these commitments from the senators themselves?" I asked. After some discussion among themselves, without being specific they said that many of the commitments had come from senators themselves and that the others came from "reliable sources close to the senators, people in the know." I was careful to say that I didn't think they were lying to me; rather I told them that while they no doubt believed the list was accurate, I knew it was not. One of the affirmative votes on the list was John Heinz.

I asked the group if they would excuse me for a few minutes, that I had to step out but would return shortly. They said they would wait. I went back through my office to the other conference room and settled into my chair. Heinz was still there. I leaned over and whispered to him, "Jack, I'm really grateful to you, I appreciate your support."

He sat up straight and asked, "What are you talking about?"

"We've been trying to get a count on where everybody stands if I have to take this bill to a cloture vote, and I've just been informed that you've committed to vote for cloture."

"Are you crazy?" he practically shouted. "I can't do that. There's no way I would ever vote for cloture on this bill. You know very well we've got a lot of coal in western Pennsylvania." He was visibly agitated.

"I know that, and I thought that's what you would say, but I had to check because I've been told differently."

"Well, whoever told you differently told you wrong."

"Okay. Thanks."

I started to get up. He grabbed my arm and pulled me back down into my chair. "I want to vote for a clean air bill, but I can't vote for this one. You know what my problems are. You fix them and I'll be with you." I did know what his problems were. I wasn't sure I could fix them, but I was going to try.

I returned to the other meeting. As close to verbatim as I could, I recounted my conversation with Heinz to the environmental leaders. I told them I didn't question their good faith or their sincerity, but I was certain that there were about fifteen other senators on their list who were in the same boat as Heinz. I understood and appreciated the role that groups like theirs played in the legislative process. They kept the pressure on to counter the pressure from outside groups on the other side of the issue (who, of course, justified their actions on the same grounds). But I asked them not to make it personal. "Max and I and John and Dave are all trying to do the right thing. We want a good, strong bill. I know you don't agree, but I'm telling you that what we're doing is the only way we can get it done." They denied that they were making it personal, and they made it clear that on the central issue they were not persuaded. They repeated their demand for an immediate vote on the Committee bill. I was disappointed. They were disappointed. They hadn't convinced me, and I hadn't convinced them. The meeting ended. As bad as things had been, I knew they were about to get worse.

In my years in the Senate, and beyond, I've occasionally gotten front-page headlines in Maine newspapers. But to the best of my knowledge, only once have I been the subject of a headline across the entire top of the front page of the *Portland Press Herald*. That happened on February 22, 1990, when the headline read, " 'Deals' on Clean Air Attacked — 13 States Say Mitchell, Others Are Diluting Bill."

A group of state environmental officials called on Senate Majority Leader George J. Mitchell Wednesday to stop making "back-room deals" with opponents of the clean-air bill because they're "cutting the heart out" of the legislation.

305

The group charged that Mitchell and other leaders of the clean-air fight are so anxious to get the bill through Congress that they have tentatively agreed to "unacceptable" concessions on smog control provisions with Senate opponents and White House officials.

At a press conference Wednesday, Thomas C. Jorling, commissioner of New York state's Department of Environmental Conservation, released a letter signed by 13 state environmental officials — including Dean Marriott, Maine's commissioner of environmental protection — urging Mitchell not to agree to the compromises.

The article triggered a series of similar attacks, all of which stung. I was angry and fumed about the irony: Jorling had been a Republican staffer on the Environment and Public Works Committee; now here he was getting headlines by criticizing me for negotiating and making compromises with a Republican president. I was aware that Jorling was being encouraged and helped by others who were supposedly friends of mine; some of them compared me unfavorably to Muskie. My offices in Maine and Washington got a few more calls than usual and soon critical letters started to arrive. I knew that when I returned to Maine that weekend, as I did every weekend, I would face a barrage of questions. I was confident that I could handle them — not convince everybody, of course, but at least fair-minded people would understand. But I was downcast and worried. I'd been arguing for a long time with my opponents; now I was arguing with my friends. The bill was so complicated, so hard. What if we couldn't reach agreement with the White House? And even if we did, could we survive the barrage of amendments that would be fired at the bill, from both sides?

Lost in negative thoughts, I said less than usual at the negotiations that day. It must have been noticeable because late in the afternoon Max leaned over and asked, "Are you okay?" "I'm okay," I answered. "But I have to tell you, this is the hardest damn thing I've ever done." He laughed and nodded in agreement. I made an effort to perk up, to stave off my rising sense of self-pity. I interrupted the discussion, moved it to an item on the agenda in which I was particularly interested, and started asking questions.

The last dark days of February passed slowly, but we persevered, and day by day, issue by issue, we made progress. As we neared the end of the month, and of the negotiations, two major hurdles remained: cap-and-trade and coal miners. Bush had proposed and his team argued strongly for an emissions trading system that he could sell to the business organizations as a market-based solution to the problem of clean air. The environmental organizations and their allies were adamantly opposed. The Committee members were split. But after some internal debate most accepted my argument that we wouldn't be here were it not for the president's decision to reverse Reagan's policy against clean air legislation; if we expected the president to move toward us on some issues, we had to be willing to move toward him on others; this one was especially important to him.

On the coal miners we had struggled for years to find the right balance, without success. Byrd had participated in a few of the negotiating sessions but, unsatisfied by what was on offer, withdrew to enlist the support of other senators and to draft his own legislation. It provided for substantial benefits to coal miners who lost their jobs as a consequence of the legislation. The amounts went far beyond those provided to workers in other industries who might lose their jobs for similar reasons. The administration quickly took the position that the estimated $500 million cost of the Byrd amendment would cause the bill to exceed the president's proposed budget for it. As a result, if Byrd's amendment passed, the president said he would veto the bill. The fate of the clean air bill in the Senate thus would turn on the Byrd amendment.

There were other amendments, of course. The environmentalists continued their criticism of the compromise bill. They heavily lobbied for three major amendments, each of which would have strengthened the bill, but adoption of any of them would have killed it because Bush had committed to a veto if any of the amendments was included in the final version. I was thus placed in the extremely uncomfortable position of publicly and aggressively opposing amendments that, in other circumstances, I might have supported. This further antagonized the environmentalists, who stepped up their criticism of me. Tim Wirth, a Democrat from Colorado, and Pete Wilson, a Republican from California, proposed to strengthen the requirements on automobile emissions. Wilson then joined with John Kerry, a Massachusetts Democrat, in proposing to strengthen the controls on smog. Frank Lautenberg proposed a strengthening amendment on toxic emissions. His amendment was especially painful for me to oppose, because we were such good friends and because he had worked so hard and so constructively on clean air and other important environmental legislation. In each case my argument was simple: "Do you want to make a statement or make a law?" While the amendments may have been good policy if considered independently, if adopted they would kill the bill. It might make a senator feel good to sponsor or vote for the amendment, and it certainly would help his or her voting record with environmental groups, but it would not advance the cause of clean air or improve the health of the American people. That argument was persuasive enough to cause the defeat of all three of the amendments. Although the margins were not great, they were misleading. Some of the senators who voted for the strengthening amendments did not in fact support their provisions. They were against the bill and hoped to kill it by supporting the amendments, in the hope that one or more would pass and induce a presidential veto.

Finally the Byrd amendment was reached. As I rose in the Senate chamber to speak against it on March 29, head throbbing and nose running, the gallery was full, the chamber was packed. I knew that I had already lost a majority of the Senate's Democrats. That morning many of them had informed me that they were going to vote with Byrd. It felt like a rapid series of hammer blows, each hurting more than the one before. Most of them said some variation of "You know how much I like and support you, and I really do support clean air, but I just can't take a chance on this one. I've got a big project pending in Appropriations." I understood and appreciated their predicament. Although I was deeply disappointed, I kept my hurt feelings to myself. I simply thanked each senator for his or her consideration, shook hands, and turned to receive the next bit of bad news. There would be other votes, tomorrow, next week, next month, on which I would need their help. That's the reality of being Senate majority leader. You always have to keep in mind the next battle, and the one after that. You can't afford permanent enemies.

Ninety-nine senators were present that day, so we needed fifty votes.* I tried hard,

* Senator Johnston had to attend a funeral and was necessarily absent. He announced that if he were able to be present he would have voted for

311

but I couldn't get a reading on every single senator, so when the clerk started to call the roll I knew that we would win or lose by one vote, but I didn't know which way it would go. I closed the debate by pointing out the problems with the amendment and urging senators to cast a vote for clean air. In his closing remarks, made just before I spoke, Dole emphasized to Republican senators the importance of the vote to the president. With so many Democrats lining up behind Byrd, and several Republicans who served on the Appropriations Committee going with him as well, we needed every available Republican vote. As the roll call progressed, I heard Steve Symms of Idaho vote yes. I knew he opposed the whole effort and strongly disagreed with the substance of Byrd's amendment, so this was just an attempt to induce a veto by the president. I walked toward Dole to urge him

---

the Byrd amendment. This had no effect on the outcome. If he had been present and voted no, there would have been a tie, fifty to fifty. The presiding officer of the Senate was Vice President Dan Quayle; he would have broken the tie in a manner consistent with the president's position, so the outcome would have been the same: the amendment defeated by one vote.

to talk with Symms, but before I got there Dole had already collared him. As the end of the vote neared we were down by two votes, fifty to forty-eight. Only Joe Biden had not yet voted. Dole had to persuade Symms to switch, and I had to persuade Biden to vote no. Biden, a friend with whom I'd worked closely on major anticrime legislation, had already made it clear to me that he would like to support Byrd's amendment. But he didn't want the whole bill to go down. He needed to be assured that the veto threat was genuine. I tried to get the president on the phone to deliver that message directly to Biden. Bush wasn't available, but his chief of staff, John Sununu, was. After the vote Biden addressed the Senate to explain his decision:

I had indicated to Senator Byrd that my sympathies were with his position — I, like him, would like to help the coal miners — and if this were not a deal buster, if this would not kill this bill, I would vote with him. But if it would, I would not.

I heard a good deal of discussion characterizing whether it would or would not kill this bill. I acknowledge that the phone call I received was incredibly timely, but, nonetheless, I received a phone call and spoke to Mr. Sununu. I asked him point blank: First, did they see this as a deal buster and, not going around the barn; second, would they, in fact, guarantee to me they would veto this; is that what they were saying?

And the answer was yes. First, they thought it was a deal buster because it pushed up the total dollar cost of this bill which he said they agreed to. And, secondly, he guaranteed me the President was going to veto the bill. I was not ready to take the chance because it has been too many years since there has been a clean air bill, and I believe passage of a bill this year is necessary to deal with acid rain and other pollution problems that are hurting my State and so many others in this country.[16]

Immediately after Biden voted Symms switched his vote to no. It was over. By a vote of fifty to forty-nine the Byrd amendment was defeated.

I had prevailed on that vote, but of the fifty-three Senate Democrats other than Byrd and me, only fifteen had joined me in voting against the amendment. I was profoundly grateful to each for their courage, especially three of them who were most vulnerable. Pat Leahy of Vermont and Wyche Fowler of Georgia were members of the Appropriations Committee, where they dealt daily with Byrd. Although not a member of that Committee, Joe Biden had conspicuously cast the deciding vote. After it was over, I thanked Leahy and Fowler, then walked across the chamber to Biden. "Congratulations," he said, "you earned it." I grabbed his arm and pulled him close. "Joe," I said, "you've got guts."

As on all Senate votes, the clerk who called the roll recorded each vote on a long rectangular tally sheet. The next day Byrd took that tally sheet, had it framed, and hung it next to the door leading into his Appropriations Committee office. For years thereafter anyone who entered his office was reminded of that vote.

After the result was announced I extended my hand to Byrd. We shook hands wordlessly. It was a grim moment, the low point in our relationship. After that our interests and views most often coincided, and I continued to seek his advice regularly, especially on the rules and procedures of the Senate. As a result our relations steadily improved. Four years later, just before I retired from the Senate, I visited him in his office, where we had a warm and cordial talk. When I left, our relationship was the best it had ever been. Twenty years later, at Byrd's funeral, Joe Biden, by then the vice president, jokingly told the story of his vote on the Byrd amendment to the clean air bill. Amid the laughter I thought about how the passage of time really does smooth over the jagged edges of our lives, leaving us with memories that tell the story as we'd like to remember it.

On April 3, 1990, the Senate passed the clean air bill by a vote of eighty-nine to eleven. The outside groups reacted predictably: the environmentalists said it was too weak; the affected industries said it was too strong.[17]

We made many concessions to the White House to get the bill through the Senate. But, to my dismay, the White House undertook a major effort to further weaken the bill in the House. It wasn't a violation of our agreement; Roger Porter made it clear at the very end of our negotiation, when we had an agreement but before we took the bill to the Senate floor, that the White House was not bound to it once the bill passed the Senate. But while it was not a violation of the agreement, I felt it was inconsistent with the spirit of our negotiation. I had already spilled a lot of political blood to get the agreement and would have to make a costly personal effort during Senate consideration of the bill, speaking and voting against my friends and their amendments. It was too late for me to abandon the course I had chosen. We had the agreement and I had to honor it, which I did. But I didn't feel right about the way it ended.

One of the most potent arguments used against me by the environmental groups and the Democratic senators who shared their views was that I had started the Committee bill down a slippery slope: the White House would water down the bill when it reached the House, and then again in the inevitable conference between the House and Senate. My answer, which few of them found persuasive, was that the White House was miscalculating its chances in the House and in the conference. I had given the White House full access to the Senate process. But the House leadership excluded the White House from their inner deliberations. They could do that because in the House, unlike the Senate, the majority, if united, need not concern itself with those in the minority. Of course there were plenty of House members, Republicans and some Democrats, who kept the White House informed, but being kept informed is much less valuable than being at the negotiating table as a full and equal partner.

Word spread and reached the press about the White House's intentions. Because it was inevitable that whatever bill the House passed would be different from the Senate bill, a conference committee, composed of senators and representatives, would resolve the differences. Ordinarily the conferees are committed to the provisions of their body's bill: senators advocate for the Senate bill, House members for their bill. Eventually they both compromise. I was confident that the House bill would be at least as strong as the Senate bill, even stronger in some areas, so I wanted to give the Senate conferees the greatest possible latitude to yield to the House provisions whenever they believed it would strengthen the bill.

At one of our last meetings I proposed to Porter that our agreement be binding all the way through the conference committee. If he accepted, I was prepared to fully honor the agreement. I thought the Senate bill was strong enough to be a good law. But if he declined, the Senate would have more freedom in the conference to work for an even stronger bill. As expected, he declined. I really liked Porter personally and had (and still have) total respect for his ability and integrity. I'm sure he believed it when he told me that the reason for declining my offer was that the administration didn't want to offend the House by supporting the Senate bill. No doubt that was valid, but I believed there were other reasons, also valid, one of which was a desire to bring the bill back closer to what the president had initially proposed. As a result of our exchange, which all of the Senate supporters of the bill were aware of, it was clear to everyone that we had in good faith negotiated an agreement, we offered to make it permanent, and the White House declined, as they had every right to do. So once the bill passed the Senate we were on our own. The administration could work to weaken the bill, and I could work to strengthen it. I thought the White House was making a grave mistake, that they were wrong in thinking they could, through Dingell, get a weaker bill. I now had an even greater incentive to see that the final bill was as strong as possible.

In the Senate the Committee had reported a bill in November 1989, the internal discussions took place in February 1990, floor debate took place in March, and final passage occurred on April 3. In the House, by contrast, the internal discussions came first and stretched over a period of several months, the Committee reported a bill on April 5, floor debate took place in May, and final passage occurred on May 23. At every step in the process Dingell and Waxman competed to control the outcome, right down to the last day of debate on the House floor. My confidence that Dingell and Waxman would resolve their differences was based on my personal experience with both men and on several other factors, including the circumstances facing Dingell. His seniority and extraordinary ability had enabled him to amass substantial prestige and influence in the House, which he used aggressively to protect his constituents. But he knew his limits. On this issue, one limit was the fact that a majority of Democrats in the House favored strong action on clean air. He could delay, he could modify, but he could not stop it. Most important, I did not believe that he wanted to stop it. I thought the White House and the business groups misjudged Dingell and were engaged in wishful thinking that he would somehow kill the bill. Like all members of Congress he rationalized differences between the interests of his district and those of the nation. But I thought that in the end he would do what was best for the country and would not risk his own position to try to defeat a bill that he believed was in the overall national interest. To the contrary, he would do his best to shape it and, then, when it passed, proclaim victory.

Speaker of the House Tom Foley put strong pressure on Dingell and Waxman to resolve their differences. After a contentious battle over a provision on alternative fuels that continued to the last minute (an alternative fuel provision had, also at the last minute, made it into the Senate bill), Dingell and Waxman joined together to work for approval by the full House. The bill passed by an overwhelming margin, 401 to 21.*

The House-Senate conference to reconcile the differences between the bills got off to a slow start. The bill was so large and important that many different committees and members wanted to be in on the action. As a result the House conferees, totaling 130 and representing seven committees,

* Eighteen years later, after a bitter contest, House Democrats voted to elect Waxman as chairman of the Energy and Commerce Committee, displacing Dingell, who had become chairman in 1981. In 2014 both announced their retirement.

were not even appointed until June 28, more than a month after the House passed its bill. The first formal meeting took place in July, and little happened until the Congress reconvened in September, following its summer break. The process picked up quickly thereafter, and a compromise bill was agreed on October 22. The conference proceeded and concluded about as I had hoped and predicted. Baucus skillfully guided the Senate conferees. Although some disagreements lingered on the House side, Dingell and Waxman worked out their differences. The House yielded to the Senate's stronger acid rain provisions, but on almost all other issues the Senate yielded and the stronger provisions of the House bill prevailed. As a result the conference "succeeded in strengthening the bill sent to President Bush."[18] It was the best possible result, from my perspective. Four days later the House approved the conference committee report 401 to 25. The next day, Saturday, October 27, the Senate agreed, eighty-nine to ten. Late that evening I left the Capitol with a mix of feelings: exhaustion, relief, elation, accomplishment. My ten-year clean air effort was over.

After the bill was signed into law, several White House aides said that their decision not to extend our agreement had been a mistake.[19]

The following year several of the environmental organizations asked me to address their annual conferences, at which they lauded my efforts on behalf of the environment; some of them gave me plaques describing me as their "Man of the Year" for my work on clean air legislation. I swallowed my anger and resisted the temptation to gloat. I knew that before I left the Senate I would want and ask for their help on other issues. I attended, accepted my plaques, and spoke earnestly about the importance of protecting the health of Americans.

More meaningful validation came with the passage of time. Twenty-two years later the Environmental Protection Agency reported, "Since 1990, nationwide air quality has improved significantly for six common air pollutants."[20] In 2011 the Natural Resources Defense Council, one of our nation's leading environmental organizations, concluded, "The Clean Air Act is a genuine American success story and one of the most effective tools in U.S. history for protecting public health." Among many other health benefits, the NRDC estimated that the 1990 amendments saved nearly two million lives. It had been a long and hard struggle, but it was worth the effort.

1

With Barbara and Robbie, 1939

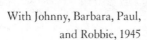

2

With Johnny, Barbara, Paul,
and Robbie, 1945

Mama and Daddy, 1950

3

I arrived late for the team picture at the Boys Club and didn't have time to change.

First Row, left to right: G. MITCHELL, J. HANDY, Captain M. JORDAN, W. BART-LETT, R. BROWN. Second Row, left to right: Coach COOMBS, J. HEBERT, B. FRASER, M. WEINER, Manager G. EMERY.

Basketball at Bowdoin, 1951

LEFT: U.S. Army counterintelligence agent, Berlin, Germany, 1956

BELOW: Being sworn in as a U.S. district court judge by Frank Coffin, chief judge of the U.S. Court of Appeals in the First Circuit, 1979

8

Welcomed to the
U.S. Senate by
President Carter as
Senator Ed Muskie
looks on, 1980

9

At a Senate committee meeting, 1984

Campaigning in Maine, 1988

10

With Senator Ted
Kennedy

11

Leaving a White
House meeting

12

Sharing a laugh with
Senators Bob Dole
and Robert Byrd

13

With President Clinton, 1994

President Clinton awarded me
the Medal of Freedom, the
highest civilian honor of the U.S.
government, at the White House
on St. Patrick's Day, 1999.

Announcing the investigation into the use of performance-enhancing
drugs in Major League Baseball, with Commissioner Bud Selig, 2006

17   As U.S. Envoy for Middle East Peace, with Vice President Biden, President Obama, and Secretary of State Clinton, 2009

18

Meeting with President Abbas, Prime Minister Netanyahu, and Secretary of State Clinton, September 2010

19

Our children keep us young. In Maine, 2005.

20

Heather, Andrew, Claire, and I returned to the Northern Ireland Assembly building, March 2012.

THE STATE OF ALTOONA

In addition to the Clean Air and Clean Water acts, the Senate Committee on Environment and Public Works dealt with other important issues, one of which was transportation infrastructure. Every few years Congress reviews and reauthorizes the laws that control the raising and spending of hundreds of billions of dollars on our nation's highways, bridges, and transit systems. The money comes from the federal tax on the refining and sale of gasoline. It is then redistributed to the states in accordance with a complex formula that is always the subject of much contention, as members of Congress battle to increase their state's share. Each time the measure moved through Congress while I was in the Senate, it generated unforgettable displays of aggressive behavior, statesmanship, and good humor. Also on display were the unique talents of Daniel Patrick Moynihan and Bud Shuster.

Before entering the Senate from New York, "Pat," as he was widely known, worked in both Democratic and Republican administrations. If there had been a title of resident intellectual in the Senate he would have been a top contender for it (along with Paul Sarbanes of Maryland). Widely read, Moynihan could (and did), at the merest hint of a question, expound on the foreign policies of the Russian czars of the eighteenth century or the domestic policies of the British Labour Party in the nineteenth century. As a member of the Committee, he regarded the periodic free-for-all over the funding formula as grubby but necessary business. I worked with him and others on the Committee to resolve the nasty fracas over the allocation formula in a process that at first seemed hopeless but always, somehow, got worked out. While competitive and political, the atmosphere was not as toxic as it is now; bipartisan cooperation was common then. Among my fond memories is working with Moynihan and the leaders of the counterpart House Committee to resolve differences between the two bodies on one of the transportation bills.

Bud Shuster was a senior Republican

member of Congress representing a district in central Pennsylvania centered on the city of Altoona. In an arena in which political aggression was the norm, Shuster stood out as superaggressive in fighting for his district. Yet although he was at times blunt, even gruff, he understood the need for compromise in enacting legislation.

The process that later grew rapidly and earned infamy as "earmarks" was then still a relatively minor part of the bill when measured in dollars, although critically important for oiling the squeakiest wheels. No wheel squeaked louder or more often than Shuster. He was there to make sure that the people of central Pennsylvania got their fair share, which to him meant quite a bit more than anyone else's definition of *fair*. But of course there is no objective definition; everyone decides what is fair through the prism of self-interest.

It took nearly two years and an override of a presidential veto to get the mammoth bill through the Senate, and then through a conference with the House, made necessary because the House and Senate bills were not identical. Through it all Moynihan maintained his composure and good humor as we reached agreement with one state after another. After the bill became law we went to the Senate press gallery to engage in the pleasant process of self-congratulation. We were feeling very good when someone asked Moynihan which state fared best in the battle over the funding formula. Without hesitation, and with only the sparkle in his eyes betraying humor, Moynihan answered, "The State of Altoona." I have always regretted that I wasn't present when Shuster was told of Moynihan's comment; his laughter must have shaken the Capitol dome.

"An Investment in Our Nation's Future"

For several years I devoted a great deal of time and effort to Maine projects. One of them was in Brunswick, for many years the daily scene of Maine's worst traffic jam. In the late afternoon thousands of day-shift workers from the Bath Iron Works got into their cars to drive home, as did thousands of military and civilian employees of the Brunswick Naval Air Station, located just a few miles away. And they all came together with the always heavy traffic on U.S. Route 1, a busy summer tourism route, which passes through Brunswick and Bath. On the many occasions I visited the area, or any town within a radius of thirty miles, people expressed concern, frustration, even anger over the daily gridlock. After years of debate and study, state and federal officials came up with a plan to deal with the problem: it included a bypass highway around Brunswick and new approaches and ultimately a new bridge in Bath to replace the old structure that crossed the Kennebec River there. The cost of the bypass was estimated at $15 million and improvements for the Bath bridge at $10 million.

I lost count of the many meetings members of my staff and I had with other members of the Senate committee and relevant House members on this project. I was assisted by Grace Reef, an able and hardworking member of my staff who never took no for an answer. Her determination and skill were evident by the time she was twelve years old. A skilled baseball player, she was denied the opportunity to play in the Little League in her hometown of Portland. She sued the national organization, won, and became the first girl ever to play in the Little League.[21] She was as tenacious and successful on the Brunswick bypass. It was a long and difficult struggle, but by 1987 the project was included in the Senate transportation bill. It was, however, not included in the House bill, so Grace and I had to work very hard at the conference to keep it in.

During the process the Reagan administration expressed opposition to funding for mass transit and to some of the projects in the bill. At one meeting with some of the conferees, an administration official identified a list of projects the president wanted deleted from the bill. We had no way of knowing how much involvement, if any, the president himself had in the details. I thought it unlikely. To my dismay Brunswick was on their hit list, as were many of the projects proposed by congressional leaders. Then an eagle-eyed congressional staff member noted that under the administration proposal most of the projects in the president's home state of California remained in the bill. The official was asked to explain why the projects in our states were unacceptable to the president, but those in California remained in the bill. In response he said, with a straight face, "We approve those we believe to be investments in our nation's future."

After much wrangling we reached a compromise, but because of continuing disagreement over other provisions, including mass transit funding, the president vetoed the bill when it reached his desk. At first we failed by one vote to override it, but a second try succeeded. Grace and I had to do another round of meetings but were able to keep Brunswick in, and I heaved a huge sigh of relief when the bill became law.

Not long afterward I was invited to speak

to a business group in Brunswick. I accepted gladly, eager to get credit for my work on the bypass. In the question-and-answer period after my speech, one man delivered a sharp denunciation of "out-of-control pork-barrel" spending by the Congress. When he finished I asked him if he considered the Brunswick Bypass to be "out-of-control pork-barrel" spending. "No," he replied. He calmly cited the important work on navy ships at the Bath shipyard and the Atlantic Ocean submarine patrols by navy planes from the Brunswick Naval Air Station, and concluded by describing the $15 million to be spent on the bypass as "an investment in our nation's future." From California to Maine the refrain is the same: My project is an investment in our nation's future. Yours is pork.

Among other large projects we were able to keep in the bill were two of great immediate significance to Maine: full funding for a new bridge over the Fore River connecting Portland and South Portland and for a new bridge over the Kennebec River connecting Waterville and Winslow. Both bridges were subsequently constructed and have had a positive effect on the communities and the state as a whole.

There was a smaller project of less immediate significance that has had an even larger impact on the state. Passenger rail service to Maine was discontinued more than fifty years ago. By the time I got to the Senate Maine was one of only two of the forty-eight states in the continental United States without such service. Wayne Davis, a Maine man with large vision and uncommon energy, led an effort by a coalition of Maine groups and individuals seeking to restore passenger service. I had worked with and gotten to know Graham Claytor, a resourceful executive who was then running Amtrak. Grace Reef and another talented young member of my staff, Sandy Brown, were able to gain inclusion of funding for the first in a series of feasibility studies, all of which were positive and promising. Claytor then authorized the track improvements and running equipment (all of it used but clean and functional), and passenger rail service was restored. The results have been spectacular, exceeding even the most optimistic projections. Today the Amtrak *Downeaster* carries thousands of passengers each day from Portland to Boston and back, and service has been extended north from Portland to Brunswick.

It is undeniable that the legislative process was later abused. The number of projects in the highway and other bills rose from dozens to hundreds to thousands in a few decades. The type of project expanded with the number and the costs, and the "earmark" era resulted. Yet it also is undeniable that many of the projects were appropriate, even necessary. No one has yet been able to figure out how to objectively decide which is appropriate and which is not in a society in which "an investment in our nation's future" is widely used to justify a project for my state but not for yours. Perhaps the most useful approach would be to subject each project to a separate vote in the House and Senate; while that method would itself be imperfect, at least it would require the approval, out in the open, of a majority of members of each house of Congress for each project.

READ MY LIPS

I woke up earlier than usual on the morning of June 26, 1990. Nelson Mandela was to address a joint session of Congress that day, after which I would host a luncheon in his honor. I had a lot to do to get ready for the day, including a decision on the sensitive issue of which senators would sit at Mandela's table. I had just gotten out of bed when the phone rang. It's early, I thought as I reached for the phone, it must be important. It was.

A White House operator asked if I could speak with President Bush's chief of staff, John Sununu. He was cordial and direct. The president wanted me to come to the White House for breakfast that morning. Would I be willing to do so? "Of course," I replied. "I'll be there in an hour." I asked who else would be there. From the Congress, Tom Foley, the Democratic speaker of the House, and Dick Gephardt, the majority leader. Treasury Secretary Nicholas Brady, Budget Director Dick Darman, and Sununu would accompany the president. He didn't have to say anything else. I knew what the meeting would be about.

Bush had been elected president on November 8, 1988. On the same day I was reelected to the Senate and Foley and Gephardt were reelected to the House. But our differences on taxes and the budget had begun before election day.

Three months earlier, in New Orleans, Bush had accepted the Republican Party's nomination for president. He brought the huge crowd at the Louisiana Superdome to its feet with a dramatic promise: "My opponent won't rule out raising taxes. But I will. And the Congress will push me to raise taxes and I'll say no. And they'll push, and I'll say no, and they'll push again, and I'll say to them, 'Read my lips: no new taxes.' " The last six words were spoken slowly, with emphasis and passion. They ultimately came to define his campaign. Although he didn't use the word *Democrats,* everyone knew what he meant; both houses of Congress were controlled by the Democrats.

Bush offered his supporters two comforting reassurances: that the Democrats would want to raise taxes, again and again, and that he would say no, again and again. I recall having a sinking feeling as I watched him speak those words on television. While I understood the political imperative — he was behind in the polls — I felt the pledge was unwise, poor policy that would constrain him and affect the economy. "If he wins," I thought, "there's going to be a tough fight on the budget." And there was. It began early in Bush's term and continued for two years.

Going back at least to Reagan's presidency, the Republicans had pummeled the Democrats on taxes, especially federal income taxes, with considerable political success. After gaining a substantial reduction in personal income tax rates in his first term, Reagan initiated an intensive debate on tax reform in his second term. Among other changes, he proposed that the top marginal income tax rate on individuals be reduced to 35 percent.* The House approved a tax reform bill in 1985, but the legislation stalled in the Senate Finance

* In 2014 individuals filing a joint return were subject to a top marginal tax rate of 39.6 percent on that portion of their taxable income that exceeded $406,750.

Committee. Faced with the possibility that the failure of the president's tax reform bill would occur on his watch, the chairman of the Senate Finance Committee, Bob Packwood, a Republican from Oregon, worked with the congressional Joint Committee on Taxation to devise a bold alternative. At first this new approach only attracted the support of a bipartisan, core group of six Finance Committee members who met privately to fine-tune an alternative.* As an early and committed supporter of tax reform, I participated in this core group. After intense discussion, we agreed on a broad reform package. Packwood took the lead and, with considerable skill, got it through the Finance Committee on a unanimous vote. A feature of the proposal was that the top marginal income tax rate on individuals would be reduced to 27 percent (later in the process increased to 28 percent) and that rate would apply to capital gains as well as ordinary income; the capital gains differential was to be eliminated. I told

* Members were Packwood, Republican senators John Chafee of Rhode Island and John Danforth of Missouri, and Democratic senators Daniel P. Moynihan of New York, Bill Bradley of New Jersey, and I.

Packwood and the other members of the group that while I would join them in bringing the bill to the full Senate for debate, I disagreed with this provision. I felt then, as I do now, that the top marginal tax rate should be in the mid-30s. I made it clear that I would offer an amendment in the Senate to restore what President Reagan had originally proposed: a top marginal rate of 35 percent. So, when the Senate debated the tax reform bill in June 1986, I offered an amendment that was based on Reagan's initial proposal: a top rate of 35 percent with capital gains taxed at a lower rate. Then and later, in 1989, when the capital gains tax debate was renewed, I made it clear that I supported the capital gains differential only if certain conditions were met. I believe that in a fair and progressive tax system, a properly crafted differential can provide a modest benefit, especially if targeted to new and small business. But that should occur only in a manner that does not have a serious adverse effect on the budget deficit.

Since my amendment was in many crucial respects identical to what the president himself had proposed, and a lower rate on capital gains had been and remains a critical element in Republican tax policy, I hoped I might gain some support from the administration and some Republican senators. But there was none. The Reagan-Bush administration opposed my amendment. While a slim majority of Democrats voted in my favor, only two Republicans did so; that overwhelming Republican opposition led to the amendment's defeat. During the debate on my amendment Senator Packwood sharply criticized the entire concept of a capital gains differential: "The biggest loophole for the rich is back. It is capital gains now that we put the rates up to 35 percent. That is a higher rate than most people are willing to take and still invest in risky ventures providing so-called venture capital. So we have brought the capital gains differential back. It is the biggest single loophole for the income class above $200,000."[22] He was joined by Senator Chafee:

The important point I wish to make is that under current law, because of the shelters and because of capital gains, 67 percent of the rich — 60 percent of those are now paying less than 20 percent of their income in taxes. In other words, although the top rate is 50 percent, they are not paying it. Sixty-seven percent are paying less than 30 percent of their income in taxes, and

43 percent of the very rich — 43 percent of all those with incomes over $200,000 — are paying less than 20 percent of their incomes in taxes. Between shelters and capital gains, they avoid taxes and they cruise along very happily at rates far below the maximum, which is 50 percent.[23]

To say that I was surprised is an understatement. Here were the Republican chairman of the Senate Finance Committee and a senior Republican member of that Committee directly criticizing a tax provision that is a pillar of Republican policy (and that also had the support of many Democrats). Their arguments were directly contrary to what Republicans had said in the past, and often would say again in the future, about the importance of a lower tax rate on income derived from capital gains than on ordinary (or earned) income.

Chafee was a close friend of mine; we worked together on the Clean Air Act and many other environmental issues. Later, after my amendment had been voted down and the bill had safely passed, I asked him what happened. How was it possible that President Reagan and Vice President Bush opposed a capital gains differential? "They want the top rate to be as low as possible," he explained. "That means more to them than anything. But once they get what they want on the tax rate they'll come back for a lower capital gains tax as soon as they can, just like you guys will come back on rates."

That's exactly what happened. In 1988, when he campaigned for president, Bush strongly advocated a lower tax rate for capital gains. There was a jarring dissonance between what Bush said in 1988 and what Packwood and Chafee, with the support of the Reagan-Bush administration, had said during the Senate debate in 1986. Packwood had called it "the biggest loophole for the rich." Bush now said it was the way to encourage economic growth. I assumed the earlier decision was merely tactical, as is common on all sides in legislative battles, to accept some provisions you don't like to get other provisions more important to you.

Bush strongly advocated for a reduction in the rate on capital gains, but his proposal did not meet the criteria on which I had based my support for a capital gains rate differential. While it may have generated a short-term increase in federal revenues, within a few years it would have significantly increased the budget deficit, so I opposed it. A long and intense struggle ensued. The president's proposal passed in the House by

deficit. The differences are now familiar to most Americans: President Bush was opposed to any new taxes; we believed that the deficit reduction package had to be balanced: it should include both spending cuts and tax increases.

Month after month our disagreement played out on the stage of national politics. The White House approach was clear and consistent with the president's dramatic speech at the convention: The Democrats will insist on raising taxes and I will say no. The White House was willing to talk with congressional leaders, but the outcome was known and stated in advance. Sununu later made it public and clear: "We're allowing them to bring their good arguments for taxes to the table. They were not persuasive last time, and they are likely not to be persuasive again. But if they want to come to the table and say they put tax increases there, it is their prerogative to put them on the table, and it's our prerogative to say no. And I emphasize the 'no.' "[24] It was a skillful political strategy. The president was generally popular; he had extended his hand to us in friendship during his inaugural address, a gesture many found appealing. Later, when the first Gulf War broke out, his popularity soared to over 90 percent.

He tried to use his popularity, and his now famous pledge, to get us to drop our demand for a balanced approach and yield to his position of dealing with the deficit solely by cutting spending. We shared his concern about the budget deficit, but his words, actions, and negotiating position led us to conclude that his primary concern was to spur the economy by reducing taxes on the relatively small number of Americans with the highest incomes. Their taxes had been cut in the Reagan administration, and the deficit and debt rose dramatically. Now Bush wanted to reduce their taxes even more, even though the stated goal was reducing the deficit. We believed that a balanced approach was necessary to achieve economic growth and job creation, which all agreed was the most important objective.

The struggle continued in various forms. The cherry blossoms came and went, as did the April showers. A year and a half had passed and the midterm congressional elections were just a few months away.

To deal with the president's approach we needed a strategy. But there were then 315 Democratic members of the Congress, House and Senate, each elected independently, each believing that he or she

346

had the answer to our nation's fiscal problems, each seeking an outlet for his or her views. So it would be an overstatement to describe our approach as a strategy. The president had to lead, especially on taxes. We had to exercise restraint, to wait for that to happen. It was, in effect, a default position, the only course for which we had any hope of garnering some degree of consensus from our Democratic colleagues. Though obvious and simple, it was extremely difficult to implement because it required patience, fortitude, and restraint, three qualities in short supply in our political process. Voters like their representatives to be independent, so most members, at least rhetorically, proclaim themselves to be independent-minded. It seemed to me that it would be impossible to get all of the Democratic representatives and senators to refrain from making budget proposals, especially those that included tax increases, at a time when they were bombarded by the press and public with demands to do so. Still difficult, but not impossible, would be getting the Democratic leadership in the House and Senate to do so. So Foley, Gephardt, and I led an effort to persuade our colleagues to let the president take the lead. Both were able, experienced leaders. I liked and respected both and worked closely with them. We had no differences on this issue, which was important because our approach was subject to intense criticism. We were reminded often that when it suited our purposes we had been quick to proclaim that we were elected independently of the president; why weren't we acting independently now? Why weren't we leading? The answer, of course, was clear, and later publicly confirmed by Sununu: the White House was using the well-worn and successful Republican playbook of portraying Democrats as tax-and-spend liberals while they were the guardians of fiscal sanity. No doubt they also believed that what they were proposing was best for the economy, but we strongly disagreed. We viewed our policies as best for the economy in the long run.

It's hard to get members of Congress to act; it's even harder to get them to say nothing, especially when they are repeatedly asked to speak out. The lure of the camera and of the headline is great. But, somewhat to my surprise, we largely succeeded. It was imperfect; a few committee chairs occasionally didn't comply with our request. But I knew our approach was working when I was visited by Dick Darman.

He was highly intelligent, articulate, with a wry sense of humor and an occasionally sharp tongue. I liked him and we got along well. I sometimes wished he was on our side. There had been many press accounts, and even more private discussions, about Darman's unhappiness with Bush's no-tax pledge. He was reported to have tried to keep the pledge out of the president's speech, describing it as "stupid and dangerous."[25] But Bush was in a tough election battle and already was suspect to conservatives, so to placate them he made the fateful pledge. Now, nearly two years later, Darman was trying to get him off the hook. We sat in my office in the Senate majority leader's suite and chatted amicably about our predicament. Darman suggested a high-level meeting from which "an agreement on a tax increase would emerge." "What do you mean, it will 'emerge'?" I asked. He extended his arms, placed his hands palms-down on the table, and raised them slowly, making a fluttering motion. As he did so he said, "Well, it will just emerge." I smiled at his ingenuity and replied, "Well, I'm sorry, but you know the politics of this very well." I then repeated his fluttering gesture. "That's just not going to work. The president has got to be clear on it. Then we'll support it." We parted amicably, still in disagreement.

Inevitably the administration's internal differences emerged publicly. At a meeting in early May Bush had suggested that we initiate talks on the budget "with no preconditions." We would not and could not decline an invitation from the president, so we accepted. The press interpreted the invitation as a softening of his no-tax pledge, and dissension broke out among Republicans. But I took no chances. I told Darman that our position was unchanged. We were not going to walk into a trap. He assured me that was not the case. Almost immediately afterward Sununu told reporters that while Democrats could propose tax increases at the negotiations, the president would reject them. It was "Read my lips" all over again. Sununu's comments uncorked the dissension that had been building among Republicans. The president's spokesman, Marlin Fitzwater, emphasized that "no preconditions" meant just that, and some Republican members of Congress criticized Sununu; Vice President Quayle spoke out in Sununu's defense.

The White House had a problem familiar to everyone who has participated in controversial high-level political negotiations: it was trying to convey two different messages to two different audiences at the same time. To the president's right were the many members of his party who thought he was not conservative enough; they were passionate about his no-tax increase pledge. To his left were others in his party, the business community, and independents; many of them regarded his pledge as purely political and economically unsound. Sununu was the point man to those who demanded fidelity to the pledge; Darman was trying to assure those who demanded flexibility. It ultimately became evident that it was impossible to please both sides.

The discussions that began in mid-May 1990 were fatally handicapped in three respects: the Democrats were extremely apprehensive and suspicious; the Republicans were increasingly in disarray; and the president, the House speaker, and I did not participate personally. We designated representatives to attend, in my case two trusted and very able senators, Jim Sasser of Tennessee, the chairman of the Budget Committee, and Wyche Fowler of Georgia, a member of the Appropriations Committee. The talks proceeded off and on for several weeks.

On June 20 Darman presented to the

negotiators what he termed a new proposal. But when we examined it we found that the only thing new in it was the insertion of the word *new* in the description. Our expectations declined even further. Darman, clearly alarmed, initiated a flurry of activity to try to breathe life into the talks. He met with the chairman of the Senate Finance Committee, Senator Lloyd Bentsen of Texas, and the chairman of the House Ways and Means Committee, Representative Dan Rostenkowski of Illinois. Bentsen spoke by phone with the president, then met over that weekend with Nick Brady, the secretary of the Treasury, an ally of Darman and a close friend of the president. Bentsen briefed me on his discussions. He said he had been clear and consistent, that the president had to take the first step on taxes, and he thought they had gotten the message. Early in the following week I met again with Darman and Brady. Foley, Gephardt, and I remained in close contact. We sensed that the internal tensions so evident in the White House would soon be resolved. We were determined to maintain our position and our discipline. Then came Sununu's early morning call.

I immediately called Foley, who confirmed that he and Gephardt would attend the breakfast meeting. We decided to meet at the Capitol in forty-five minutes and ride to the White House together. On the way we agreed on our approach: Foley would speak first and in detail, then Gephardt and I would follow with brief comments. There was no difference in our positions and we would be careful not to let any emerge in the discussion. Sununu had been clear about his expectations. We had to be equally clear about ours.

Over a breakfast of scrambled eggs, toast, and coffee, the discussion was civil, even low key. The president was accompanied by Sununu, Darman, and Brady. Bush spoke first. He calmly stressed the importance of dealing with the growing budget deficit, the threat that high interest rates posed to the economy. He had described the problem before, in public, and there was nothing with which we disagreed. We all knew that we had a problem; we had to work together to solve it. Darman followed with a fact-filled presentation that supported and amplified the president's. Foley responded. Speaking as calmly and persuasively as had the president, he set forth our position on the scope and significance of the problem. He also broke no new ground. He concluded by repeating what we had said many times: we were prepared to strongly support the president once he took the lead in making clear that a balanced approach, which included taxes, was needed to address the problem. I and then Gephardt spoke very briefly, supporting Foley. There was a short pause. Then the president said, "Okay, let's go ahead." That was it. There had been no loud voices, no banging on the table, no threats or ultimatums. It was as though we had ratified a prior decision, not reached one during our meeting. The president then turned to Sununu and Darman and asked them to go into the next room and draft a statement. For the few minutes they were gone the rest of us engaged in pleasant, social conversation, as though nothing of significance had happened or was about to happen.

Sununu and Darman returned so quickly with a typewritten statement that I assumed they had prepared it in advance. They handed out copies. I read mine quickly. It was just four sentences long:

STATEMENT BY THE PRESIDENT

I met this morning with the Bipartisan leadership — the Speaker, the Senate Majority Leader, the Senate Republican

Leader, the House Majority Leader, and the House Republican Leader — to review the status of the deficit-reduction negotiations.

It is clear that both the size of the deficit problem and the need for a package that can be enacted require all of the following: entitlement and mandatory program reform; tax revenue increases; growth incentives; discretionary spending reductions; orderly reductions in defense expenditures; and budget process reform — to assure that any Bipartisan agreement is enforceable and that the deficit problem is brought under responsible control. The Bipartisan leadership agree with me on these points.

We have further agreed that the budget negotiations should reconvene promptly with a view toward reaching substantive agreement as quickly as possible.

Before anyone else spoke I said, "Mr. President, this is very positive. But before we respond I'd like the opportunity to meet for a few minutes privately with my colleagues." The president agreed and Foley, Gephardt, and I went into an adjoining room, where we had a general discussion. We each had a positive reaction, but we also had some concerns. In the second paragraph, the only substantive part of the statement, I thought the words *to me* should be added after "It is clear," so there could be no doubt that it was the president himself who believed that tax revenue increases were required. The second was the phrase itself: *tax revenue increases.* Our preference would have been to delete the word *revenue.* "But," I said, "I think they believe this will get them off the hook with their right wing. So they'll probably insist on it. We should let them have it because it won't save them. They won't get anywhere trying to explain it away by the use of the word *revenue.*" Foley and Gephardt agreed. We also suggested a minor change in the last paragraph. After a further brief discussion we reached full agreement; I took out my pen and wrote the changes on the typewritten draft.[26]

We returned to the breakfast table and I read our proposed changes aloud. I told the president that if he agreed to make that statement public we would return to the Capitol building and within five minutes of its release we would hold a joint press conference at which we would express our agreement with and support for his statement. I then handed him my copy so he could see the changes on paper. He read it, looked up, and repeated what he had said earlier: "Okay, let's go ahead."

The storm broke quickly. Some Republican leaders tried to hold back the tide by arguing that the statement was not a change in policy. But, as we anticipated, their words were drowned out by the protests of disbelief and dismay that reverberated across the country. For all the attention the statement received, Americans would have been justified in thinking that the budget crisis had been resolved. But in fact the struggle continued and even intensified. The president's statement had acknowledged that "tax revenue increases" were necessary, but he had not been specific about which taxes. This led to a long and intense disagreement. The president was stung by the strong reaction to his reneging on his "Read my lips" pledge. This increased his determination to exclude any increase in income taxes from the negotiations and from any agreement. He might agree to other tax increases, but at this point he was adamant on income taxes. He obviously was well aware, as we all were, of how Reagan had handled the issue.

In 1981, his first year in office, Reagan had proposed and gained early enactment of a substantial reduction in federal personal income tax rates. Then, in the summer of 1982, with interest rates and the deficit rising, he supported legislation that cut federal spending and increased taxes. But it was personal income tax rates that were crucial to Reagan, and those were not included in the 1982 bill. On the day the House passed the bill, Reagan said, "I want to thank the Members of both parties . . . who made today's victory possible. . . . A bipartisan majority bit the bullet and voted for the revenue increases and spending cuts we so urgently needed to get deficits and interest rates down, and Americans back to work." He was questioned by reporters who referred to the bill as a tax increase and asked if he was concerned about losing conservative support. In response Reagan said, "To even have referred to this as a tax increase, I think, was wrong, because it was an adjustment of the tax cut that was passed last year."[27]

Describing the tax increase as "revenue increases" and "an adjustment" of the previous year's tax cuts enabled Reagan to maintain that he had never raised taxes. Bush now had a similar problem, but in much more difficult circumstances.

Our negotiations continued for several

more months. There would be many more controversies and many headaches before an agreement was reached. Through the summer and into autumn frustration rose, as did the deficit projections. When we began, the deficit in the next fiscal year was projected to be less than $150 billion; now it was over $200 billion and climbing. In mid-September I joined about two dozen of the other negotiators — congressional leaders and White House aides — at nearby Andrews Air Force Base in what proved to be a vain hope that isolation would induce compromise. But the differences were narrowed only slightly, and after ten days we returned to the Capitol, where the process ground on.

From the time I entered the Senate I returned to Maine almost every weekend, to be with my family and to meet constituents. The disagreement with the president over taxes and the budget was widely reported, of course, and my weekend meetings with constituents grew increasingly contentious. At one such meeting a large crowd, disproportionately elderly, gathered. As was my practice I made no opening speech; I wanted to hear from them, I said, as I invited statements and questions. The first person to speak was an elderly man, well-dressed and articulate, who thanked me for coming and said he wanted to make a statement and then to ask a question. His statement was a sharp denunciation of me for what he described as "excessive partisanship" and an unwillingness to compromise. "The people of this country want you to work with the president," he said to growing applause. "Stop bickering, get together and compromise, settle this like gentlemen." When he completed his statement many in the crowd stood and applauded vigorously. Then he said, "That's my statement. Here's my question: All we get from the TV and newspapers is politics. What are you people arguing about? What are the issues?"

I briefly explained, as best I could, the major issues: taxes and spending cuts, including Medicare. When I finished he jumped to his feet, pointed his finger at me, and said, with much more emotion than before, "Senator, this is a democracy. You represent us. And we're telling you now, loud and clear, you go back there and don't give an inch on Medicare. We've earned it. Neither you, the president, or anyone else can take it away from us." With that the entire crowd stood and gave him an ovation that far exceeded in length and intensity their previous applause. So I went back to Washington with two clear messages from that group of constituents. The problem, of course, was that the messages were somewhat contradictory.

Finally, after a few more weeks of contentious wrangling, we reached agreement in early October on a package that would have reduced the deficit by $500 billion over five years. It included some painful and politically difficult provisions. Federal excise taxes were raised on beer, cigarettes, gasoline, and a host of so-called luxury goods. The cap on income subject to the Medicare portion of the payroll tax was increased, so those with higher incomes had to pay more. At the same time the Medicare premium paid by all of the elderly was increased. Bush had prevailed on personal income tax rates. Try as we might we could not get him to agree to an increase in the top marginal rate above 28 percent. However, from the president's perspective the package was still disappointing because it did not include a reduction in the tax rate on capital gains, which also remained at 28 percent. Spending was cut on a range of programs, including defense, farm support, student loans, and civil service pensions.

As soon as the details were released many

members of Congress, in both parties, who had demanded deficit reduction came out against it. Everyone is for reducing the deficit in concept, but not everyone will support the painful specific actions necessary to do so. In the House Newt Gingrich led the opposition to the package because it included some tax increases, thereby defying the president and Bob Michel, the Republican leader in the House. Many Democrats also opposed the bill because they were concerned that the tax increases would hit lower- and middle-income households harder than those with higher incomes; to offset that effect they felt the top income tax rate should be higher than 28 percent. The president delivered a nationally televised speech in favor of the package, and in what was billed as the televised "rebuttal" I supported the president and the package. Tom Foley, Dick Gephardt, and Bob Michel led the effort in the House. But when the vote in the House took place, on October 5, a majority of Democrats and a majority of Republicans voted no; the bill was defeated, 254 to 179.

Exhausted, apprehensive, angry, we resumed the negotiations. Foley and his Democratic House leadership team went back to the drawing board. They concluded that there was no possibility of getting support from most House Republicans, so they put together a package that would attract most of the Democrats. It included a top marginal tax rate of 33 percent, with a surtax of 10 percent on incomes in excess of $1 million, for an effective top rate of 36.3 percent. Since there were only fifty-five Democrats in the Senate we could not pass the House bill. We needed sixty votes to overcome a filibuster. So we started with the bipartisan package that the president and we supported but the House had just defeated. With a few changes I thought we could pass it in the Senate.

As the dispute dragged on, across the country the political tide had begun to shift, slowly at first, then with gathering momentum. Throughout the negotiations each side had regularly requested analyses of the effects of their proposals from the Congressional Budget Office and the Treasury Department. The closer we got to the end of the process, these analyses, in the form of "distribution tables," made it increasingly clear that the president's proposals — mainly to keep the top marginal income tax rate on earned income at 28 percent while lowering the rate on unearned income through capital gains to

15 percent — when combined with increases in excise taxes on gasoline, alcohol, tobacco, and other items, would have the effect of providing a tax cut for the wealthiest of Americans while raising taxes for almost everybody else. The media picked up on this conclusion and hammered away at it. The midterm elections for a third of the Senate and all of the House were just weeks away. Republican congressional leaders, concerned about the adverse effect on their candidates, became increasingly frustrated with the White House's rigid insistence on its position. Harsh words were exchanged in private, and the tensions made their way to the press. "By Tuesday, September 25 the animosity between Congressional Republicans and the White House was barely disguised."[28]

Foley and Gephardt then successfully led the Democratic bill through the House, and we squeezed the compromise package through the Senate. That was a difficult and unpleasant task for me. As I had on the Clean Air Act a few months earlier, I opposed amendments offered by Democrats even though I personally favored some of them. I believed we had no choice. We had to compromise. A failure to act could have been disastrous for the economy. So I argued, "We must recognize what the realities are." I pointed out that the president had committed himself to vetoing the House bill that raised the top marginal personal income tax rate from 28 to 33 percent. "I don't agree with the president, I think he's wrong. But that is the reality." Long after midnight weary senators passed the bill, fifty-four to forty-six.

Shortly thereafter I told Darman that while I accepted the president's veto threat on a 33 percent rate, even though I strongly disagreed with it, there was room above 28 and under 33 for a compromise in the conference committee that would be needed to iron out the differences in the House and Senate versions of the bill. On the two biggest issues of the year, Clean Air and the budget, I had been out front, on the Senate floor, in opposing Democratic amendments that I personally favored because I believed that compromise was necessary and I thought the president was sincere and acting in good faith. I admired his courage in reversing himself on his tax pledge and had said so publicly, even though he had created the problem for himself by making the pledge. But we had been at this budget effort for nearly two years, during which time the administration was increasingly focused on provisions that would reduce the tax burden on the wealthy; we didn't doubt his sincerity in believing in the theory that this was the best way to spur the economy, but we strongly disagreed with the validity of that theory. It may have made sense when the top marginal rate was 90 percent, or 70. But it made no sense when the top marginal rate was in the mid-30s. And, I emphasized, it was President Reagan who initially proposed a 35 percent rate. Their approach to that issue had to change, I told Darman. Otherwise the whole painful effort had been in vain. We knew and agreed that there had to be cuts in spending. But there had to be a balanced plan. Darman made no substantive comment in response. At least I had gotten my message across and I knew Darman would repeat it to the president.

Whatever the reason, the conference committee soon reached a compromise that was balanced, though unpleasant in some respect to both sides. It included an increase in the top personal income tax rate from 28 to 31 percent and new limitations on the ability of high earners to claim personal exemptions and itemized deductions. Taxes went up on gasoline, alcohol, tobacco, and so-called luxury goods. There were reductions in a range of programs, from Medicare to farm subsidies. Late on the evening of Friday, October 26, 1990, the House passed the conference report, 228 to 200. The next day, Saturday afternoon, the Senate approved it, fifty-four to forty-five. On November 5 President Bush signed it into law.

When measured against the needs of the country it was a modest result. When measured against the difficulty of adopting anything that inflicts sacrifice on any segment of society it was a significant accomplishment. I hoped that from the pain and bitterness of our experience we all had learned valuable lessons that we could apply to better effect in the future. But obviously that didn't happen.

Two Minor Bills That
Had a Major Impact

On the many occasions I've been interviewed about my service in the Senate, almost all of the questions understandably have focused on major, highly publicized matters like the Clean Air Act and the several battles on the budget. I was involved in many other legislative efforts, however, two of which were, in my view, noteworthy because of the major and continuing effects they have had.

One has come to be known as the Low Income Housing Credit. I have already described briefly the tax reform effort of the late 1980s, initiated by President Reagan. The motivating principle was that the tax code had become far too large and complex. Filled with credits and preferences, it distorted economic decisions and inhibited the working of the free market economic system which had proved so beneficial to our society. The thrust of reform was to eliminate all, or as many as politically possible, of the many distorting preferences. The motive was valid and the method sound. As a result the code was trimmed. But, as with all human efforts, it was imperfect. Some preferences that should have been eliminated were retained, while others that should have been retained were eliminated.

Why should any preference be retained? A good question to which there is a good answer: because there are some areas of our economy where there is no market in which profit-seeking enterprises can operate successfully. One such market is in the provision of housing for families with very low income. This was not clear, or at least not accepted as clear, when the Tax Reform Act of 1986 was being considered and debated. I was convinced it was a valid position, and I led the affordable housing effort in the Finance Committee and in floor debate. But I had a hard time convincing other members of the Committee. That was understandable because the very idea of a new or expanded credit was contrary to the primary objective of tax reform.

The Housing Credit is a complicated program but has a simple construct. It is designed to substitute equity capital for debt capital that is typically used to build and acquire real estate. The equity capital is raised from corporations, which receive a return in the form of tax credits on their investment. Almost all real estate — whether a single-family home, an apartment building, or an office building — is largely financed by borrowing money, which requires monthly interest payments to service the debt. But there is much less capacity to borrow money to finance affordable housing because the cash flow from rental income is limited to make the property affordable to lower-income families. There must be a substitute source of capital to keep debt low; that is where the Housing Credit program comes in. It enables a developer to raise equity capital from corporate investors, largely banks, who receive a return from the tax credits on their equity rather than from interest payments on debt. The Finance Committee's initial tax credit proposal included some unrealistic limitations on the Housing Credit that would have made the program unusable. Among other problems, the finance bill would have prevented the use of the new tax credit program with any other federal housing subsidy.

Bob Rozen, a very able member of my

Senate staff, spent a lot of time working with the affordable housing community and the Senate Finance and Joint Tax Committees. As a result during the debate on the Senate floor I offered an amendment with nineteen cosponsors, five of them Republicans. The amendment made a number of changes to the Finance Committee bill, including changes to facilitate use of the new program with existing affordable housing programs offered through the Department of Housing and Urban Development and with tax-exempt debt, and to encourage participation in the program by nonprofit organizations. The amendment was approved unanimously in the Senate. But this was a new concept, and more design work was needed in a short period of time to make sure the program that emerged from the tax reform conference committee with the House would be an effective tool to develop affordable housing. In conference we modified the basic subsidy credit rates in the program, changed the income rule to target farther down the income scale, and refined the rules for use of the program with other housing programs.

When tax reform was enacted, with a temporary three-year life for the Housing

Credit, many in the industry doubted it would work. That was a reasonable concern because it was a new approach that had not been the subject of hearings, academic study, or industry debate. In the first year of the program's existence, only about 20 percent of the Housing Credit authority was used, mostly by developers who had projects in the works that for the most part had sufficient subsidies to develop without the credit. The states were ill-equipped to manage the allocation of tax credits. It was clear the program needed to be reviewed and reimagined if there was going to be any chance to extend it beyond its 1989 expiration date.

In 1987 Senator John Danforth, a moderate and articulate Republican from Missouri, joined me on this effort. We put together an industry task force to review the program and make recommendations for improvement. The task force proposals were largely enacted into law in 1989, along with a temporary extension of the program. The 1989 changes kept the basic design of the program but reworked many aspects of the law, especially giving more responsibility to state housing finance agencies to manage the program by establishing annual housing needs assessments, creating competition among developers for credits, and providing effective oversight of the financing and management of developments. These changes helped make the program successful, and further improvements were made in 1993, when the program was made permanent.

Over the years the program has had strong bipartisan support in Congress and in the affordable housing community. The Housing Credit is now the primary tool by which the federal government supports the production and preservation of affordable housing in this country. Since enactment, about 2.5 million affordable apartment units have been developed, averaging about 100,000 units annually. The Housing Credit is a job creator, generating about $7.1 billion in economic income and about ninety-five thousand jobs each year. Over the first twenty-four years of the program's existence it financed more than sixteen thousand properties across the country. During that period, according to a recent study, only ninety-eight properties experienced foreclosure, an extraordinarily low aggregate foreclosure rate of about .006 percent.

The Housing Credit is proof that it is possible to design a federal program to meet a clear public need and to do so in an efficient and effective manner. It also demonstrates that bipartisanship can pay significant policy dividends. Some of the most important and enduring acts of Congress, including the Tax Reform Act of 1986 itself, have been the product of vigorous bipartisan negotiation and have enjoyed strong bipartisan support.

The other minor bill that had a major effect dealt with major oil spills. Shortly after I entered the Senate I was surprised to learn that there was no comprehensive federal law protecting against or responding to oil spills in American waters.* Maine had such a law (as did three other states), enacted in 1969 in reaction to an oil spill along our coast. For a long time Portland was the fourth largest oil-importing port in the country, being at one end of a large pipeline through which crude oil was pumped to Montreal for refining and use in eastern Canada. Concern about spills in and around Portland harbor led the Maine Legislature to enact the law.

The realization that almost all of the

---

* There was limited and inadequate coverage under two earlier laws: The Federal Water Pollution Control Act of 1972 and the Clean Water Act of 1977.

harbors in the United States were largely unprotected led me to join with other senators in introducing legislation in 1981 to establish a national protection and response program. That bill would have imposed strict liability on an owner or operator of a vessel for the discharge of oil into the navigable waters of the United States; the discharger would be responsible for the costs of cleanup of the oil as well as for damage to another person's real or personal property, loss of income or loss of use of natural resources; a fund would be established through a fee on each barrel of oil produced in or imported into the U.S. to provide cleanup costs and compensation for damage from oil spills when the damage exceeds the limits of the owner's liability or the responsible party cannot be found. Later bills added a provision requiring, over a long phase-in period, double hulls on all oil tankers entering U.S. ports.

The effort was complicated by the fact that some members of Congress (especially in the House, where similar legislation was considered) who supported the concept of a national program insisted that it preempt existing and future state laws on the subject. I refused to accept preemption because I feared that the industry would persuade friendly members of Congress to support a weak national law that would eviscerate stronger state laws like Maine's. The debate over this issue was contentious, even acrimonious at times. Despite our best efforts we were unable to gain enactment into law of the legislation. I then introduced updated versions of the legislation in 1986 and 1988 with the same negative result.

On March 24, 1989, thousands of miles from Washington, DC, in the cold waters of the North Pacific Ocean, in just a few hours the politics of oil spill legislation changed irrevocably. There had been major spills before. In December 1976 the *Argo Merchant* ran aground off Nantucket Island, spilling 8.5 million gallons of fuel oil. Luckily, it was blown out to sea. Two years later the *Amoco Cadiz* went aground off the coast of France, losing its entire cargo of 67 million gallons of oil.

But the *Exxon Valdez* spill took place in the biologically rich waters of Prince William Sound. The effect, and the reactions, were larger. It changed the attitude of Americans and, therefore, of the president and members of Congress. It became politically impossible to oppose legislation that had been stuck in Congress for nearly a decade. The Senate unanimously approved the oil spill legislation and it became law on August 18, 1990. While oil spills continue to occur, they are fewer in number and most are far less damaging than they would be if the law had not been enacted.

ONE ROAD NOT TAKEN, ANOTHER OPENS

When I decided, over Christmas 1982, that I would limit my tenure in the Senate, I did not imagine that in just six years I would become the majority leader and the intensity of work would increase to a level that is hard to describe or understand. After I became majority leader, I was daily besieged by requests from senators. Many asked that votes not occur at certain times because they had other commitments, almost all of them related to fundraising. I got to my office early every morning, where, waiting on my desk, was a list of calls and messages: "Don't have a vote between noon and two because I'm attending a fundraising lunch"; "I've got a reception at four, protect me for an hour." A reception at five, another at six, and then a long list of dinners. No votes please. Protect me. I was of course familiar with the receptions since I was invited to most of them and attended many, urging

378

donors to help reelect that evening's beneficiary.

On one occasion I exaggerated to make a point. I took a large monthly calendar divided into hourly increments and blacked out most of the slots, leaving only a few slivers of white showing. I showed it to a group of senators and said, "The blacked-out areas are the times that I've been asked not to have votes because one or more of you have scheduled fundraisers. The white areas are when there are no requests not to have votes. As you can see, they cover only two to six o'clock in the morning, Tuesday through Thursday. So if I accede to all of your requests the Senate can vote only in the middle of the night in the middle of the week!" The reaction was good-natured, with a lot of bantering back and forth. As the meeting ended a good friend stood and said, "You've got a tough job, but nobody forced you to run for majority leader." I nodded my head in agreement, smiled, and said nothing. But I thought, "He's right. Nobody forced me to run for majority leader, or for the Senate. I didn't just volunteer; I worked hard to win. And I've got to recognize and accept that fundraising is a big part of life in the Senate." In the two decades since I left the Senate it's gotten a lot bigger.

Many men and women in many walks of life constantly struggle to balance the demands of work and family; many, among them several senators, appear to have achieved a balance that is right for them and their families. I was not one of them, and I have no one to blame but myself. Too often work won in the competition for my time and attention, and family or other personal needs lost.

One concrete example illustrates the dimensions of the personal challenge. Not long after I entered the Senate I was invited to a conference on the aspirations of Maine's young people. It was disheartening to hear that, on balance, they were low, especially in the rural, less populated, and less prosperous areas. I was asked to talk about my personal history, and later in the day a group of education officials urged me to tell that story in high schools throughout the state: "Our kids need to hear from someone with a background like theirs, who's been successful, who they can relate to." It seemed like a good cause: to use my position and experience to help lift the aspirations of young people whose lives were similar to my early life. In addition, I soon realized, I could benefit politically by getting around the state, especially into the rural areas which tend to be Republican and where I might otherwise have difficulty getting an audience. So, over time, two members of my staff — Mary McAleney, my administrative assistant, and Diane Smith, who handled my schedule — devised a plan in which I would speak at the graduation ceremony at every high school in Maine. It was a daunting task. Maine's population of about 1.3 million is spread over thirty-three thousand square miles, and its 140 high schools all held their graduation on the same three weekends in June. But through a long process of planning and development that took over a dozen years, I made it to every one. The personal cost was high. Each year for the first three weeks of June I was in Washington for five days tending to Senate business; on weekends I scrambled back and forth across Maine, to speak at four or five graduations. Along the way we increased the goal: I would try to visit each school twice, once for graduation and once for an assembly or special class. I did make it to every one for graduation, but, although I made the second visit to most, I hadn't reached them all by the time I left the Senate. The burden of travel was heavy, especially since I was trying simultaneously to visit each manufacturing plant, service club, hospital, and more. For the last three graduations I attended, on islands off the coast, I chartered a small single-engine plane and, hopping from island to island, made three graduation speeches in one day. In retrospect it is now clear to me that at some point in the process the healthy objective of visiting every high school became an unhealthy obsession.

Over the Christmas break of 1993, eleven years after I made my decision to limit my time in the Senate, I felt the time had come. I had been majority leader for five years. As far as I could tell, I remained in good standing with the people of Maine. No serious opposition to my candidacy for reelection had emerged. I had earlier set a fundraising target of $2 million for my campaign for reelection and had quickly reached that goal, so I had stopped raising money.* By February I felt certain enough to plan an

* This led to an unusual experience. Some contributions were received after the goal was reached, so the checks were returned. Most donors were pleased that I had set and kept to a limit. But, to my surprise, I received quite a few phone calls from donors angry that I hadn't accepted their contribution: "What's the matter, Senator, isn't my money good enough for you?"

announcement. It had been five months since I'd met Heather, and I knew that before long we would marry. That reinforced my decision. Heather did not object to my seeking reelection; to the contrary, she encouraged me to do whatever I wanted. But I was wary; my first marriage had been adversely affected by my participation in political life, and I didn't want that to happen again.

There also had been a major political change. In November 1992 Bill Clinton was elected president. Shortly after the election he invited Foley, Gephardt, and me to Little Rock, Arkansas, to talk about how to proceed once he took office. We had a pleasant dinner with the president-elect and Mrs. Clinton, followed by a long, informal discussion. Although I had met him before, this was our first in-depth discussion. I liked him from the start. He was extremely well-versed in the major issues he soon would have to confront, and he had well-thought-out plans on how to do so. Among those issues were the budget, welfare reform, and health care reform. He would have to determine not just the substance of his legislative proposals in those difficult areas but also their timing and sequence. I left Little Rock reassured about his energy and ability to handle the awesome duties of the presidency and also about his positions on the many issues with which he and we would have to deal.

His inauguration was a time of promise for Democrats. The youthful, energetic combination of Clinton and Gore raised expectations to a dangerously high level that would be difficult to meet. His first few months brought everyone down to earth. None of us had anticipated the speed and skill with which congressional Republicans would catapult to the forefront the policy of "Don't Ask Don't Tell" on gays in the military. With congressional Democrats divided and the administration unprepared, there was an early stumble. Differences of opinion within Congress and between the administration and Congress on an economic stimulus package that spring generated more difficulty. But gradually the president and his team gained their footing and went on to a successful first term, in particular in the adoption of a budget and economic program that narrowly overcame unified Republican opposition but, once enacted, laid the foundation for spectacular economic growth, creating budget surpluses and more than 22 million new jobs. His welfare reform program was enacted, but his health care package was not. It was a record that ultimately enabled him to easily win reelection in 1996.

That was in the future, however. In early 1994, I considered my own plans. I had worked closely with the president for two years and found it painful to leave in the middle of his first term. A few of my close friends suggested that I run for reelection and, if I won (which then seemed very likely), serve for two years, to the end of Clinton's first term, then retire. I rejected the suggestion as unfair to the people of Maine. If I ran for reelection to a six-year term I would have to serve it out; anything less than that would have been dishonest. So, after long and careful consideration, I decided to retire from the Senate.

In late February I informed a few members of my staff and scheduled a public announcement for the first week in March. By coincidence I was invited to a small private dinner with President Clinton the night before. As the dinner drew to a close I asked to speak privately with him. After the other guests had left we sat in his small office in the residence of the White House. There we talked for about two and a half hours. When I told him of my decision he tried to talk me out of it. Anticipating that he would do so, and knowing how persuasive he is, I had made arrangements to start the process of delivering copies of the videotape in which I announced my decision to every television station in Maine, so I told him it was too late; no matter what he said I could not change my mind. Eventually he accepted that my decision was final and he asked, "If in the future something comes up where I think you can be of assistance, would you be willing to help? Or are you just turned off of politics?" I told him that I enjoyed public service and would be happy to help if he thought I could be useful. My answer was as abstract as his question. But within a month he became very specific.

On April 6, 1994, Associate Justice Harry Blackmun announced his intention to retire from the Supreme Court. The speculation about his successor began immediately, and my name was among those mentioned. Early the next week President Clinton called and told me that he had decided to nominate me to succeed Blackmun. I thanked him and told him that I was honored and flattered. As a lawyer and a former federal judge I regarded membership on the Supreme Court as the pinnacle of professional accomplishment and an opportunity for important service. In response to a question from the president I said I didn't think I'd have any trouble getting confirmed by the Senate; while there inevitably would be some opposition I didn't think it would amount to much. He agreed. But I also told him that I was concerned about the effect my departure from the Senate would have on the legislative battle over health care, which was just heating up. It was the administration's highest priority in that session of Congress.

Less than five months earlier I had introduced the president's health care reform bill in the Senate; Dick Gephardt, the House majority leader, had simultaneously introduced it there. The bill was the product of many months of study and drafting by a large team led by the president's wife, Hillary Rodham Clinton. Among many other provisions it included a requirement that employers (other than small businesses) provide health insurance for their employees. The employer mandate made it clear that the president intended to build on and reform the current system, not sweep it away and replace it with something entirely new. Employers had been providing health care coverage to their employees since World War II. With millions of men serving in the armed forces and demand rising to meet the material needs of a worldwide conflict, employers competed vigorously for workers. Unable to offer the traditional incentive of higher pay because of wartime wage and price controls, they began to offer other benefits, including health insurance coverage. The system grew to the point that most Americans who had health insurance received it through their employment.

Despite this history, most Republicans in the Senate, and some Democrats, were strongly opposed to an employer mandate. A month after the bill had been introduced, just before Christmas, twenty Republican senators, including their leader, Bob Dole, introduced their own health care reform bill; they were joined by four Democrats. It did not include an employer mandate; instead it proposed what was then the relatively new concept of an individual mandate. Rather than requiring employers to provide coverage to their employees, the bill put the burden on each individual to obtain such coverage, through employment or otherwise. The principal author of the Republican bill was Senator John Chafee of Rhode Island. Chafee and I had often worked together on two major committees,

Finance and Environment and Public Works.

When we returned in January 1994 for the second session of Congress, health care reform was the most important and most controversial issue confronting us. There were numerous conferences and endless meetings, some partisan, some not. Chafee and I saw each other often and discussed health care regularly. Although there were many areas of disagreement, I believed that there was a realistic chance for reform if both sides were serious and prepared to compromise. I thought if Democrats could be persuaded to make a major gesture (one possibility was dropping the employer mandate and accepting the individual mandate) we might receive in return major concessions from Republicans. Chafee too wanted to get to a compromise; though he was keenly aware of and stressed the many difficulties, I believed he shared my hope and my sense of possibility, so I felt there was a reasonable chance that we could get a meaningful health care reform bill through the Senate that summer. As I considered the Supreme Court offer, I didn't want to exaggerate or dramatize my importance, but I was the principal sponsor of the administration's bill and had led the

Democratic effort for reform. My departure would significantly reduce our chances of success.

For a few days there was speculation in the press about a scheme in which I could be nominated and confirmed but then delay my departure from the Senate until health care was completed. I regarded that as nonsense. I had no idea if anyone at the White House had such thoughts, but I did not. It would have been disruptive and harmful to try to do that. My choice was straightforward: I could decline the president's offer and stay in the Senate for the rest of the year to fight for health care reform, or I could leave the Senate for the Supreme Court. While I believed I could do a good job on the Court, I knew that there were many others who could serve as well if not better; among them was Stephen Breyer, the man ultimately chosen. So I told the president that because I thought there was a reasonable chance we could pass a good bill in the Senate, I would stay to finish the fight for health care reform. While heartened by my assessment of the chances for reform, he was disappointed by my decision. I told him that I wanted to end any distraction and get the issue out of the way quickly. He agreed and consented to my promptly making my decision public. On April 12, six days after Blackmun made his announcement, I made mine.

In the next few months it became clear that my assessment of our chances on health care had been unrealistic. The health insurance companies had launched a huge and successful campaign against our bill, stressing its complexity. As opposition solidified and spread, Senate Republicans became less and less open to compromise and Democrats became increasingly apprehensive. Through the spring and into the summer support for the president's bill hemorrhaged slowly on both sides. We hit what seemed at the time like rock bottom when the Senate Finance Committee gathered in July to "mark up," or draft, the bill. On the way into the Committee hearing room, where we would spend days debating and voting, I said to Chafee, with a smile, "I'm going to introduce your bill as an amendment and force you guys to vote on it." He was not amused. "Oh, don't do that," he replied. "You'll embarrass me but you won't gain anything." The Republicans had moved so far away from the center on the issue that not one of them, not even Chafee, would now vote for the bill they themselves had introduced seven months earlier. Chafee was right, of course. We would embarrass him and his colleagues, but it wouldn't help us pass a bill. He also knew that, given our close friendship and our history of working together, I would not do anything to embarrass him.

We got the bill out of the Committee and, with great difficulty, on to the Senate floor for debate. To no avail, I kept the Senate in session during what would normally have been the August recess. The debate was heated. Angry words were exchanged. Tension rose. Tempers flared. What particularly inflamed Democratic senators, myself included, was the inconsistency between the public position and the personal behavior of Republican senators. Even though the administration's bill did not provide for a government takeover of the health care system, but rather built on the existing private system, over and over and over again Republican senators hammered away at "government health care." With dramatic flourishes they warned of how terrible it would be for the American people. And yet those same senators had chosen to accept and were receiving "government health care" for themselves and their families. After deploring "government health care" in powerful speeches on the Senate floor they would walk a few steps to the Senate Physicians Office in the Capitol, where they were greeted by a government receptionist, prepared by a government nurse, examined and treated by a government doctor. When surgery was required they went to a U.S. military hospital where government surgeons opened them up and sewed them back together. Their message to the American people was, in effect, Do as we say but don't do as we do. Yet, whatever Democrats said, it was clear that our concern did not resonate with the public. The Republicans were increasingly unified and solid in opposition, while I was unable to unify the Democrats. Each day, with increasing frequency and intensity, I was beseeched and assailed by my fellow Democrats with contradictory requests: "Pull the plug"; "Keep going." The outcome was inevitable long before I took the bill down and put the Senate into recess.

The president was deeply disappointed, as I was. We hadn't handled it well. Try as we might, we were unable to significantly reduce the bill's length or complexity, rendering it vulnerable to the criticism that it was too complicated to ever work in the real world. In addition many of the interest groups who supported the bill were more interested in improving their position (and their finances) than they were in overall reform. But the circumstances were such that even with the best handling it may well have failed. The scars from that battle were so deep that it was a quarter century before it was again joined.

I didn't have much time to feel sorry for myself. A heavy agenda awaited us when we returned to session in early September, and I was extremely busy trying to bring the last session of my Senate career to a successful close. We finally adjourned on December 1. Heather and I had scheduled our wedding for December 10, and I had to think about what I would do with the rest of my life. In November I was asked by a high administration official if I would serve in a full-time diplomatic position. I declined, telling him that if I were going to stay in government full time I'd continue as a senator. A few weeks later I was asked to serve as special advisor to the president and the secretary of state on economic initiatives in Ireland. The lengthy and ambiguous title reflected the president's concern that the British government not be offended. That government had long resisted efforts by the government of Ireland to involve others, especially Americans, in efforts to end the conflict in

Northern Ireland. Clinton stressed that my duties would be limited in time and subject matter. I was to organize a White House conference on trade and investment in Northern Ireland, to be held in May 1995. It seemed perfect: a brief, interesting assignment to ease my transition to private life.

Heather and I were married on December 10. I left the Senate on January 2, 1995, and was sworn into my new position one week later. In early February I was in Northern Ireland for what was scheduled to be five months. It turned out to be five years.

NORTHERN IRELAND

OMAGH

As the late Saturday afternoon breeze quickened, sailboats large and small made their way into Northeast Harbor, a small village on Mount Desert Island off the coast of Maine. The guests on the porch of the grand home overlooking the harbor basked in the warm glow of the sun as it dipped slowly toward the mountains in the west. I was scheduled to speak to them later in the evening, but, unable to focus on the present, I sought out the host and asked to speak as soon as possible. "I'm sorry," I explained, "there's a problem in Northern Ireland, and I've got to get back to my cottage to take some calls." It's hard to give a good speech when your mind is three thousand miles away, but I did my best to conceal my haste to leave.

The first call had come just before Heather and I left to drive to the event from the summer cottage we had rented that August.

The overseas connection was bad, the news worse. What little I understood was deeply disturbing: "A bomb . . . many killed . . . will call later." An agreement had been reached four months earlier, on April 10, 1998, Good Friday, ending two years of negotiation and many centuries of conflict. It had been approved by the voters in a referendum in May by overwhelming margins in the Irish Republic and Northern Ireland. After more than three years of effort, the negotiations I chaired, involving the British and Irish governments and ten political parties of Northern Ireland, had concluded in agreement, and the people had added their approval. Now, just a few months later, on August 15, men of violence sought to undo all that had been accomplished, using the only arguments they had left: murder, death, destruction.

There had been three and a half years of seemingly endless negotiations, argument, disagreement, killing, near despair. Then, on Easter weekend, it had all ended suddenly in a way that few anticipated: with a peace agreement. Now that peace was threatened. Or was it? As I raced back to the cottage I was nervous and worried. Could it all have been in vain?

It also was a warm Saturday afternoon in

Omagh, a medium-size market town in the western part of Northern Ireland. On this as on other Saturdays, as they had for centuries, people came from the surrounding towns and villages, from Killyclogher and Gillygooley, from Dromore and Carrickmore, from Fivemiletown and Sixmilecross, to buy and sell, to shop and swap, to visit, to see and be seen in one of the most ancient and pleasurable rituals of life in every human society. Just after two-thirty in the afternoon the first of three warnings was phoned in to a local television station. But there was confusion about the precise location, and the police, believing that a bomb had been placed at the local courthouse, began moving people away from that building. Many ran or walked down Market Street, on which many shops were located. What they did not know, could not know, was that they were racing *toward* the bomb. On Market Street, about four hundred yards from the courthouse, a maroon Vauxhall sedan was parked. It had been stolen that day in Ireland, its license plates replaced by Northern Ireland plates, packed with a five-hundred-pound bomb and driven to Omagh, where it now sat and waited for its victims. As the people raced toward and around and past the car, some of them brushing it as they ran by, it exploded in a huge burst of flame and thunder and hot flying metal. Those closest were mowed down like stands of grain by a giant scythe, and suddenly there was blood and burning flesh everywhere. After a moment of stunned silence, as the flames came to life and the smoke rose, the shrieking and crying and moaning began. Then came the gasps and tears and curses of those who, unhurt, first came on the grisly scene. Then came the sirens and the ambulances and the medics and those who tried to help, to comfort, to save.

When the grim accounting was completed twenty-nine people had been killed and nearly three hundred injured, many of them horribly and permanently maimed. A small group of dissidents who called themselves the Real IRA was responsible. They were opposed to the Good Friday Agreement because it did not provide everything they wanted: an immediate and full British withdrawal from Northern Ireland and a fully united Ireland. Even though the Agreement had been approved by 95 percent of those voting in the Republic of Ireland and by 71 percent in Northern Ireland, the men of violence wanted their way, 100 percent. When they didn't get their way they responded by killing and maiming innocent men, women, and children.

In the horror of death and destruction on the narrow streets of Omagh was laid bare the utter senselessness of sectarian violence as a way to solve the political problems of Northern Ireland. It hadn't worked before, and, once again, it didn't work now. It did not spark the reversion to sectarian conflict the murderers so badly wanted. To the contrary, the people and political leaders of Northern Ireland, stunned and horrified by the carnage, came together in opposition to continued violence. First Minister David Trimble, a unionist, joined with Deputy First Minister Seamus Mallon, a nationalist, in condemning the barbaric act and pledging to revive the effort to resolve their differences through democratic and peaceful means, not through violence.

Within days I received a call from the White House asking me to join President Clinton on a visit to Omagh to meet with survivors and the families of those who did not survive. A week later we were in a municipal recreation center in Omagh packed with hundreds of people. The mood was somber; it was a time to grieve. The president and Tony Blair, prime minister of the United Kingdom, spoke briefly and were well received. Then we were asked to meet separately with individual survivors and families. In a corner of the room I talked with several of them, one family at a time. I had been through other grieving events before, but none so laden with tension, sorrow, and the sheer number of people present. It was a long and warm evening, moving and unforgettable. I had been in Northern Ireland for nearly four years and I identified with these people. Although I had not previously met any of those with whom I spoke, I felt I knew them and their neighbors. Two especially moved me.

Michael Monaghan was thirty-three, with dark hair and an open pleasant face. He had to work to contain his emotions as he described to me his visit to Omagh that day with his wife, who was pregnant, their eighteen-month-old daughter, and his wife's mother. Three generations of women from one family, wiped out in a single, senseless moment. I could not match his restraint when he told me that his two-year-old son, Patrick, asked him every day, "When's Mommy coming home?"

Claire Gallagher sat erect, her hands folded in her lap, her long fair hair flowing over the white dress she was wearing.

Fifteen years old, a tall, aspiring pianist, her attractive face was largely concealed behind two huge white patches that covered the gaping holes where her eyes had been. Both had been destroyed in the blast. She reached out for my hand, tentatively and slowly. I placed my hand in hers and she held it tightly through our conversation. Calmly and steadily, as though we were old friends, she talked about her life, before and after. I could not see her eyes, as she could not see mine, but I felt that I could see her soul, and the soul of Northern Ireland: strong and brave, badly hurt by sectarian violence, but determined to leave the bitter past behind.

When I left Northern Ireland three months earlier I had no idea when, if ever, I would return. I had come home to my wife and new, young son, never dreaming that within three months I would return to a Northern Ireland in mourning. As I eased my hand from Claire's grip and stood, drenched in sweat and emotion, I realized that my ties to Northern Ireland never would be severed. Her parting words reinforced my feelings: "Keep going, Senator. You can't let the peace process fail." Michael Monaghan had said almost the same words to me earlier, as had others with whom I spoke. In their moment of greatest grief their thoughts and words had been with others who they hoped would not have to go through what they were going through. I am and always will be an American, and proud of it, but a large part of my heart and my emotions forever will be in Northern Ireland. I didn't know how or when, but I knew I would return.

The opportunities came before and after Omagh. In early July 1997, I had received an honorary degree from the Queen's University of Belfast, Northern Ireland. I've received more than fifty honorary degrees, all of them meaningful and for which I am grateful. But none means more to me than Queen's. The ceremony was brief but warm, marked by the reading of a thorough and thoughtful citation prepared and read by one of the university's law professors. Two years later, in May 1999, to my pleasant surprise I was invited to serve as chancellor of the university, a largely honorary position. I served with great pleasure for ten years. Established in 1845, now serving seventeen thousand students, the university plays a crucial role in the life and development of Northern Ireland. My position as chancellor enabled me to return to Northern Ireland several times each year, and with each visit I learned more and more about the history and people of Northern Ireland. I was filled with regret in January 2009 when I was required to resign as a result of my appointment as President Barack Obama's special envoy for Middle East peace.

In the summer of 1999 I became deeply involved in Northern Ireland yet again. On July 15 I was in London, at Buckingham Palace, to receive a knighthood from Queen Elizabeth, a tribute to my prior service in Northern Ireland. My knowledge of British protocol is limited, but my understanding was that, since I am not a British citizen, the designation bestowed on me was purely honorary. Nevertheless the ceremony was memorable and gratifying. The queen was extremely gracious. We reminisced briefly about her visit to Washington in 1992. After meeting with the president she had addressed a joint session of Congress. As I had with Nelson Mandela two years earlier, I cohosted a luncheon in her honor in the Capitol. I introduced her to the other senators around the table, one of whom was Robert Byrd. As I pointed toward him and mentioned his name I told the queen, "Senator Byrd is a keen student of British history and can recite from memory the name and date of rule of every one of your predecessors." The room was crowded and noisy; Senator Byrd mistakenly thought that I had asked him to recite, so he began, starting in AD 500. After he got through about a half century of kings and dates the queen politely interrupted and, with a smile, said, "Oh, Senator, they were all long before my time." Byrd took the hint, smiled, and thanked the queen for coming to visit, and we sat down to a pleasant lunch and a discussion filled with talk of British history. Now, seven years later, we were with the queen in her palace. My Scottish Canadian wife and her mother, Shirley MacLachlan, were particularly impressed, as was my sister, Barbara, who accompanied us. Shirley had a pleasant chat about her hometown, Montreal, with the queen. I told the queen that Barbara's birthday was the next day, and the queen warmly wished her a happy birthday. Barbara was so impressed that she has since stopped recognizing her birthdays and now refers only to the one that she and the queen of England celebrated together.

By a highly unfortunate coincidence, on that very day the Northern Ireland Assembly, which had been established pursuant to the Good Friday Agreement, collapsed. So rather than attend a celebratory dinner, as planned, I spent the evening receiving telephone calls from officials from Britain, Ireland, and the United States. Within twenty-four hours I had talked with the prime ministers of the United Kingdom and Ireland, Tony Blair and Bertie Ahern, and agreed to their request to return to Northern Ireland to try to put the process back together. By the end of the next day I had met with David Trimble, then the leader of the Ulster Unionist Party in Northern Ireland, who happened to be in London; I also talked by telephone with other party leaders. From then until December of that year I was fully reengaged. Thankfully this effort took months, not years. By the end of the year we had managed to patch together an imperfect but ultimately successful solution to a very difficult and complicated series of issues. Many more years of effort were required on the part of the people and political leaders of Northern Ireland to resolve those issues, but they have kept at it and the process has moved forward. It is still a work in progress, as differences, disputes, and occasional violence continue.

For the survivors and the families of the victims at Omagh the tragedy endures; the confusion that preceded and immediately followed the bombing continued in the aftermath. Only one man was convicted of a criminal offense, and that conviction was overturned on appeal. Although four men were held liable for damages in a civil trial, to this day no one has been imprisoned for a crime that took twenty-nine lives and permanently damaged hundreds of others.

ANDREW'S PEACE

Late in 2011 I received a telephone call from Trevor Birney, an independent television producer in Northern Ireland. I had met him once before, when he interviewed me in London in connection with a documentary film on Northern Ireland that he was producing. "Have you made your return trip to Northern Ireland with Andrew?" he asked.

I was surprised by the question, so I paused before answering. "No, not yet."

"Have you thought about it?"

"No. Not lately."

"Well, if you're willing to make the trip now I'd like to make a documentary on it for the BBC. We would locate some of the sixty-one children born in Northern Ireland on the same day as Andrew and try to line up visits with them for Andrew and you. Would you be interested?"

There was another, longer pause. "Gee,

Trevor, that would be really nice, but I have to think about that before answering. I don't know if the time's right. And I have to talk to my wife and children."

"Will you do that and call me back?"

"Okay, I'll talk to them and think about it, and then I'll call you back."

The conversation brought back some emotional memories. In one chapter of my book *Making Peace,* I described the profound effect my son's birth in 1997 had on me and my work in Northern Ireland:

On Thursday, October 16, Andrew Mac-Lachlan Mitchell was born. He weighed seven pounds fourteen ounces at birth. He was healthy. We were happy. Heather had some problems which required her to return to the hospital a few days later, and this delayed my return to Belfast, but it meant we were able to spend a few more days together.

Late in the middle of one night I sat watching Andrew sleeping. I began to imagine what his life would be like, lived, as it would be, almost entirely in the twenty-first century. I then started to think about how different his life would be had he been born a citizen of Northern Ireland. I wondered how many babies had been born in Northern Ireland on October 16. What would *their* lives be like? How different would those lives be had they been born Americans? I picked up the telephone and called my staff in Belfast. After getting a routine briefing, I asked them to find out how many newborns had been delivered in the province on October 16. It didn't take long to get the answer: sixty-one.

For the next several days, the thought stayed with me. It was with me as I got up late on another night to comfort Andrew. Heather and I had such high hopes and dreams for our son. Surely the parents of those sixty-one babies had the same hopes and dreams. The aspirations of parents everywhere are the same: for their children to be healthy and happy, safe and secure, to get a good education and a good start in life, and to be able to go as high and as far as talent and willingness to work will take them. Shouldn't those sixty-one children in Northern Ireland have the same chance in life that we wanted for our son? Could they get it if Northern Ireland reverted to sectarian strife? There would always be the risk of babies being torn from their mothers' arms by the sudden blast of a bomb. When a mother sent her children off to school in the morning there would always be the nagging fear of random violence, the chance that she might never again see them alive. Why should people have to live like that? This conflict was made and sustained by men and women. It could be ended by men and women. And I knew those men and women. They were there, in Stormont. I had been with them for a year and a half, and I was now determined to stay with them to the end. I was also more determined than ever that these negotiations end with an agreement. For the sake of those sixty-one children, and thousands of others like them, we had to succeed. All of the doubts I had about my role in Northern Ireland vanished. No matter what, I would see it through, all the way to an agreement.

I felt an overpowering urge to touch my sleeping son. I picked him up and held him close for a long time. He couldn't hear me, but I told him that for him and for his sixty-one friends in Northern Ireland I was somehow going to get this job done, and when I did I would refer to it as Andrew's Peace.

I ended the book with these words:

The Good Friday Agreement was, for me, the realization of a dream that sustained me for three and a half years, the longest, most difficult years of my life. After the agreement was approved, I talked with several of the men and women who had negotiated it; we were all overcome with exhaustion and emotion. As we parted, I told them that I have a new dream.

That dream is to return to Northern Ireland in a few years, with my young son, Andrew. We will roam the countryside, taking in the sights and smells and sounds of one of the most beautiful landscapes on earth. Then, on a rainy afternoon (there are many in Northern Ireland) we will drive to Stormont and sit quietly in the visitors gallery of the Northern Ireland Assembly. There we will watch and listen as the members of the Assembly debate the ordinary issues of life in a peaceful democratic society: education, health care, agriculture, tourism, fisheries, trade. There will be no talk of war, for the war will have long been over. There will be no talk of peace, for peace will by then be taken for granted. On that day, the day on which peace is taken for granted in Northern Ireland, I will be fulfilled.[1]

Over the following decade I visited Northern Ireland often and occasionally made reference to that passage in my book. But I had not considered, in a serious and sustained way, making the trip I had dreamed of. Now, in response to Trevor's call, I did so. I talked with several friends in Northern Ireland and the United States to obtain a current and in-depth picture of the situation there; most of the comments were positive. I asked some directly if they thought it an appropriate time for the trip. All answered in the affirmative. I talked about it at length with Heather and with Andrew, who was then fourteen, and our daughter Claire, three years younger than Andrew. Heather and Claire were positive, but Andrew was reticent. Unlike his father, who like most politicians enjoys the spotlight of publicity, Andrew prefers privacy; he neither seeks nor enjoys being the focus of attention. But he is also thoughtful of others, so when I told him it would mean a lot to me, he agreed to go.

It was one of the most enjoyable weeks of my life. After two days of filming in New York, we traveled to Northern Ireland. It was in March, spring break at the schools Andrew and Claire attended, so I warned them to bring sweaters, raincoats, and umbrellas; I knew from experience that the weather would be cold and windy and wet. To my amazement, and to our children's delight, the weather was clear and sunny for the entire week, with not a drop of rain. Although it was occasionally cool and windy, we thoroughly enjoyed the crisp and clear days. By coincidence, school vacation coincided with St. Patrick's Day. As a result most of Northern Ireland's political leaders were in the United States. Over the past few decades American presidents have hosted receptions on St. Patrick's Day to which the prime minister of Ireland and a host of other politicians, north and south, regularly flock. It is one of the peculiar ways in which, on occasion, "being Irish" means more in the United States than in Ireland.

But that had no effect on our visit. We were there primarily to meet with the families of children born on October 16, 1997, and to visit the Northern Ireland Assembly. Trevor and his producer, Michael Fanning, arranged visits to four families; they were as diverse as Northern Ireland itself. The Robinson Family is Catholic; they live on a farm in the rural western county of Fermanagh. The parents, Martin and Mary, welcomed us into their home as though we'd known each other all our lives.

Their son Conor graciously showed Andrew around the farm. The Robinsons welcomed and supported the Good Friday Agreement; they believed it ended years of discrimination and created a new sense of community. From Fermanagh we traveled to a suburb east of Belfast, to meet the Best family. Peter is an architect, Heather a teacher. Their son, Alexander, took Andrew to visit his school, which in many ways is similar to St. Bernard's, the school Andrew then attended. The Bests are Protestants who supported the Agreement, believing that it would help to move Northern Ireland away from the violence of its past. We then traveled to County Down, where we met the Stephenson family. They were warm and gracious in their welcome. As a police officer, Ian is in constant danger; understandably that has affected their view of the Agreement. They believe that it inappropriately rewarded bad behavior and has not resulted in a durable peace. Their daughter Lucy, born on the same day as Andrew, and their other children took Andrew to a local recreation center, where he participated in archery lessons. The children had a good time, as did their parents.

In the twenty-two months of negotiations

at the Stormont Estate, site of the Northern Ireland Assembly, I had grown indifferent to its beauty and majesty. As the iron gate swings open you drive in and start up a slowly rising hill, exactly one mile long, to the impressive granite Parliament building, set at the top of the hill. Now, for the first and only time in my life, I took that drive with my wife and children. My indifference vanished. I asked the driver to slow down so we could take in the scene for a few seconds longer. The sky was blue, with a few clumps of heavy white clouds, but it was windy, so we didn't pause long when we got out of the car at the foot of the broad stairway leading to the front entrance. After a brief welcoming ceremony Heather and Claire were whisked off on a tour of the building while Andrew and I were ushered into the visitors' gallery of the Northern Ireland Assembly, the democratically elected body that governs the people of Northern Ireland. The impressive exterior of the building is surpassed by the inspiration of its interior, especially the Assembly Chamber, in the beauty of the royal blue leather benches and the dark wood paneling. We were conspicuous as we took our seats; there was no one else in the gallery, and several well-intentioned attendants made a fuss over my return. We listened as a government minister reported to the members on a conference he had attended in Brussels. It was as dry as dust and as boring as only a government report can be. I recalled the words I had spoken to the delegates at the peace negotiations fourteen years earlier: "We will watch and listen as the members of the Assembly debate the ordinary issues of life in a democratic society." This, finally, was happening. And my son was there to share the moment with me. I was silent but very emotional.

A half hour passed; to me it seemed an instant, but not to Andrew. He leaned toward me and whispered, "Dad, this is really boring. Can we go now?" I smiled, hugged him, and said, "Of course." As we stood I said to him, "I know it's boring to you, but that's the point. To me, it was soothing, like music to my ears."

Our last visit was the most emotional. We traveled to Omagh to meet with Claire Gallagher and her family. The fifteen-year-old girl has become a tall woman of thirty. Her hair was short, and she no longer had large patches covering her empty eye sockets. Her face still bore the scars of that terrible day of the car bombing in 1998, but her spirit was as strong as ever. She was accompanied by her father and mother, her loving husband, Ryan Bowes, and two beautiful small children, Oran, four years old, and Connor, two. As much as anyone could, given what she had lived through, Claire led a normal and happy life. It took time for her to accept the reality that she would never see again, but she adjusted and graduated from the Northern Ireland equivalent of high school. Although she had several college scholarship offers from institutions outside of Northern Ireland, she chose to stay closer to home, so she attended and graduated from Queen's University in Belfast. She then married Ryan and had two children, all the while improving her skills in serving others who are blind. She now works as an eye care liaison officer at the Royal Institute of Blind People. As she had when we first met, on that sweltering night in Omagh fifteen years earlier, she reached out for my hand and held it as we talked. As calm and methodical as she had been then, she told me about her fifteen-year journey to her current life. It is a tale of power and emotion, of how a person deals with the most unexpected and terrible of tragedies. Surely she had periods of sadness, regret, even depression over the misfortune of timing and the severity and awful nature of her injuries, but in our meetings she never let those emotions show. Calm, steady, consistent, Claire is a shining exemplar of the strength of the human spirit, an inspiration to me and to many others, in Northern Ireland and the world. My admiration for her was one of the factors that led Heather and me to name our daughter Claire on her birth in 2001.

Henry Kissinger's Poster

After I returned from Northern Ireland I wrote a book about my experience there. When it was published I attended many promotional events, among them several sponsored by Irish-American groups. I received so many such invitations I concluded that in the United States there are more Irish-American organizations than there are Irish-Americans. I accepted as many as I could and enjoyed every one of them. As I traveled among them, there developed an informal competition as to who could give me the longest, most favorable introduction; most were exaggerated and some included incidents that I myself had previously not been aware of. The proper reaction, of course, would have been to show humility and to ask them to keep the introductions short and factual. But I had an improper reaction. I encouraged them, even scolded those who left out any relevant part of my personal history. Dangerously, I began to believe what was said about me and developed an inflated sense of my importance. By the time I got to the last group, the Irish-American Society of Stamford, Connecticut, I could barely squeeze my swollen head through the front door. The first person I encountered was an elderly woman who rushed up to me and vigorously shook my hand. She was excited and told me in emotional and gushing terms how she had driven three and a half hours just to meet me because I was such a great man who had done so much good around the world. She then handed me a pen and a large poster and asked if I would sign it. I looked at the poster and told her I'd be happy to sign it, but first I thought there was something I should tell her.

"What is it?" she asked.

"I'm not Henry Kissinger," I replied. The picture on the poster was of Kissinger.

"You're not?" she shouted. "Well, who are you anyway?"

When I told her, she was visibly disappointed. "That's terrible," she said, "I drove three and a half hours to meet a great man and all I've got is a nobody like you."

"I'm sorry to disappoint you," I said. "I wish there was something I could do to ease your pain."

She thought for a moment, then said, "Well, there is."

"What is it?" I asked.

She leaned toward me. In reaction I leaned toward her and she said, in a low, conspiratorial voice, "Nobody will ever know the difference." I must have looked puzzled, so she then said, "Would you mind signing Henry Kissinger's name on my poster?"

"Of course," I said, and I did.

So today, somewhere in eastern Connecticut, that poster is hanging, a constant reminder to me not to take seriously the introductions I receive.

No Time for Retirement

9/11

On the evening of September 10, 2001, I spoke at a forum sponsored by St. Bartholomew's Church on Park Avenue in Manhattan. The large crowd listened politely as I talked about some of the foreign policy challenges facing our nation. Following my remarks there was a lively discussion on many topics, including the use or threat of acts of terrorism to achieve political goals. We all were unaware, of course, of the tragedy that would strike the following morning.

Heather and I thought it would be a memorable day as we left home in the morning to take Andrew to his first day of preschool. We were among several excited parents who watched with smiles and tears as our three- and four-year-olds marched into a classroom for the first time. Then I left for the airport and the day became tragically memorable.

It was unusually warm for mid-September. From the backseat of the taxi I couldn't hear the radio over the hum of the air-conditioning. As we approached the Triborough Bridge on the way to LaGuardia Airport, the driver's eyes locked on mine in his rearview mirror. "There's been an accident. They're saying a plane hit the World Trade Tower. Can that be?" I asked him to turn off the air conditioner so I could hear the radio. We listened in silence for the few minutes it took to get to the airport.

I was headed for Washington, where I was to deliver a speech on my experience in Northern Ireland at the Meridian Center, a respected nonprofit organization with which I had been involved during my earlier service in the Middle East. In the few seconds it took to step from the car to the terminal it became clear that something was wrong; large numbers of people were surging out of the terminal. I pushed past them to find even more people headed for the exits. Among them I spotted a police officer and asked him what was happening. "All flights have been canceled," he replied. "The airport is being closed." Outside again, I joined the crowd trying to find a way back into Manhattan. After several attempts I found a limo that looked available, but when

I jumped into the backseat I discovered a young woman sitting there. She and the driver agreed that I could join them.

As the car moved slowly in dense traffic, she told me that she was scheduled to be married that week but might now have to postpone the wedding. That was a far more serious problem than my having to cancel a speech. Neither of us could get a signal on our cell phones, but I tried to reassure her that her fiancé would figure out why he couldn't reach her once he heard the news. As we drove onto the Triborough Bridge that news became more ominous. The first tower was burning, and the second had been struck. Just before our car reached the peak of the bridge the traffic came to a complete stop. Minutes later a radio newscaster explained why: the entrance to Manhattan from the bridge was closed, and all traffic was being routed north, away from Manhattan. We sat in silence and listened to the radio. I looked out the back left window and, incredibly, saw the towers clearly across the several miles that separated us from them. We watched the first tower collapse as we listened on the radio to eyewitnesses describing that collapse.

Between the Triborough Bridge and the Hudson River there are eight bridges that cross the Harlem River into Manhattan. We joined thousands of other cars and drivers trying to find one open to traffic into Manhattan, but we were not successful. As we moved west, along the north shore of the Harlem River, we encountered one closed bridge after another: Willis Avenue, Third Avenue, Madison Avenue, 145th Street, Macombs Dam, Washington, University Heights, and finally Broadway. In each case there was an agonizingly slow approach through bumper-to-bumper traffic moving inches at a time, only to get close enough to learn that the bridge was closed, then head to the next one. Our anxiety mounted, especially the driver's, who became visibly nervous. As we stopped at the Broadway Bridge and learned that it too was closed, we knew we were out of options. The driver turned to us and said, politely but firmly, "I'm sorry, but I have to go home. I'm a Palestinian and I've got a wife and child in New Jersey. I'm going to go upriver to the Tappan Zee Bridge and go home. You're welcome to come to New Jersey or you can get out here. But I'm not going to keep trying to get to Manhattan." The woman said she would go to New Jersey and try to reach her fiancé from there. I decided to get out. The bridge is at

Broadway and 220th Street. At that time my wife and I lived in an apartment at Broadway and 66th Street. "I'm on the street where I live," I told them, "about a hundred fifty blocks away. The bridge has got to open at some point, so I'll walk home if I have to." I paid the driver, shook hands with both, and wished them well on their onward journey. I took my suitcase and walked onto the bridge.

There I joined a crowd of several hundred men and women who stood on the north end of the bridge, unable to cross. Their path was blocked by a single uniformed police officer who stood in the middle of the bridge. The crowd was anxious but orderly; nobody tried to dash across, although it was obvious that the lone officer could not have prevented large numbers from making it across. By now the sun was high in the sky, the temperature and humidity had risen, and I was very hot and uncomfortable. I tried repeatedly to reach Heather by phone but was not able to do so. She had our four-year-old son and eight-month-old daughter to care for. Andrew was in prekindergarten on the east side of New York; I wondered whether Heather had managed to get him and bring him home while caring for baby Claire. I had

confidence in her judgment and resourceful-
ness, and I felt sure they would be home by
the time I got there.

After about forty minutes the police officer suddenly, and without explanation,
walked off the bridge. The buzz of the
crowd stopped. It was so quiet that I heard
the noise of a fire engine on the Manhattan
side. Suddenly one man ran across, then
another, then the whole crowd, all running
as if afraid the officer would return. Within
minutes we were all in Manhattan, racing
down Broadway.

I sprinted a few blocks to make certain I
was clear of the bridge. I was sweating and
breathing heavily, so I stopped and sat on
the curb to rest and figure out what to do. I
estimated that I was about seven or eight
miles from my apartment. It would be difficult and tiring, given the heat and my
suitcase, but I was confident that if all else
failed I could walk home.

I decided to go down Broadway on the
street, as close to the curb as I could get,
and try to simultaneously walk and flag
down a taxi or empty limousine. Several
blocks and twenty minutes later a limousine
driver kindly stopped to pick me up. His car
wasn't empty; there were three women in
the backseat, also trying to get down

Broadway. Traffic was light, so we proceeded quickly until we reached the intersection with 168th Street. There we encountered a roadblock manned by several police officers. One of them flagged the car to a stop. "I can't go no further," the driver said, so we all paid and thanked him and got out. I took my suitcase out of the trunk and stepped onto the sidewalk. As I did so a police officer standing there called to me: "Senator Mitchell?"

"Yes."

"Where are you going?"

"I'm trying to get to my apartment. It's at Broadway and 66th Street, near Lincoln Center."

"The subway has just reopened. The C line is running. Go in there, get on, and that'll take you down Central Park West."

As he spoke he pointed to an entrance to the subway, just a few feet away. I thanked him, went down the steps, and in a few minutes boarded a C train, which took me to Central Park West and 72nd Street, about eight blocks from my apartment. The subway car was not full, so I easily found a seat. As I sat down the man next to me asked, "Aren't you Senator Mitchell?" He introduced himself as David Barstow, a reporter for the *New York Times*. He said he was covering the reaction to the attacks on the towers and proceeded to interview me. I recounted my experience, a summary of which appeared in the *Times* the next day.

As I left the subway station at 72nd Street, to my surprise and shock, I could clearly smell the smoke and fire even though I was miles away from the stricken towers. My anxiety rose as I got closer to home, so I ran the last few blocks. I was exhausted but enormously relieved when I walked into our apartment to find Heather and the children, anxious but safe. It had taken me nearly six hours to get home from the airport.

In the aftermath, like most Americans, I followed closely the news reports on the events of 9/11. As the scope and horror became clear, I shared the pain and sorrow of the victims and their families. But I had no idea that I soon would be directly involved. In late November I received a telephone call from Berl Bernhard, a close friend and a founder of the law firm at which I was then a partner. He told me that, through their connections to Dartmouth College, he had been a longtime friend of David McLaughlin, the chairman of the board of the American Red Cross. Immediately after 9/11 the Red Cross had begun assisting the victims and had

436

simultaneously launched the Liberty Disaster Relief Fund, a major fundraising drive. As the money poured in, controversy developed over allegations that the Red Cross planned to use some of the funds for blood banks, community outreach, and other needs not directly related to the attacks. McLaughlin, Chief Executive Officer Harold Decker, and the board were searching for someone to serve as an independent overseer of those funds, which were already substantial and rising rapidly. Berl had suggested they ask me. He is an old and extremely close friend. Unless it was physically impossible for me to accept, there was little chance that I would say no to him on this or any other request. Besides, I wanted to do it. I welcomed the chance to help people who had suffered so much.

My responsibilities, as McLaughlin and Decker later spelled out, were to help the Red Cross devise the most effective way to distribute the Liberty Disaster Relief funds and services to those affected by the 9/11 attacks in response to the numerous demands. There were many interests to consider: the intent of countless donors from across the country and around the world, the immediate and long-term needs of recipients, and the appropriate role for the Red Cross to play given the involvement of many other charities and government programs. I accepted on condition that I would have full access to all relevant information and complete independence in making my recommendations, conditions that the Red Cross agreed to and then adhered to throughout the process. I did not require the Red Cross to agree in advance to adopt my recommendations, only that I would have full independence in making them and that the Red Cross would give them serious consideration. As it turned out, they did accept and adopt all of my recommendations.

In early December I began meeting with representatives of victims' organizations, other donors, Red Cross officials, first responders, and many individuals and families that had been directly affected by the 9/11 attacks. I was determined to hear from and give primary consideration to the views of those who were most directly affected. Over the next two months I listened to hundreds of people tell me their personal stories. They were all moving, some deeply heart-wrenching, and they brought home to me again the variety and complexity of human life.

As I listened to their stories it became

increasingly difficult to figure out what was fair. The word has many meanings; I learned in this process that it had a different meaning for almost every victim of 9/11. To cite but one of many examples: one of my meetings was with a group of women whose husbands had been killed. We were seated close together in a small circle. The women were serious, even somber; they were all well-informed and articulate. I asked each of them to tell me what she thought was fair. The first to speak was a tall, well-dressed, well-spoken woman, who said that she thought the money should be distributed in equal amounts to the families of those killed in the attacks. That sounded fair. But the woman seated next to her said that she had a child, so she thought she should get more than the widows who had no children. That too sounded fair. Another woman said she had four children, so she should get four times as much as the woman with one child. Yet another said she had only two children but one of them was severely disabled, so she should get more for that. They all sounded fair. Another said that her husband had been a waiter at the restaurant in one of the towers; that should be taken into account in providing her with a larger payment than the woman whose husband had been a wealthy investment banker and had left her with a large savings account and a generous life insurance policy. So it went, for hours, as each struggled with her grief, her needs, her embarrassment at talking about money with a man she had just met and a group of women she barely knew.

As complicated as it was, the discussion didn't even touch on many related problems: What about those who were injured but not killed? What about those who were neither killed nor injured but suffered property damage or loss of income? The questions piled up much faster than the answers. The effort was complicated by the proximity to Christmas; most of the discussions took place in December and January, when many of the families were experiencing their first Christmas and New Year without their loved ones and emotions were high.

I had parallel meetings with as many donor groups as possible — they were giving money and deserved some say in how it was used — and also with representatives of other service organizations to try to come to grips with the inevitable problem of overlap and inefficiency. Finally we confronted one of the most difficult challenges: striking the right balance between getting the money to those who needed it as quickly as possible and doing so in a way that minimized the inevitable fraud from false or inflated claims.

The learning process was intense and emotional, but also very informative and rewarding. By late January I was ready to act. Four months had passed since the attacks, two months since I was asked to get involved. I benefited enormously from the assistance of several members of our firm, DLA Piper, especially Berl Bernhard and Jim Pickup. Jim is a Californian who moved to Washington to serve on the staff of a member of Congress, then entered the private practice of law. He is calm, methodical, and extremely bright — perfect qualities for the difficult task we faced.

We knew that no matter what we did, it was inevitable and understandable that not everyone would be fully satisfied. Therefore our objective was to distribute the available funds in a way that was most fair and best met the needs of those who had suffered a loss. We sought to achieve four objectives:

- Meet the needs of those who suffered losses.
- Honor the intent of the donors.
- Provide assistance in a manner

consistent with the mission and traditions of the Red Cross.

- Ensure that all the money donated to the Liberty Fund would go to those who suffered loss on September 11.

We were also mindful that needs, logistics, and financial realities change over time, particularly in the first year, so we were flexible with respect to specific targets, although our broad goals remained constant. We later monitored implementation closely, and through the year 2002 submitted four quarterly reports on our progress toward meeting the plan's objectives, which were substantially achieved.

By the time I made and announced my decision on how to distribute the funds, the Red Cross had raised about $850 million, some of which had already been distributed. We estimated that almost three thousand people had loved ones who were killed or seriously injured; those families each received about $109,000. About fifty-five thousand people had been directly affected; they received assistance in accordance with their needs. The previous bombing tragedy in Oklahoma City had demonstrated that mental health needs arise over time, so we held back $80 million, to be combined with donations from other charities, to provide long-term assistance.

I was deeply gratified when my recommendations received broad support from the victims' organizations, the donors, other service providers, and the press and public. As contributions continued to arrive, the amount distributed by the Red Cross ultimately exceeded $1 billion. I maintained close supervision for nearly a year, and our quarterly reports, all of which were released publicly, were well received.

My experience with the Red Cross gave me a better insight into the many good works performed by that noble organization. Because I met so many of those affected by 9/11, and hopefully provided them with some assistance, the event continues to hold special meaning for me. It provided glimpses of the worst and the best of human behavior.

DISNEY

I thought it would be like the many other fundraising events I'd attended over the previous two decades: a prayer, a greeting, a short presentation by an official of the organization, then I would stand and talk about the contribution this organization was making to the community, the nation, possibly the world. I always tried to make my presentation relevant and interesting by telling a few stories and commenting on current national affairs, but my mission was clear and unchanging: to support the host organization.

But this event was different. Other than my speech, few words were spoken. Instead there was entertainment: songs, dances, video clips, all involving well-known stars affiliated with the Walt Disney Company. I was surprised and impressed. As I applauded with the rest of the large, appreciative crowd, I reflected on how I, a senator from Maine, had come to be at a well-decorated hotel ballroom in Los Angeles speaking in behalf of the University of Southern California.

In March 1994 I announced that I would not seek reelection to the Senate. I then received many calls and letters from friends and supporters. Most simply thanked me and wished me well; a few asked me to endorse causes in which they were interested, and some invited me to attend a wide variety of events. Whenever I could, I responded favorably. One such call was from Yoshi Honkawa, a nationally known leader in health care policy. I had gotten to know him well in the health care debates that year. He also was then serving on the board of trustees of USC. He implored me to come to Los Angeles to speak at the university's annual dinner.

To my pleasant surprise, it turned out to be an enjoyable engagement, not at all a chore. The Disney entertainment was arranged by Stanley Gold, another member of the university's board who also was a member of the board of directors of the Walt Disney Company. When we met and shook hands that evening I could not have known that over the next dozen years I would become deeply involved with him, and with Disney.

Several Disney executives were at the dinner, among them the company's chief executive, Michael Eisner. He was one of the most highly regarded business leaders in the country, well known for his creativity and innovation. In our brief meeting he made a strong first impression; tall, outgoing, articulate, with a lively sense of humor, he radiated confidence, authority, and success.

Just a few days later, back at my desk in Washington, I received a phone call from Eisner, asking if we could meet on his next trip to Washington. We did so, and a series of meetings followed, with him and then with several members of the company's board of directors. One such meeting was held at a dinner at Stanley Gold's home.

Earlier that year the president of the Walt Disney Company, Frank Wells, had died in a helicopter crash. An outstanding lawyer and business executive, Wells had been a steady and trusted partner to Eisner. Now, to my surprise, Eisner, with the backing of the board, offered me the position of president of the company when I left the Senate. I told him that I needed time to talk with Heather and to think about the offer.

It was flattering, and financially attractive, but I had several concerns. In the last few months of my Senate service, I received a large number of offers, from law firms, banks, other businesses, and universities, so I wasn't thinking about the Disney offer in isolation. I wanted to wait until the Senate adjourned for the year before making a decision; I didn't want there to be the fact or perception of any favoritism on my part to a future employer. Also Heather and I were to be married in December. Where we would live depended on where I would work; that was the subject of much discussion between us.

Ultimately I declined the offer from Disney and all others not related to the law. I had been trained as a lawyer and had enjoyed the practice of law; I had been a U.S. attorney and a federal judge. It was a subject I knew, liked, and was comfortable with. So, although the compensation was far less than what Disney and many others offered, I decided to join the Washington firm of Verner, Liipfert, Bernhard, McPherson and Hand.*

But it was with considerable regret that I told Eisner of my decision. I liked him and

* See note on page 250.

447

the other Disney executives and board members I had met, and working at the company, a national icon, would have been challenging. Eisner said he understood, and we parted on cordial terms.

A few weeks later he called me again. By then I was at Verner, Liipfert and at President Clinton's request had begun my work in Northern Ireland. Eisner said he understood and accepted my decision not to join Disney as a full-time executive, but now there was a vacancy on the board of directors. Would I consider that? I said I would. It didn't take long. I told Heather of the offer and that I would like to accept. When she agreed I called Eisner. I served on the Disney board from 1995 to 2006. It turned out to be a great and mostly enjoyable experience.

I quickly established a good relationship with other members of the board. I had many warm discussions with Roy Disney, Walt's nephew, who was also a board member, and his wife, Patty; we shared an interest in and a love for Ireland, where they owned a home and where I was then working much of the time. During that time I also served on other boards for varying periods; each was a unique opportunity and a hugely beneficial education. I learned a great deal about every aspect of operations at large and medium-size businesses. I met, observed, worked with, and learned from several extraordinary executives, men and women who started, created, built, and ran highly successful enterprises. Fred Smith invented the concept of express mail and created Federal Express; he is one of the most talented leaders I have ever met. Tom Stemberg created and built Staples. Barry Sternlicht did the same with Starwood Hotels and Resorts. There were others. And there was Michael Eisner and the Walt Disney Company.

As with most large human institutions, at Disney there were successes and failures. In the early years of my service on the board the successes were many, the failures few. I served for three years on the governance and nominating committee, then for a similar term on the audit committee. The company itself and its operations are interesting, of course, and I enjoyed learning about all aspects of the business side of the entertainment industry. In 2002 I was elected to be the board's first presiding director. As the title suggests, I presided at the board's meetings and served as a liaison, to the extent one was needed, between the CEO and the members of the board. Each of the members was highly successful in his or her own life, most of them outside the entertainment industry, so part of the fascination of the job was to meet and learn from a wide range of talented people.

In 1984 Eisner had become the chief executive of a company that was struggling artistically and financially. That year Disney had revenues of $1.45 billion and net income of $98 million. With energy, creativity, and a keen sense of the public's taste, Eisner led a sharp and successful expansion. By 1995, when I joined the board, revenues had risen to $12.15 billion and net income was $1.38 billion. New theme parks were opened and new attractions added at existing parks. The company entered the cruise ship business, as well as the live stage show business, creating long-running hits like *The Lion King** and *Beauty and the Beast*. The animated movie division churned out a series of hits, and the live-action movie business flourished. ABC television was acquired in 1996 and with it the spectacularly successful ESPN sports network.

In the first ten years of Eisner's tenure

* In 2014 *The Lion King* became the largest grossing show in Broadway history.

Disney's stock price rose by 870 percent. It was a heady period for the company's executives and the members of the board. To a newcomer to the board and the business, all seemed harmonious. Although Roy Disney rarely spoke at board meetings, Stanley Gold, who represented Roy's interests, spoke often and at length; Gold was strongly supportive of Eisner's leadership, and the two men appeared to be very close personally.

Inevitably the rate of growth and profitability slowed. In the first decade of Eisner's term revenues had grown at an average annual rate of 21 percent, but in the second decade they fell to 10 percent; average net income growth went from 27.6 to 6 percent. And within that second decade was a stretch of several years when there was little growth. Disney's net income declined in five of the six years from 1998 through 2003.

When things go badly, especially when they do so quickly, it is human nature that smiles turn to frowns, the happy talk turns angry, and a blame game begins. What in retrospect appears to have been a turning point was Disney's acquisition of Fox Family Worldwide, the principal asset of which was a Saturday morning cartoon show called *Power Rangers*. The transaction was announced just days before the tragedy of 9/11; Disney paid $3 billion and assumed $2.3 billion in debt. That turned out to be far more than the acquired assets were worth.

Following that acquisition it became increasingly clear that the acquired assets (subsequently renamed ABC Family), were not performing anywhere near the projections. I do not know whether that was the straw that broke the camel's back for Roy Disney and Stanley Gold, or whether there were other grievances more important to them. But they turned against Eisner and became increasingly critical of him, first in board meetings and then in public. That in itself was jarring because until then Eisner and Gold seemed so close, professionally and personally. It was clear that the company had overpaid for an underperforming asset, an acquisition that Eisner had conceived and pushed hard for. But the criticism was obviously galling to Eisner, and to other members of the board, because Gold had been such an aggressive supporter of the transaction. He didn't acknowledge that later, when he went public with his criticism, and to the company's critics, who included analysts and shareholders, it didn't matter. What mattered was that the company wasn't doing well, and when a company doesn't do well, a natural reaction is to change its leadership.

It was a widespread practice at the time (and still is, although less so) for the CEO of a large corporation to also serve as chairman of the board. But in the period during which Disney's growth slowed, several of the organizations that monitor and advocate on corporate governance urged that the positions be separated. For many of them, Disney became the poster child for this issue, and they were loud and insistent in urging that someone other than Eisner be appointed to serve as Disney's board chairman.

The process of separation had already begun in December 2002, when I was elected to the newly created position of presiding director. But as the bad news continued (Disney's revenues were essentially flat in 2001 and 2002) the demand intensified. The year 2003 was difficult, and it ended on a down note when Roy and Stanley resigned from the board to devote themselves to a full-time public campaign.

That campaign reached its peak of intensity on March 3, 2004, at the company's annual shareholders meeting, held that year in Philadelphia, the city of brotherly love. But it was neither brotherly nor loving when over three thousand shareholders gathered in the grand hall at the Philadelphia Convention Center. Gold unleashed a stinging attack on Eisner and received applause for it. He also criticized me, but only briefly; I was just collateral damage. To Gold I was too close to Eisner and thus part of the company's problem. I had never had a disagreement, personal or professional, with Roy or Stanley. But to them the fact that the rest of the board had refused to join their public campaign to remove Eisner was evidence of our lack of fitness. They wanted allies, not neutrals, and certainly not friends of Eisner.

Although they had drawn applause during the discussion, Roy and Stanley fell short in the voting. Since all shareholders are eligible to vote on the election of directors, those present at the meeting represented a small portion of the total. Eisner received 55 percent of the votes cast for his reelection to the board, and I received 75 percent, both enough to be reelected but both well short of an overwhelming vote of confidence.

The board met immediately following the shareholders meeting. Earlier Eisner had become convinced that he could not retain both positions, of chief executive officer and chairman of the board; a few days before the meeting he had asked me to agree to serve as chairman. I had declined, reasoning that to do so just prior to the shareholders meeting would appear to be a panicked attempt to foreclose criticism at the meeting; besides, I told him, I was already so overwhelmed at my law firm and with other activities that I doubted I had the time to serve effectively as chairman.

Now, in the aftermath of the shareholders meeting, he renewed the request, this time accompanied and supported by the full board. I hesitated, torn between wanting to be of help to a company I had come to love and the concern that I was already too busy and that this would be a long and painful effort not likely to end well. After an inconclusive discussion with the full board, Eisner requested a brief recess and asked to speak with me alone.

We went into an adjoining room where we talked for a half hour. I liked and admired him; he had been remarkably successful in re-creating the company and making it profitable. I felt that Stanley and Roy had been excessively personal and unfair in their criticism. But their concerns were not unfounded. The company had not been doing well, and now the management and the board were being held accountable. As is often the case with strong leaders, as the criticism mounted Eisner became more defensive and less willing to accept it.

In the end I couldn't say no. I realized that I would have to shed some of my other activities, and, although I enjoyed serving on other boards, I resigned from some of them. Over the next three years, serving as chairman of the Disney board was, by itself, a full-time job; since I also was practicing law full time, it was a very hectic period in my life. The complexity was eased somewhat by the fact that the company's New York office was just one block from the apartment in which Heather and I lived. I took an office there and enjoyed the shortest commute to work I've ever had, before or since. But the short commute had no effect on my main concern: how to help the company return to growth and profitability and, in that context, determine whether Eisner should continue as CEO.

In fact the turnaround had already begun. In 2004 the company's revenues rose by 14 percent, its net income by 83 percent; in 2005 the figures were 4 and 11 percent, respectively. But was that enough?

As with almost all major public figures,

Eisner has received both praise and criticism, but, to the best of my knowledge, no one has ever described him as unintelligent. He is in fact brilliant, creative, and provocative, especially in his chosen field of entertainment and the arts. He also has a keen business sense. Despite his deeply held feeling that he could and should continue as CEO, ultimately he realized that the issues raised by the internal struggle through which he and the company had gone would not subside; rather they would continue to hamper him and the company to which he had devoted much of his life. In the end, although he still felt strongly that Disney would be best served if he remained as CEO, he accepted the reality of change.

That led to the question of succession. A prime candidate was Bob Iger. His entire work life had been in television, beginning as a weatherman at a small local station and gradually working his way to the top. He was running ABC when it was acquired by Disney in 1995. Over the next decade he worked diligently alongside Eisner and was the clear heir apparent. Eisner himself strongly favored Iger. But the board was unanimous in insisting on a full search for a new CEO, including examining external candidates. It meant no disrespect to Iger, who was highly regarded by most board members. But it was essential, especially in view of the turbulence through which the company was going, to seek out and hire the best possible candidate; that required a wide-open national search.

Rather than appoint a search committee of a few board members, I decided to have the full board participate in the search process. It was at times acrimonious, and it took a long time, but in the end it proved to be the right approach. Throughout the process every member of the board was fully informed and had an equal opportunity to participate in and influence the decision.

There were several candidates, some of them clearly qualified by ability and experience to serve as CEO, and early on there was some support for several of them. But the more deeply into the process the board went, the more support for Iger grew. In early March 2005 the board concluded the process in a series of long and intense meetings, during which I advocated strongly for Iger. At the very end of the very last meeting the decision became unanimous. On March 12, a Sunday afternoon, at a telephonic press conference, I announced to hundreds of reporters that Bob Iger would succeed Michael Eisner as CEO, effective October 1, 2005.

I thought we had finally navigated our way through the turbulence to a safe landing. But not quite. The hostility that Stanley and Roy harbored for Eisner and Iger was so intense that it clouded their judgment. Just a few weeks later they filed a lawsuit challenging Iger's election. In it they alleged that the board had falsely represented that it would engage in a bona fide CEO selection process, including serious consideration of external candidates, and that this false representation caused Roy and Stanley to refrain from running a competing slate of directors at the 2005 annual shareholders meeting. They sought from the court an order voiding the 2005 election of directors, compelling a new election, and prohibiting any change in Eisner's and Iger's employment contracts. The suit was wholly lacking in merit and proved to be the final act in a long and painful episode.

Iger quickly demonstrated his good judgment and common sense. He called Roy and invited him to lunch. Roy soon returned to the company as a consultant and was named a director emeritus, and the lawsuit was dismissed. All involved, including and perhaps especially Roy, were relieved that the dispute was finally over. I will always believe that Roy himself was uncomfortable with some of the words spoken and actions taken in the dispute.

In the decade since Iger's arrival the company has performed extremely well. For fiscal year 2013 revenues were $45 billion, net income was $6.6 billion, and by the end of fiscal year 2014 the stock price rose to around $90. For the past thirty years the Walt Disney Company has been led by two outstanding executives. For two decades Michael Eisner was a creator and builder; for the past decade Bob Iger has been an innovative manager. Each was the right man at the right time.

Helping to manage a great company through a difficult transition was an experience I will forever treasure. And there was personal pleasure as well. When I became chairman of the board, Andrew was six years old and Claire three. On many joyous occasions we traveled to Orlando and to Anaheim, where together we laughed our way through the rides and held our breath on the roller coasters; learned the words to "It's a Small World"; had our pictures taken with Mickey, Donald, and Goofy; checked out the lions and giraffes; and demonstrated that you're never too young, or too old, to have fun.

THE OLYMPIC GAMES

The Olympic Games are among the premier sporting events in the world. Thousands of skilled athletes from every corner of the globe gather for two weeks of competition watched by billions on television. Legends are created, reputations are made, and billions of dollars change hands. But, as with other inspiring and glittering human institutions, there is also a seamy underside.

On January 9, 1991, Norman Seagram, Arthur Eggleton, and Paul Henderson appeared before the leaders of the International Olympic Committee (IOC) in Lausanne, Switzerland. Eggleton was then the mayor of Toronto; Seagram and Henderson had been leaders of Toronto's bid to host the 1996 Summer Olympic Games. They failed, despite what they regarded as a superior presentation, the product of a five-year, multimillion-dollar campaign.

On reflection, and after inquiry, they

concluded that they had been victims of a corrupt process in which the votes of IOC members had effectively been bought. In polite but blunt language, the Canadians pried open the lid on a mess teeming with improper gifts, including cash payments, in exchange for votes. In strikingly prophetic language they warned of the consequences of such behavior continuing unchecked. The IOC peered into the mess, then replaced the lid and looked away. And what the Canadians feared soon came to pass.

I was in my law office in Washington on a Friday afternoon when Bill Hybl called. A short, friendly, enthusiastic man, with an open face and manner, Bill was the chairman of the U.S. Olympic Committee. He wanted to see me, and I agreed. When we met he asked me to serve as chairman of the USOC's Ethics Oversight Committee. I had always loved sports, and I knew I would enjoy the opportunity to be involved in what I thought would be an interesting and constructive role. Bill assured me that it was a part-time responsibility and that I'd be assisted by an able staff. Although I was still involved in Northern Ireland, which meant that I was out of the country much of the time and was concerned that it would be difficult to find the time to do the job right,

I accepted. Not long afterward a scandal erupted in Salt Lake City.

From 1989 to 1991 Salt Lake City had competed to host the 1998 Winter Olympic Games. The city's Olympic Bid Committee made what its members felt was a persuasive effort and presentation. Included was the expenditure of over $250,000 on travel, hotel, entertainment, gifts, and payments of money to members of the IOC, their relatives, or friends. But when the IOC met in Birmingham, England, in June 1991, it chose Nagano, Japan. Stunned and disappointed, the Salt Lake City Bid Committee resolved to try again for the 2002 Winter Games. In an effort to improve their chances, they reviewed the process they had just gone through and concluded that Nagano's effort had been more sophisticated and extravagant. To win next time they would have to step up their game. And they did.

In a process of "gift creep," they moved from goodwill gifts to strangers to payments specifically intended to get votes; from small, inexpensive items they graduated to lavish gifts, and ultimately to payments of substantial sums of money to individual IOC members. The Salt Lake City committee didn't invent the culture of corruption;

they stepped into it and came to believe that in order to win they had to match or exceed their competitors in the petty and grubby process of buying votes. As so often happens, in their zeal for victory good men and women left their judgment and conscience at the door in the comforting belief that "everybody does it." And they prevailed.

When the scandal broke publicly, Hybl moved quickly and urged me to do so as well. He asked me to chair an independent commission to make recommendations that, if adopted, would help to prevent such abuses in the future. The target date for the commission's report was the end of February 1999, barely two months later. That precluded an exhaustive factual inquiry, which in any event would have been impossible because criminal investigations were under way in the United States and most of the participants refused to talk to an independent commission. Lacking subpoena power, we could not compel them to testify or to produce relevant documents. What we needed, and what we were able to get, was a sufficient factual basis to enable us to craft meaningful recommendations for reform.

I was joined on the commission by four outstanding members. Ken Duberstein had served as President Reagan's chief of staff and is a business consultant in Washington. I had known Ken for several years and liked and respected him. I had not previously known the other three members: Donald Fehr was the executive director and general counsel of the Major League Baseball Players Association; Roberta Cooper Ramo was a partner in an Albuquerque law firm and had previously been president of the American Bar Association; Jeff Benz was a lawyer in a San Francisco law firm and had been a national champion figure skater. In an intense setting and a tight time frame we worked well together. There were no substantive disagreements, and our report was unanimous. That result was facilitated by the outstanding lawyer we retained to assist us, Richard Hibey, an experienced trial lawyer and former prosecutor, who was a partner in a Washington law firm.

Although we did not identify the particulars of every improper transaction, we had more than enough information on which to base our recommendations. The Canadians had laid it out clearly eight years earlier. Our recommendations were made to both the USOC and the IOC. They were intended to eliminate the practices that contributed to the buying of votes; to strengthen oversight by both organizations over the site-selection process; and to make fundamental structural changes to increase transparency and accountability to the public.

To his credit, Bill Hybl provided the commission with full support and complete independence. He also urged the USOC to adopt our recommendations, which it did promptly and in their entirety. The IOC made meaningful changes in its site-selection process, in some respects going further than our recommendations. But while the IOC's response was generally positive, it was less forthcoming on structural changes and it remains a relatively closed and tight-knit organization.

For me it was another lesson in the complexity of human behavior. At the Olympic Games the best and the worst coexist: superb athletes, thrilling performances, and spectacular ceremonies alongside greed, theft, hypocrisy, and falsehood. This doesn't detract from the greatness of the performances, but it does remind each of us how high we can soar and how low we can sink.

BASEBALL

In the past few years a remarkable transformation has taken place in Major League Baseball. In the midst of the 2013 season, in which he won the Cy Young Award, Detroit Tigers' pitcher Max Scherzer told reporters that players were "tired of guys who blatantly try to break the system" and expressed support for the development of "a fairer system that correctly punishes players . . . so that players don't feel the need to cheat."[1] Mike Trout of the Los Angeles Angels, the 2013 American League Rookie of the Year, said, "To me, personally, I think you should be out of the game if you get caught. It takes away from the guys that are working hard every day and doing it all natural."[2] David Hernandez, a pitcher for the Arizona Diamondbacks, was emphatic: "I think you should be out of baseball. It sounds harsh but at the end of the day you're making it harder on

467

somebody else who is trying to make it in the game. You're essentially ending somebody else's career if you're cheating and putting up numbers. You should be done. It's not fair to all of us who have played the game the right way. I think there should be stiffer penalties from the get-go. Apparently 50 games isn't enough to stop players from cheating. A lot of us feel that way around here. Basically you're cheating us, the players. Not only the fans, but us, the union."[3] Boston Red Sox infielder Dustin Pedroia and Los Angeles Angels pitcher C. J. Wilson made similar comments.[4] Later that year other players were outspoken in their criticism after Jhonny Peralta signed a lucrative contract with the St. Louis Cardinals following a fifty-game suspension for his involvement with the Biogenesis clinic that had been implicated in providing performance-enhancing substances to players.[5] The Major League Baseball Players Association acknowledged that players were "disgusted" that some were continuing to use such substances despite years of efforts to eradicate them from the game.[6]

On March 28, 2014, Major League Baseball and the Players Association announced that they had reached agreement on what they described as the "most significant improvements to the disciplining and testing provisions of the Joint Drug Program since 2006." Those provisions include the following:

- The number of in-season random urine collections will more than double beginning in the 2014 season (from 1,400 to 3,200). These are in addition to the mandatory urine collections that every player is subjected to both during Spring Training and the Championship Season. This represents the largest increase in testing frequency in the Program's history.
- Blood collections for hGH detection — which remains the most significant hGH blood testing program of its kind in American professional sports — will increase to 400 random collections per year, in addition to the 1,200 mandatory collections conducted during Spring Training.
- A first-time performance enhancing substance violation of the Joint Drug Program will now result in an unpaid 80 game suspension, increased from 50 games. A player's second violation will result in an unpaid 162-game suspension (and a loss of 183 days of

pay), increased from 100 games. A third violation will result in a permanent suspension from Baseball.

- A Player who is suspended for a violation involving a performance enhancing substance will be ineligible to participate in the Postseason, and will not be eligible for an automatic share of the Player's Pool provided to players on Clubs who participate in the Postseason. (Such Players are already ineligible to participate in the All-Star Game.)
- Every Player whose suspension for a performance enhancing substance is upheld will be subject to six additional unannounced urine collections, and three additional unannounced blood collections, during every subsequent year of his entire career.
- The Arbitration Panel will have the ability to reduce a Player's discipline (subject to certain limitations) for the use of certain types of performance enhancing substances if the Player proves at a hearing that the use was not intended to enhance performance.[7]

In announcing the agreement, Tony Clark, the executive director of the Players Association, said, "Experience proves that increased penalties alone are not sufficient; that's why the Players pushed for a dramatic increase in the frequency and sophistication of our tests, as well as comprehensive changes in a number of other areas of the program that will serve as a deterrent. Make no mistake, this agreement underscores the undisputed reality that the Players put forward many of the most significant changes reached in these negotiations because they want a fair and clean game."[8]

These statements and actions represent a welcome change from the Players Association's earlier long-standing opposition to drug testing. Whatever may have occurred in the past, it is clear that the players and their union, to their great credit, are now committed to an effective program with strong penalties for violations. Among other results it has enabled me to again view baseball as I did when I was a young boy growing up in a small town in Maine — not quite as innocent, perhaps, but still with hope for the future.

As far back as I can remember my brothers, my friends, and I played baseball. It started as soon as I could hold a bat and throw a ball: pickup games, Junior League (the rough equivalent of the modern Little

League), American Legion summer league. I wasn't good enough to make the varsity team in high school or college, so I played in a variety of softball leagues, then and later in college and the army.

After playing baseball all day we listened to and talked baseball in the evening. My brothers and most of my friends followed and rooted for the Boston Red Sox, although a few supported the New York Yankees. We all were up to date on the many statistics of baseball: the standings, the batting averages, the pitching records. As with baseball fans everywhere our discussions were endless and inconclusive, especially when the subject was Ted Williams or Joe DiMaggio. Although our support never wavered, we agonized over Boston's close loss to St. Louis in the seventh game of the World Series in 1946 and their rout at the hands of the Cleveland Indians in a one-game playoff for the American League Championship in 1948. As year after year passed without a championship the intensity of our support increased even as our expectations declined.

On many summer days when there was no game or team practice my friend Ron Stevens and I would walk the short distance to the Colby College diamond, where the two of us played our version of a full baseball game. We had one bat, a few old baseballs, and one glove each. He stood at home plate as I pitched the balls to him. After he hit all of them we trotted out to pick them up and continue the game. When he made three outs it was my turn at bat. We called each batted ball: ground out to the second baseman, single to left field, fly out to right field. These were, of course, highly subjective judgments, so there was a lot of debate about each call. On and on we went, through seven innings, which was the usual length of Junior League games. Since there were just the two of us our games took a very long time, often a full morning or afternoon.*

* One summer day, while playing baseball, Ron's life changed. I was pitching and he was catching for our team. A foul tip struck his throwing hand and dislocated his right index finger. Late that night he suffered his first epileptic seizure. We spent so much time together that I was instructed by his parents and his doctor how to respond when he had a seizure in my presence. I loved him so much that I found unbearable the thought that I might have contributed to his condition by throwing the pitch that dislocated his finger. But I was reassured by his father that there was no way

It was not until I was in high school that I got to see my first Major League game. As a birthday present, my brother Paul and his wife, Yvette, took me to Fenway Park to see the Red Sox play the Yankees. I was deeply impressed by the size and beauty of the park. I had played in and watched a lot of local baseball games at which the attendance ranged from zero to a few dozen. To be among a crowd of thirty thousand people watching a game was for me an unforgettable experience.

The teams were tied at the end of nine innings. In the top of the first extra inning Joe DiMaggio came up to bat with the bases loaded. After taking a couple of pitches he swung and hit a hard line drive to left field. The crowd leaped to its feet in anticipation, then heaved a collective sigh of relief when the ball veered just outside the foul pole as it cleared the thirty-seven-foot left field wall

---

of knowing whether there was any relationship between the dislocated finger and the seizure. Advances in medical science enabled Ron to control his epilepsy through a program of drugs created for that purpose. He went on to a successful life in business. Although our paths diverged and we saw less of each other later in life, he remained the best friend anyone could ever have.

known to baseball fans everywhere as "the Green Monster." But we were barely back in our seats when, just two pitches later, DiMaggio hit one harder and longer. There was no doubt this time as the ball sailed out of the park, high over the head of Joe's brother Dominic, the Red Sox center fielder, for a grand slam home run. In the home half of the inning the Red Sox went down meekly, retired in order. To complete our anguish Ted Williams struck out to end the game. But to me it was still a great day, one I'll always remember, especially to be able to see both DiMaggio and Williams in my first Big League game.

Paul's memory of the day is not of the game. He recalls that when we ate before the game, I (then a finicky eater) took so long picking the onions out of my plate of spaghetti that we were almost late getting to Fenway. Aside from the game, what I remember most vividly about the trip is that we stayed overnight at a hotel in Boston; that was an exciting first for me. There was only one bed and it wasn't very large, so it was a night of close encounters. Paul slept in the middle, and I had only a narrow sliver of mattress on one side. The next morning he complained that I had kept him up all night; he rejected my explanation that I had to hang on to him to keep from falling out of the bed. Not surprisingly, that was the last time Paul took me to a baseball game.

It was a long way from there to the inner sanctum of Major League Baseball. That came much later, on the morning of March 10, 2006. Just as I opened the door the phone rang. I was in Anaheim, California, at a hotel in Disneyland, about to leave for the annual meeting of shareholders of the Walt Disney Company. A large crowd was expected. As chairman of the company's board of directors I would preside over the meeting, so I didn't want to be late. My first instinct was to ignore the call, but as the ringing continued I paused; it might be an emergency at home. I picked up the phone.

"Hi George, it's Bud Selig."

"Hi Bud, what's up?"

"I need your help."

Selig, the MLB commissioner, told me that he was deeply concerned about the problem of the use of performance-enhancing substances by the players. The recent publication of a book on the subject by two San Francisco writers had generated widespread publicity and growing criticism of baseball.[9] Selig asked me to conduct an investigation to find out, as best I could, what had happened, and to make recommendations to improve the League's drug-testing program. He had been pleased at the results of the Blue Ribbon Commission a few years earlier and felt that I could do the job that was needed now.* The Blue Ribbon Commission's report had a major and positive effect on baseball. Many of our recommendations found their way into the collective bargaining agreement that was entered into between the thirty clubs and the Players Association in 2002. It was the first such agreement reached in Major League Baseball without a work stoppage since 1972, and there has not been a work stoppage since. Clearly Selig was hoping for a similar result on performance-enhancing

* In 1999 Selig appointed a Blue Ribbon Commission to evaluate the economic structure of Major League Baseball and to make recommendations to improve competitive balance in the sport. I was one of four independent commissioners; the others were Richard Levin, then the president of Yale University; Paul Volcker, the former chairman of the Federal Reserve Board; and George Will, the author and syndicated columnist. When the report was completed I was asked to present it at a news conference. *The Report of the Independent Members of the Commissioner's Blue Ribbon Panel on Baseball Economics,* July 2000.

substances. But there were significant differences in the two situations.

"Bud," I said, "I'll be happy to talk further with you about this, but there's one thing I need to be clear at the outset. This won't be a committee, like the Blue Ribbon Commission, this will be just me. I'm your friend, but you understand that if I do this I must have complete independence to follow the evidence wherever it leads and to report on what I find, whatever that is."

"I understand," he said, "and I agree. You have my commitment that you will have my full support and total independence." Neither he nor I could know then what I would find, conclude, or report. But, to his credit, he never wavered in those commitments.

It took several lengthy meetings to work out the details. I was retained by the commissioner and in turn retained the law firm of which I was then chairman, DLA Piper. I put together a formidable team, led by three of the most able lawyers I have ever met: Charlie Scheeler headed up the investigation, John Clarke was assigned to draft the report, and Peter Pantaleo served as my principal advisor. When the commissioner announced my appointment at a press conference at MLB headquarters in

New York on March 30, 2006, we hoped that we could complete our work by the end of the year.

Within days of the announcement our optimism vanished. We still thought we could finish by the end of the year, but we no longer knew which year. It quickly became clear that the players' union was surprised and upset by the commissioner's decisions to have an investigation conducted and to appoint me to head it. Our research made clear that baseball and drugs went back a long way, and the issue created animosity between the club owners and the commissioner, on one hand, and the players and their association, on the other.[10]

Although I anticipated the union's negative reaction to my appointment and to the investigation, I was surprised to learn, through a few public and many private comments, that some owners and even some officials within the commissioner's office also were opposed to the investigation. Selig had acted despite the negative views of the Players Association and contrary to the views of some of the owners. It was courageous of him, but it didn't bode well for me and my colleagues. Lacking subpoena power, we could not compel the cooperation of witnesses or the production of documents.

How were we supposed to conduct a meaningful inquiry and submit a credible report when all of the players and some of the owners were opposed to the investigation?

We began by reaching out as broadly as possible:

- I initiated a dialogue with the Players Association.
- We initiated an effort to establish a baseline of usage, based on existing data from players' preseason physicals, without identifying any individual players.
- We attempted to make contact with the players, current and former, who had been publicly implicated in the BALCO * scandal, and their attorneys.
- We tried to engage with all current players.
- We reached out to the federal prosecutors who were handling the criminal investigation of BALCO.

* The Bay Area Laboratory Co-operative was then at the center of a widely publicized investigation of the use by Major League baseball players and other athletes of illegal performance-enhancing substances.

- We began to conduct interviews with officials from each of the thirty clubs, including owners, general managers, managers, coaches, trainers, and other club employees.

I went directly to the head of the Players Association. I had met Don Fehr, its executive director, when, at the request of the U.S. Olympic Committee, I chaired a commission investigating allegations of impropriety and corruption by members of the International Olympic Committee in connection with the selection of Salt Lake City as the site for the Winter Olympic Games in 2002.[11] Fehr, who had been active in Olympic matters for many years, was a member of the commission. We worked closely together, along with the other commission members. I liked and respected him and had the impression that the feeling was mutual. Our several discussions on the baseball investigation were cordial but unproductive. He and the players were upset that Selig had not consulted with them about the investigation or about my being chosen to head it. He insisted that the Players Association had come a long way from its initial opposition to drug testing in any form, and he emphasized that the owners had not pushed hard for tougher testing in the collective bargaining process. I responded that, while any conclusions were necessarily preliminary and tentative, based on the many estimates I was aware of it appeared that a minority of players were users. The Players Association had an obligation to all of its members, including the majority who did not use performance-enhancing drugs and who, as a result, were faced with the unacceptable choice of using or of being placed at a competitive disadvantage. He never explicitly rejected that argument, but he emphasized his obligation to all players, including those about whom as yet unproven allegations might be made. He never declared that the Players Association and its 1,200 members would not cooperate in the investigation, but that's the way it turned out. The Association subsequently rejected my requests for relevant documents and urged the players to refuse to talk with me.

One of the first questions I encountered after accepting this assignment was "How big a problem is steroid use in baseball?" Major League Baseball had been able to start random drug testing in the minor leagues in 2001 because the approval of the Players Association was not required, but the Association always had resisted testing at the Major League level. In August 2002, however, under enormous public pressure, the MLB clubs and the Players Association had reached a collective bargaining agreement for the years 2003–6. For the first time this agreement included a form of mandatory random drug testing. Drug testing beyond 2003 was not automatic under the agreement. The "survey testing" that was conducted in 2003 was anonymous. Despite the fact that the players knew in advance there would be tests, enough players tested positive to trigger mandatory drug testing for the 2004 season and beyond.

I reached out to many experts in the field, most of whom expressed the view that steroid use was much higher than these figures suggested. The point made most frequently was that the survey test was meaningless because the players had known about it in advance, and even then many of them had tested positive. Some also cited the case of Marion Jones, the track and field star, which became public at about this time, and other cases, to demonstrate that athletes could pass tests and yet still be illegally using steroids.* I learned during the investigation that no drug-testing program, no matter how well administered, can be expected to catch all cheaters. Many athletes and their advisors have become very skillful at evasion, and people are always creating new and — at least for a time — undetectable substances.

In an interview with a member of my staff, a cooperative club physician stated that every player is required to take a comprehensive physical each year at the beginning of spring training. These physicals include blood tests. We then spoke with a number of experts in endocrinology and learned that there are a number of markers, such as changes in cholesterol levels, that can be telltale signs of anabolic steroid use. (These markers would not, however, detect the use of human growth hormone, hGH.) Alone these markers were not sufficient to establish that a particular player used steroids. But, we wondered, could the aggregated data from the thousands of physicals conducted since the beginning of the so-called steroid era provide a reliable estimate of overall steroid use in baseball

* The Lance Armstrong case broke years later and provided dramatic affirmation of this point.

over time? If it could, that would be extremely helpful in developing recommendations to improve the drug-testing program. We could estimate the size of the problem, which would allow us to appropriately scale the proposed remedies. And we would not need to identify individual users to do so. We also could determine the effect of drug testing on overall use. Was drug testing reducing drug use? As simple as the question seems, no one knew the answer.

I retained Dr. James Heckman, a professor of economics at the University of Chicago who is an expert in constructing statistical studies from huge amounts of data. He told me that, with assistance from an expert endocrinologist, he likely could develop reasonably accurate estimates of overall steroid use in the MLB on a year-to-year basis. To do so he would use a process called latent variable analysis.* I knew Heckman was the right man for the job. In

* Latent variables, also known as hidden variables, are variables that are not directly observed but can be inferred from the presence of other variables through mathematical models. In this case steroid use, although not directly observed, could be inferred from the presence of other

2000 he was the co-winner of the Nobel Memorial Award in economics for his work on latent variable analysis.

There had never been a study like this conducted in any sport. The results would not only be important for baseball, but they could provide a window into how prevalent illegal steroid use was in all competitive sports. Such a study would have been an important milestone for years to come.

But major hurdles remained. Federal and state medical privacy laws prevent the disclosure of medical records, such as the players' physicals, without the consent of the patient. And the patients would not give their consent. Without that, the clubs could not provide the information.

For months we worked with the Players Association, the clubs, and the Commissioner's Office to solve this problem. We proposed that all of the medical data would be "de-identified"; in other words, before Heckman's team would see any data, the players' names and all other identifying information would be removed by a separate group of experts who would have no involvement in the data analysis. We agreed

---

health-related data documented in the records of the players' annual physical exams.

that under no circumstances would any individual player be named as a steroid user as a result of this study, an issue of great importance to the players and their union. But the Players Association refused to waive its members' rights under the privacy laws; as a result we could not get agreement to proceed from the Association or from the clubs. After months of negotiations we had to abandon the project.

This was my second biggest disappointment in the investigation, the first being the uniform refusal of current players to talk to me. It was not without irony. Since we could not reliably estimate overall use on a basis that did not require the identification of individual players, we had to rely even more on evidence of illegal use by individuals. This ultimately led to the identification and publication of the names of over eighty players for whom we developed credible and compelling evidence of use. Prior to the publication of my report I had many discussions with the leadership of the Players Association, and others, before making the difficult decision to name these players in the report. The Association strongly urged me not to name any players, but after receiving and considering a wide range of advice, I concluded that was not an acceptable course of action. If I had been able to receive reliable estimates of overall use from Heckman's study, it is possible that I would not have had to name individual players.

On April 27, 2006, I sent identical letters to attorneys representing four current and three former players who had been publicly named in allegations relating to the BALCO investigation, asking for several categories of documents. In compliance with the requirements of the collective bargaining agreement between the clubs and the players, I sent to the Players Association contemporaneous copies of the letters that were sent to the attorneys for the current players. The Players Association insisted on receiving copies of the letters to the former players as well. When I declined to do so the Association sent an email to players and agents advising them that our investigation was not following the rules for dealing with players as outlined in the collective bargaining agreement. That assertion was wrong. Former players are not members of the Association (or of the players bargaining unit), so the Association has no right to be included in communications with those individuals. But the message to current and former players and agents was clear: Don't cooperate with Senator Mitchell's investigation.

Over the next few months we sought repeatedly to communicate directly with all active players, within the constraints imposed by the Basic Agreement, to encourage their cooperation with the investigation. I wanted to make to them directly the argument I had made, unsuccessfully, to their representatives at the Players Association: that the majority of players who abide by the rules are the principal victims of the minority of players who cheat. In September 2007, after extensive negotiations with the Association about the terms under which such a communication would be permitted, I received consent to send a memorandum to all active players, but only on the condition that it be accompanied by a memorandum from the Association.

My memorandum was dated September 6, 2007, and was distributed to all current players shortly thereafter. It read, in part:

I have been retained by the Commissioner of Baseball to conduct an independent investigation into the alleged illegal use of performance enhancing substances in Major League Baseball. I have pledged to conduct an investigation and to complete a report that is independent, thorough, and fair. I believe it's in your interest to help me achieve those objectives.

The illegal use of performance enhancing substances is a serious violation of the rules of Major League Baseball which directly affects the integrity of the game. The principal victims are the majority of players who don't use such substances.

The memorandum from the Players Association warned the players about the perils of cooperating with me. It suggested the possibility of criminal prosecution of individual players for the use of such drugs, even though no player has ever been so prosecuted, before or since, even the many who have publicly admitted such use. The memo from the Association had its plainly intended effect: an almost total lack of cooperation by players with the investigation. Of the 1,200 players who received these memoranda, only two spoke to me voluntarily.*

In our review of public information we

---

* In May 2007 Jason Giambi publicly admitted that he had used steroids and that he had been wrong for doing so. This admission, which was consistent with earlier reports that he had admitted such use before the BALCO grand jury, cre-

learned that several players had expressed their concern about the use of steroids. These outspoken players were "clean" and above suspicion. I asked to meet with all of them; I wanted to get their views directly and to learn more about their careers. As required by the Basic Agreement, I wrote to the Players Association asking to meet with these players. I was deeply disappointed by the response: all but one declined to talk to me. These were, after all, players who had been publicly outspoken against the use of steroids in baseball, and even they refused to talk to me.

The one who did talk with me was Frank Thomas, twice voted the Most Valuable Player in the American League and later inducted into the Baseball Hall of Fame. When I spoke with him he was with the White Sox, so we met in Chicago in October 2007. There were no dramatic revelations; he conditioned his willingness to meet with

---

ated the possibility of discipline by the Commissioner's Office. Instead, the Commissioner's Office, Giambi, and the Players Association agreed that he would be interviewed by me. But they also agreed that I could not ask him to identify any other player about whom he had knowledge of illegal use.

me on the understanding that he would not identify other players. But he did express his views and he answered my questions. Although he would not name names, he was otherwise direct and forthright. He was clear in his belief that the use of performance-enhancing drugs in baseball was widespread and that it had an adverse effect on him and other players who did not use them. He was proud of his record and of the fact that he had compiled it the "hard way." To him it was a question of fairness. He didn't cheat, but he had to compete with players who did. Thomas supported the drug-testing program as a way of curbing the use of performance-enhancing drugs. I had been impressed by his athletic ability before I met him; after our meeting I was even more impressed by his integrity.

Another active player, about whom we received allegations of the purchase of performance-enhancing drugs, requested an interview, which he attended accompanied by his wife and his personal lawyer. During the interview he told me that the Players Association had urged him not to cooperate with me, but after talking with his wife and consulting his personal lawyer he decided to ignore that advice. He admitted that he had obtained performance-enhancing drugs but provided persuasive evidence, which we were able to independently verify, that he had not used them. He was not named in the report as a result.

Shortly after my appointment was announced I placed telephone calls to three men in San Francisco. The first two were Mark Fainaru-Wada and Lance Williams, the journalists who had written the book *Game of Shadows* that had generated so much publicity and concern about the use of performance-enhancing substances in Major League Baseball. I was disappointed that they refused to talk to me. I had more success with the Office of the U.S. Attorney for the Northern District of California. That office had jurisdiction over the cases that arose from allegations that BALCO had supplied performance-enhancing drugs to numerous MLB players and other professional athletes. Scott Schools, the U.S. attorney, agreed to talk with me. I offered to travel to San Francisco, but he told me that he would be in Boston in the near future and suggested we meet there. A few weeks later, over breakfast at a restaurant overlooking the Boston Common, we had a pleasant and productive discussion. I told him that, having been a U.S. attorney myself, I had at least some idea of the pressure he was under in a case that had generated so much publicity. I assured him that I would not say or do anything that might in any way hinder or jeopardize his investigation. My investigation was private and civil and had to be subordinate to his, which was public and criminal. I pledged that I would honor his requests in that regard. At the same time, I said, our investigations had at least some overlapping objectives and there might be opportunities down the road for cooperation that could enhance both. He agreed to further discussions, and I had a good feeling as we parted.

I immediately made plans to travel to San Francisco to meet with the assistant U.S. attorneys who were handling the BALCO cases. Matt Parrella and Jeff Nedrow are experienced and able federal prosecutors. Our common backgrounds — mine as U.S. attorney for Maine and then as a federal judge, Charlie Scheeler's as an assistant U.S. attorney in Baltimore — served as a basis for what proved to be the most important meeting of the several hundred we held during our investigation. Parrella and Nedrow appreciated our deference to their investigation and recognized the existence of some parallel interests. Importantly, they also introduced us to Jeff Novitzky, a federal agent; he and Charlie bonded quickly and, with Parrella, served as the point men in the cooperation that developed. They introduced us to Kirk Radomski and Brian McNamee, both of whom admitted to distributing performance-enhancing drugs to major league players. Without their cooperation and participation, our investigation would have produced far less than it did.

Our meetings with those important witnesses, and the information they provided, are set forth in detail in our final report.[12] We also obtained a great deal of information from the more than seven hundred interviews we conducted of persons, almost all of them men, involved in every aspect of professional baseball, from former players to clubhouse attendants and executives at all levels. Much of it was general; some of it was helpful, some unhelpful; and some of it plainly false. Several club officials, former players, and managers had made strong, negative public statements about drug use, but when we talked with them, almost without exception they recanted or modified their statements, claimed they were misquoted, or claimed to forget entirely their prior public statements. Others, some of whom had spent years, even decades in baseball, claimed to have been unaware of any aspect of the subject before their interviews, despite the enormous publicity that had occurred. A few actually said that they had never before heard or read anything about the subject of steroids in baseball and first learned about the issue from our questions!

Radomski and McNamee, by contrast, provided direct, eyewitness testimony and, in some cases, documents (canceled checks, receipts, letters, etc.) to corroborate their testimony. From emails we received in response to our many document requests to the clubs, we were able to verify that some clubs were aware of, or highly suspected, substance use by some of the players that Radomski identified. Several club executives openly discussed use by players they were evaluating (and in some cases went on to sign up for their team).

On the snowy afternoon of December 13, 2007, I released the report of our investigation at a press conference at the Grand Hyatt Hotel in New York. There were hundreds of reporters present, and a bank of dozens of television cameras was arranged in the back of the room. Along with my team, I was joined by Richard McLaren, a law professor and a member of the Court of Arbitration for Sport, and Dr. Gary Green, a professor of medicine at UCLA who studies the use and detection of performance-enhancing substances, both highly regarded experts in their fields.

I concluded that for more than a decade there had been widespread illegal use of anabolic steroids and other performance-enhancing substances by MLB players in violation of federal law and baseball policy. The evidence we uncovered indicated that it was not an isolated problem involving just a few players or a few clubs. Each of the thirty clubs had players who used such substances at some time in their career. Club officials routinely discussed the possibility of substance use when evaluating players. The response by baseball had been slow to develop and was initially ineffective. For decades, citing concerns for the privacy rights of players, the Players Association had opposed mandatory random drug testing of its members for steroids and other substances. But in 2002, under public and congressional pressure, the effort gained momentum after the clubs and the Association adopted a mandatory random drug-testing program. While that program was effective in reducing the detectable use of steroids, the use of human growth hormone had risen because it was not detectable through urine testing.

The report outlined the substantial information we had uncovered regarding the use of steroids and human growth hormone by MLB players. Much of that information came as the result of the cooperation of Radomski, McNamee, and other witnesses, including former players. More information was gained as the result of our other efforts, including interviews of active coaches and club personnel. While I was criticized by the Players Association for naming players who had used illegal substances, I made it clear in the report that I did so only where I had credible and compelling evidence, including in some cases eyewitness testimony or corroborating documents.

While much of the press coverage of the report focused on the players who were identified, my recommendations for reform were the heart of our efforts. I suggested improvements to the joint drug prevention and treatment program that is part of the Basic Agreement between the clubs and the Players Association, including requiring periodic reports of aggregate testing activity, making the joint program more independent, increasing the frequency of testing, and improving the collection process to ensure effective testing. I also recommended that the commissioner more aggressively investigate evidence of use or possession of prohibited substances, especially by establishing a department of investigations that would be charged with this task. Other recommendations were improvements in drug education; random, unannounced testing of clubhouse personnel; and the establishment of a hotline for reporting anonymous tips. The commissioner announced that he would adopt immediately all of my recommendations that were not subject to the collective bargaining process. Later the Commissioner's Office and the Players Association agreed to changes to the joint drug program that incorporated most of the remaining recommendations.

Looking back years later, the most important recommendation I made may have been the establishment of a department of investigations within the Commissioner's Office to gather evidence of substance use from sources other than drug tests. That department's work led to suspensions arising out of the Biogenesis clinic matter, which became public in 2013. Thirteen MLB players were suspended for the use of prohibited substances they received from that Miami clinic. As I've noted, one of the most fundamental lessons is that drug testing is not a foolproof detection method: it's more of an ongoing cat-and-mouse game between the cheaters, their enablers, and those who use science to try to prevent cheating. With this new investigative capacity, MLB has another powerful weapon in its enforcement arsenal.

Some social problems persist, despite laws and other efforts to prevent them. Every society has laws prohibiting crimes, but no one expects an end to crime; it is a serious problem that must be aggressively punished and deterred. So it is with the use of performance-enhancing substances in sports. There will continue to be those in sports who want so badly to gain a competitive edge that they are willing to cheat, and there also will continue to be those who see profit in meeting that demand. As the money offered to premier athletes continues to rise rapidly, the risk-reward ratio skews increasingly to more risk taking. All sports, not just baseball and not just professional, face a serious and continuing challenge. To its credit Major League Baseball, after a halting initial response, has moved vigorously to meet the challenge. For that, Commissioner Selig deserves great credit. Credit also should go to the players and their Association; after decades of resistance and delay, they have come to understand that their interest lies in a strong, effective, and fair program of testing and vigilance to limit the use of performance-enhancing substances to an absolute minimum. I am heartened by the fact that more players than ever are speaking out against steroid use, and I am hopeful that the tide is turning against substance use in baseball and other sports.

Since the day my report on drugs and baseball was released the question I've been asked more often than any other is this: "Given what you've learned, do you still like baseball?"

In the past few years I have learned a lot of unpleasant facts, but I'm as much a fan now as I ever was. During the season the box scores of the previous evening's games are the first thing I turn to in the morning paper. It was inevitable that I and most other fans would be saddened and disturbed to learn of the extent of performance-enhancing drug use in baseball. As in business, politics, the arts, and the professions, indeed in virtually every aspect of life, learning that our childhood heroes are fallible humans is disillusioning. As we grow up, we get over our disappointment and we understand this as just another example of the enormous complexity of life. We come to terms with the reality that we all are fallibly human. Each of us will, throughout our life, make some mistakes and bad decisions. At the age of ten life seems simple and clear. By the age of forty the contrary realization has long been obvious.

That knowledge frees us to sit in the stands on a warm summer evening, preferably with our children, taking in the sights and sounds of a great spectacle. The contrast of the deep green grass of the outfield and the white lines set on the reddish brown dirt of the infield; the ease and fluidity with which a small group of enormously talented men run and throw and catch a small, hard, white ball; the power and precision of a pitcher throwing a ball ninety-five miles an hour to a predetermined point sixty and a half feet away; the almost superhuman reaction of the batter, who has a fraction of a second to decide whether or not to swing; the electric crack as the ball meets a bat swung quickly and with stunning power; and the sudden roar as forty thousand fans jump as one to their feet.

You stand, cheering and clapping, as does your son. With a big smile on his face he turns, high-fives you, and then gives you a big hug. You hold on, longer than you should, because you know that soon he will be slipping away from you, and a moment like this may never recur. There's not a word or a thought about drugs. My answer is yes, I still love baseball.

THE MIDDLE EAST

We had just returned from a brief vacation and were waiting for our luggage at LaGuardia Airport when my cell phone rang. It was early January 2009. Ann Ungar, my assistant, called to tell me that someone from Hillary Clinton's office had called. Hillary had been chosen by President-elect Obama to be secretary of state. Could I come to her home in Washington that evening? I quickly calculated how long it would take to get to our apartment, drop off Heather and our children, then return to the airport. "Tell them I'll catch the six o'clock shuttle and be there at eight."

Shortly after the election in November, I'd had a brief telephone conversation with Joe Biden. We had served together in the Senate and worked closely on several major anticrime bills. I congratulated him on his election as vice president, and we discussed my work in Northern Ireland and whether I might serve in the new administration. I said I would of course be happy to consider it.

Two months had passed and I had forgotten about the conversation, but Hillary reminded me of it when we met. She and I had worked together on President Clinton's unsuccessful effort to reform our health care system, and she had been actively helpful to me when I was in Northern Ireland. Now she wanted to know if I would join the administration as special envoy to the Middle East.

She was accompanied by Jim Steinberg and Jack Lew, two able and experienced men who would go on to serve as her principal deputies at the State Department. I told her that I enjoyed public service and would like to accept but that I had personal concerns. I had worked on Northern Ireland for five years, and then, in 2000 and 2001, at her husband's request, I had chaired the International Commission on Violence in the Middle East.[13] Now I had two children, eleven and eight years old, and I had to talk with Heather about the personal and financial implications of returning to public service. Hillary encouraged me to have that conversation; she also made it clear that she was considering others for the position and that whatever decision she made would require the approval of the president-elect.

A week later, at Hillary's request, I returned to Washington to meet with Barack Obama. I had retired from the Senate before he arrived there, but we had met briefly. While in the Senate I traveled the country to support and raise money for Democratic candidates; on two occasions, at events in Chicago, I was introduced to the young Illinois state senator. Both times the hostess of the reception told me, "This young man is very bright and is going places. I wouldn't be surprised if someday he got elected to the U.S. Senate." Now he had done that and more. In just a few days he would be sworn in as the forty-fourth president of the United States.

We met in a low-rise government office building that had been temporarily converted into his transition office. We talked for an hour, some of it trading stories about our service in the Senate. Although our meetings in Chicago had occurred several years earlier, he recalled them; he even remembered the jokes I had told. When he asked if I would serve as his envoy to the Middle East, I told him that I would.

Heather and I had discussed it at length. Despite the burdens it would place on her, she was, as always, fully supportive. She asked whether there was any real chance of success. At that time a bitter and destructive conflict was raging in Gaza between Israel and Hamas. Emotions were high and hostile. I had been to the region often and knew most of the leaders there. I knew the chances were very low of getting an agreement between Israelis and Palestinians. But, as she had at a critical moment in Northern Ireland, Heather told me, "You'll never forgive yourself if you don't try."

So when I told Obama I would serve, I made clear there were limitations: "I can't commit to serve the full four years of your term. I spent five years working on Northern Ireland and also did an earlier tour of duty in the Middle East. I have two children who are about the same age as yours. The difference is that at my age I'm not going to see my kids become adults, have careers, get married, have families of their own, as you will. This is my time with them."

"I understand. How long can you commit to?"

"I'll commit to two years, then we'll see where things stand."

"That's fine."

We stood, shook hands, and I left. On the flight back to New York I thought of how lucky I'd been to reach this stage in my life.

Any American who is asked by the president should be ready and willing to serve our country. But I also realized that this conflict was older, more complicated, and more difficult than Northern Ireland had been. Any realistic assessment would have to conclude that the prospects ranged from slim to none. But Heather had been right. I had to try.

Two days after he was inaugurated, President Obama went to the State Department, where he and Secretary of State Clinton announced the appointment of two special envoys: Richard Holbrooke, an experienced diplomat, for Afghanistan and Pakistan, and me for Middle East peace. In my statement I tried to make clear both the problems in the region and the promise of peace.

I don't underestimate the difficulty of this assignment. The situation in the Middle East is volatile, complex, and dangerous. But the President and the Secretary of State have made it clear that danger and difficulty cannot cause the United States to turn away. To the contrary, they recognize and have said that peace and stability in the Middle East are in our national interest. They are, of course, also in the interest of the Israelis and Palestinians, of others in the region, and people throughout the world. . . . Just recently, I spoke in Jerusalem and I mentioned the 800 years [of conflict in Northern Ireland]. . . . Afterward, an elderly gentleman came up to me and he said, "Did you say 800 years?" And I said, "Yes, 800 years." He repeated the number again — I repeated it again. He said, "Ah, such a recent argument. No wonder you settled it." . . . This effort must be determined, persevering, and patient. It must be backed up by political capital, economic resources, and focused attention at the highest levels of our government. And it must be firmly rooted in a shared vision of a peaceful future by the people who live in the region. At the direction of the President and the Secretary of State, and in pursuit of the President's policies, I pledge my full effort in the search for peace and stability in the Middle East.[14]

The president wanted to make it clear that he was serious about dealing with this problem, so within days I was on a plane headed for the region. On the fourteen-hour flight I had time to reflect on the past and present of this long-standing issue.

The conflict between Israel and the

Palestinians does not exist in a vacuum. It continues — to this day — against a backdrop of resurgent violence elsewhere in the Middle East. In trying to comprehend an area where for a long time rulers and boundaries were imposed from elsewhere and where religious, tribal, and family loyalties often trump national identity, many Americans are both confused and angry. Weary after more than a decade of war in Iraq and Afghanistan, many want to turn away from what seems to be an intractable and unsolvable mess. Others want to do just the opposite: to unleash more American military power in an effort to quell the seeming chaos.

The conflicts in the Middle East are many and overlapping: Persians and Arabs; Arabs and Jews; Israelis and Palestinians; Sunni and Shiite Muslims; fundamentalists and moderates; Sunni-led governments and Sunni opposition groups, including the Muslim Brotherhood. All of these conflicts are products of history. We cannot change that history, but we may be able to alter its future course. It is in our national interest to help resolve conflicts and reduce instability in the Middle East to the extent possible, especially where we can do so by means other than military force.

In particular we should continue the active pursuit of an agreement to end the conflict between Israel and the Palestinians. While there are many reasons to be pessimistic, successful peace negotiations could end the suffering of those war-weary peoples and could dramatically improve America's credibility in the region and the world.

Any such peace effort requires understanding how the conflict started. A good place to begin is not in the Middle East itself but in London and Paris, where decisions made a century ago reverberate today.

After Britain and France suffered huge losses in the killing fields of Belgium and France in World War I, battle lines hardened and a long and destructive period of trench warfare began. From the beginning the British and French governments sought help wherever they could find it, and they saw opportunity in the Middle East. For four centuries the region had been part of the Ottoman Empire, based in Turkey. Persuading Arabs to revolt against the Ottomans, who were allied with Germany, became an important military objective for Britain. In addition the prospect of carving up and grabbing a piece of the decaying Ottoman Empire was enticing to each of the major participants in World War I.

In pursuit of these goals, the British high commissioner in Egypt, Henry McMahon, in 1915 engaged in negotiations with the emir Hussein bin Ali, the Arab tribal and religious leader in the area of western Arabia that includes the holy cities of Mecca and Medina. Although there is much dispute among historians about the nature and significance of these negotiations, the emir and his Arab allies thought they were getting a British commitment of support for an independent Arab nation, extending from what is now Iraq through Syria and the Arabian peninsula (with some exclusions), in exchange for an Arab revolt against the Turks.

Beginning well before the onset of war, Zionist leaders had sought support from Britain, then still regarded as the dominant world power. The British government's interest in the Zionists rose as its losses mounted in the war. Prime Minister David Lloyd George later testified that in his discussions with the Zionist leaders he was motivated by a desire to encourage support for Britain from the United States and Russia, both with large Jewish populations.

The culmination of all of this came in 1917, in the form of a letter from the British foreign secretary, Lord Balfour, to Baron Walter Rothschild, a leader of the Jewish community in Britain. The letter expressed support for "the establishment in Palestine of a national home for the Jewish people," subject to "it being clearly understood that nothing shall be done which may prejudice the civil and religious rights of existing non-Jewish communities in Palestine, or the rights and political status enjoyed by Jews in any other country."

Few documents have been subjected to the microscopic analysis accorded the Balfour Declaration in the ninety-seven years since it was published. The obvious questions — What does "a national home" mean? How could this be accomplished without "prejudice [to] the civil and religious rights of existing non-Jewish communities in Palestine?" — were followed by many others, some of which continue to be the subject of interpretation. The Zionists, however, believed they had received a commitment of British support for a Jewish state in Palestine.

The apparent contradiction in the positions taken by the British government in the McMahon-Hussein negotiations and the Balfour Declaration were further complicated by the Sykes-Picot Agreement, reached in 1916 (named after the British and French diplomats who negotiated it). Under the treaty's terms, Britain, France, and later Russia agreed to divide among themselves control of the lands of the Ottoman Empire after the war. Palestine was to be under international administration. Although the agreement itself was subsequently repudiated, in 1922 Britain and France received mandates from the League of Nations to govern most of the region.

While Sykes and Picot and their colleagues no doubt believed they were serving their respective national interests, neither did their countries any favor. Britain especially suffered through nearly three decades of hostility, violence, and enormous expense, as both Jews and Arabs came to regard their mandate rulers as biased or incompetent or both.

From the beginning of the mandate to its end in 1948, the British struggled unsuccessfully to contain the tensions between Arabs and Jews. As Jewish immigration to Palestine rose, Arab resentment grew, finally erupting into riots and outbreaks of violence in 1933 and, more widespread and intense, from 1936 to 1939. In response the British were militarily aggressive; there were many arrests and some executions. Politically, however, Britain made a significant gesture to the Arabs in 1939 by issuing a White Paper that renounced its commitment to a Jewish national home in Palestine and restricted immigration of Jews to the area to seventy-five thousand over five years. This, of course, angered the Jewish inhabitants, who began establishing their own political and military institutions. A militia called Haganah (Hebrew for "defense") was created, initially to protect Jewish settlements; later it played a major role in the 1948 war.

World War II was a turning point, not just in Europe but also in the Middle East. The Jewish community, known as the Yishuv, supported the Allies. The Arabs were split: some supported the Allies and a few thousand even fought with the British, but more supported the Axis powers, most notably the grand mufti of Jerusalem, who spent the war years in Germany. The earlier British decision to limit Jewish immigration into Palestine later resulted in the rejection of many Jews who were trying to flee the Holocaust. This generated widespread international criticism of British policy and added to discontent in Britain over the mandate.

At its peak the British military force in Palestine exceeded 100,000 troops — a huge expense for a country reeling from the cost and other burdens of World War II. Menachem Begin and Yitzhak Shamir, both of whom would later be elected prime minister of Israel, became the leaders of two Jewish paramilitary factions that had been organized in response to the earlier Arab uprisings. These groups began a campaign of violence to force the British to withdraw. The most publicized event was the 1946 bombing of the British military headquarters at the King David Hotel in Jerusalem, in which ninety-one people died. In Britain the desire to withdraw intensified, and in 1947 the British government announced that it would leave Palestine the next year and asked the United Nations General Assembly to decide what should replace the British administration there.

On November 29, 1947, the General Assembly adopted a resolution proposing that Britain's mandate be replaced by a plan of partition under which there would be an independent Arab state and an independent Jewish state and the city of Jerusalem would be placed under an international regime administered by the United Nations. The resolution triggered a new round of violence, resulting in thousands killed and many more injured. Ultimately the Jews accepted the plan, but the Arabs did not. By early 1948 the sporadic violence had coalesced into organized military operations. The Haganah became the Israel Defense Force, and the paramilitary groups were forced to disband and join the IDF. They were opposed by what came to be known as the Arab Liberation Army.

The British gradually withdrew their forces, a process completed on May 14. On that same day David Ben-Gurion publicly proclaimed the establishment of the state of Israel. Almost immediately President Harry Truman announced U.S. recognition.

Several Arab countries then entered the fray, but their efforts were not effectively coordinated. In response to a question about why he seemed so confident, Ben-Gurion said it was because Israel had a secret weapon: "the Arabs." By the following spring Israel had prevailed on all fronts, the fighting had wound down, and a series of armistices had been signed.

Amid the strife, however, hundreds of thousands of Palestinians left or were driven from their homes and communities, some of which were destroyed. Most ended up in refugee camps in Gaza, Jordan, Lebanon, Syria, and elsewhere. There they have remained for sixty-five years. At the same time, hundreds of thousands of Jews living in Arab countries emigrated or were expelled. The Palestinians' right of return to their homes — the living Palestinians who actually left in the 1940s and their descendants — remains one of the contested issues between Israel and the Palestinians.

In 1964 the Palestine Liberation Organization was established in opposition to Israel's existence. For the next quarter century, under the leadership of Yasser Arafat, it waged yet another campaign of violence. One of the most publicized acts was the killing of Israeli athletes at the 1972 Olympic Games in Munich by a PLO faction called Black September. Wars between Israel and neighboring Arab states broke out in 1967 and 1973. Israel prevailed in both, expanding its military superiority and its territory to include the Gaza Strip and the West Bank.

In 1977 Egyptian president Anwar Sadat made a surprise, historic visit to Jerusalem, where he met with Israeli prime minister Begin. A year later Sadat and Begin accepted President Jimmy Carter's invitation to Camp David, where they reached agreement on a framework for peace. A formal treaty between Egypt and Israel was signed on March 26, 1979. Sadat's actions angered some in Egypt, and he was assassinated two years later. President Bill Clinton later encouraged negotiations between Israel and Jordan, and the leaders of those two countries signed a peace treaty on October 26, 1994.

The first Palestinian intifada, or uprising, took place in 1987, during which Hamas was established as an offshoot of the Muslim Brotherhood in Egypt. That conflict resulted in the PLO's renouncing violence and accepting a two-state solution in 1988. In 1993 the PLO recognized Israel and its right to exist in peace and security, and in 1996 it repealed the provisions in its charter that called for armed resistance and the destruction of the state of Israel. In 2000 Arafat and Israel's prime minister Ehud Barak met with Clinton at Camp David. After they were unable to reach agreement, the second intifada broke out. It continued for four years with the loss of more than three thousand Palestinian and nearly one thousand Israeli lives.

Arafat died in 2004 and was succeeded by Mahmoud Abbas, who continues today as the president of the Palestinian Authority, the executive branch of the Palestinian government. The division among Palestinians between those who favor retaining the right of armed resistance and those who oppose violence and favor peaceful negotiation is now manifested in the competition between the Palestinian Authority, which is led by Fatah, its major political party, and Hamas. The Palestinian Authority is a secular organization and is supported by the United States. Hamas, on the other hand, seeks to establish an Islamic state, and the United States has designated it a terrorist organization. In 2007, after a brief battle in Gaza, Hamas routed the PA's military force and seized control there. As a result the internal Palestinian split became geographic as well as political: the PA controls the West Bank, with about 2.7 million residents, while Hamas controls Gaza, with a population of about 1.8 million, although the PA still has many loyalists in Gaza and Hamas has many in the West Bank.

After Hamas gained control of Gaza, the so-called quartet — the United States, the United Nations, the European Union, and

Russia — issued a statement of principles, which called upon Hamas to commit to nonviolence, recognize the state of Israel, and accept previous peace agreements. To date Hamas has refused to do so.

Those prior agreements include the Oslo Accords of 1993, which were the product of secret negotiations that gave the Palestinians a limited degree of self-governance under the Palestinian Authority. The signing of these accords, which promised a peace agreement to reach a two-state solution, sparked intense debate within Israel. Yitzhak Rabin, the prime minister who negotiated and signed the accords, was assassinated in 1995 by an Israeli who opposed them.

Ariel Sharon, who had defeated Barak in 2000, unilaterally withdrew Israeli armed forces and settlers from Gaza in 2005, but tensions have remained high between Israel and Hamas along the border. Open conflict erupted in late 2008, in 2012, and, most recently, in 2014, as Israel tried to eliminate rocket fire from Gaza and destroy tunnels between Gaza and Israel, while Hamas sought the lifting of the blockade on Gaza that Israel and Egypt have imposed since 2007.

Where does this history leave us today?

My personal experiences in the region lead me to the following conclusions about the current state of Israeli-Palestinian relations:

- The conflict has gone on for a very long time and has included a great deal of violence. As a result hostility and mistrust between Israelis and Palestinians are at very high levels. Those strong negative attitudes are intensified by a profound sense of victimization in both societies; indeed their disagreements include skepticism and even denial about some parts of the other's narrative.
- In the past, skepticism and disagreements were overcome by strong and committed leaders. Israel has had a peace treaty with Egypt for thirty-five years and with Jordan for twenty. Yet, mirroring attitudes in both societies, the personal level of mistrust between Prime Minister Benjamin Netanyahu and President Abbas is high; both often refer to the "lack of a partner," and each appears to have no confidence in the other's sincerity and seriousness of purpose and thus no confidence in the prospect of a successful outcome. As a result each has

been reluctant to take political risks that would subject him to intense domestic criticism.

- Both societies are also divided internally. The PA has committed to recognizing Israel, to nonviolence, to seeking recognition of an independent state through peaceful negotiation, and to compliance with previous agreements. Hamas refuses to commit to these principles.
- In Israel many still favor a two-state solution, but many others, including several members of the cabinet, are outspokenly opposed to a Palestinian state in the West Bank.[15]
- The PA has little to show for its commitment to a two-state solution through nonviolence and peaceful negotiation over the twenty years since the signing of the Oslo Accords. The continued lack of progress toward a state will undermine the PA's status and cause more Palestinians and other Arabs to support armed resistance.
- There have been twelve U.S. presidents and twenty secretaries of state since 1948. Each has tried to reconcile the differences between Israelis and Palestinians. In recent decades there

has been substantial continuity in their policies, which include a firm commitment to Israel's security and to the establishment of an independent and viable Palestinian state.

- The ability of the United States to control events in the world, including those involving Israelis and Palestinians, is limited. But we do have unequalled power to influence events.

The Israeli-Palestinian conflict is rooted deep in history and involves highly emotional issues: religion, national identity, territorial competition. It has gone on for so long, it has had such destructive effects, and the level of mistrust and hostility is so high that many in the Middle East and elsewhere regard it as unsolvable. It is of course easier to describe the problems in the Middle East than it is to prescribe a solution. But I disagree with those who have concluded that the conflict cannot be resolved. At some time, in some way, this conflict is going to end. It is in our interest, and surely the interests of Israelis and Palestinians, that it end as soon and as fairly as possible.

The renewed pursuit of peace is important to the region and to the United States for many reasons. As 9/11 demonstrated — and as the rise of the Islamic State in Iraq and Syria as well as Boko Haram in Nigeria remind us today — there are many evil people and groups in the world. And many of those most hostile to the United States are based in the Middle East. It is also a region where several countries are U.S. allies. Regrettably some of them are also at odds with each other.

Peace between Israel and the Palestinians and the resulting stability in the region would help to deprive the extremists of the chaos in which they thrive. It would also allow the United States to unite its allies to confront and take preventive action against the extremists on their home turf.

Beyond terrorism, the Middle East is centrally located between Europe, Asia, and Africa. Any conflict there could spill over and bring in other world powers in a way that could threaten U.S. political, economic, and military interests. Consider, for instance, that a large portion of the known oil reserves are in the region, and the continuing supply of that oil remains vital to most of the world's advanced economies, even amid the transition to a lower carbon future. Moreover the United States has long had a strong commitment to Israel's existence and security as well as, more recently, a firm commitment to the establishment of a viable, independent, and sovereign Palestinian state.

In the highly volatile Middle East, instability in one part of the region feeds instability in another part. Resolution of the Israeli-Palestinian conflict could make it possible for Israel and the Sunni-dominated monarchies to work together to combat their common foe: extremist forces across the region. Achieving these goals requires maximum effort by the United States, despite the difficulties and setbacks. The key is easy to state but difficult to achieve: it is the mutual commitment of Israel and the Palestinians to reach agreement, with the active participation of the U.S. government and the support and assistance of the many other governments and institutions that can and want to help. The international community can help best by encouraging both sides to look past their historic grievances toward a negotiation that deals with the realities of the situation today.

In a major policy speech in Jerusalem in January 2009, President George W. Bush said:

The point of departure for permanent status negotiations . . . is clear: There should be an end to the occupation that began in 1967. The agreement must establish Palestine as a homeland for the Palestinian people, just as Israel is a homeland for the Jewish people. These negotiations must ensure that Israel has secure, recognized, and defensible borders. And they must ensure that the state of Palestine is viable, contiguous, sovereign, and independent. It is vital that each side understands that satisfying the other's fundamental objectives is key to a successful agreement. Security for Israel and viability for the Palestinian state are in the mutual interest of both parties.

The president's main point bears repeating: the United States supports the establishment of a Palestinian state, but for that to happen Israel must have reasonable and sustainable security. The establishment of a Palestinian state will help Israel achieve that security. Success is in their mutual interest.

On taking office in 2009, President Obama reaffirmed that policy. When he appointed me as special envoy to the region, he further signaled his administration's desire to forge an Israeli-Palestinian peace. Now, as I made my first trip to the region in that position, it seemed that the culture of peace, so carefully nurtured during the Oslo negotiations in 1993, had largely dissipated, to be replaced by a sense of futility, despair, and, ultimately, the inevitability of conflict. Fighting in Gaza, which had erupted the prior year, had just ended. The Palestinians were deeply divided, and uncertainty around upcoming Israeli elections lay ahead. Few believed that there was any chance for rebooting peace negotiations, let alone achieving a peaceful end to the conflict.

Many had given up on the two-state solution as efforts to achieve it had not succeeded. The doubts were justified, but no critic had advanced a more credible or feasible alternative. The fact that a two-state solution had not yet been achieved was not in itself conclusive proof that it could never be achieved. Peacemaking requires patience and perseverance. In Northern Ireland, for instance, centuries of discord and violence, and many failed negotiations, preceded the Good Friday Agreement. Just a few days before it was reached, a public opinion poll revealed that 83 percent of those in Northern Ireland believed that no agreement was possible.

Of course, the history and current circumstances in the Middle East are different from those in Northern Ireland, so the benefits of comparison are limited. But it was clear to me that past failures to achieve peace do not make failure inevitable. I believe there is no such thing as a conflict that can't be ended. Conflicts are created and sustained by human beings. They can be ended by human beings.

A solution, however, cannot be imposed externally. The parties themselves have to negotiate directly, with the active and sustained support of the United States. The pain required to negotiate an agreement, while substantial for both sides, will be much less than the pain that will result if negotiations don't happen or don't succeed. As I write these words there are worrying signs, especially in Jerusalem. Always a flashpoint, the city, deeply significant to each of the three major religions in the area, now seethes with actual and threatened violence. It could erupt at any time.

If the conflict were to resume, both Israelis and Palestinians will face an uncertain future. That, of course, includes the loss of many lives. But there are other potential dangers that both parties have to recognize. For the Israelis, the first is demography. There are now about 6 million Jews living in the area between the Jordan River and the Mediterranean Sea. In the same space there are about 5.5 million Arabs, including Israeli Arabs and Palestinians on the West Bank and in Gaza. The Arab birth rate overall is much higher than the Israeli; within just a few years Arabs will be in the majority. As Ehud Barak, the former prime minister and then defense minister of Israel, has said, Israel then will have to choose between being a Jewish state and being a democratic state; it cannot be both once the two-state solution is lost. That is a painful choice Israel should not have to make.

Their second challenge is in technology. A serious military threat to Israel now comes from rockets. Hamas still has thousands of them; they're crude, lacking in guidance and destructive power, but they do create widespread fear and anxiety in Israel. No one can doubt that, in the absence of a peace agreement, over time Hamas will rebuild and improve its arsenal. In Lebanon, on Israel's northern border, Hezbollah already has thousands of rockets aimed in its direction; public estimates in Israel are between thirty thousand and fifty thousand. These rockets are somewhat more effective, although also limited in range. Even as I flew across the Atlantic, Hezbollah was engaged in an effort to upgrade their systems. Most threatening to Israel, however, Iran has developed rockets that can reach Israel from inside Iran itself. The Iranians don't yet have the precision needed to strike specific targets, but they could cause vast destruction in cities.

The United States is fully committed to Israel's security. We have honored that commitment in part by providing enormous political, financial, and military support. In his first term President Obama authorized hundreds of millions of dollars of additional aid to Israel to accelerate development and deployment of the Iron Dome antimissile system. Although its early use has been promising, it is unknown whether that or any system will be able to intercept the number and quality of missiles that might be launched in an all-out conflict. Israel's security might then be seriously threatened.

Israel's third challenge is its potential isolation. Although strong in the United States, especially in Congress, its support is declining elsewhere in the world. In 2011 the UN Security Council voted on a resolution that demanded that "Israel, as the occupying power, immediately and completely ceases all settlement activities in the occupied Palestinian territory, including East Jerusalem and that it fully respect its legal obligations in this regard." Fourteen of the fifteen members of the Council, including the United Kingdom, France, and other U.S. allies, voted in favor of the resolution; the United States voted against it and used its veto power to prevent its adoption. Although the resolution was not voted on in the General Assembly, an overwhelming majority there supported it; only the United States and Israel were opposed. In November 2012, despite intense opposition by the United States and Israel, 138 of the 193 countries in the world voted for a UN General Assembly resolution that elevated Palestinian status in the United Nations to nonmember observer state, a status shared only by the Vatican. Only nine countries opposed the resolution, while forty-one abstained.

In October 2014 the prime minister of Sweden announced his government's intention to recognize a Palestinian state, becoming the first major Western European government to do so. Similar sentiments were expressed in Ireland, Spain, Britain, and France. The British Parliament voted 274 to 12 to recognize a Palestinian state, although the vote was symbolic (it was nonbinding on the government, which continues to oppose recognition). During the debate in the House of Commons, Richard Ottaway, a member of the governing Conservative Party and chairman of the Foreign Affairs Committee, said that he had "stood by Israel through thick and thin, through the good years and the bad," but now realized "in truth, looking back over the past 20 years, that Israel has been slowly drifting away from world public opinion. Under normal circumstances I would oppose the motion tonight; but such is my anger over Israel's behavior in recent months that I will not oppose the motion. I have to say to the government of Israel that if they are losing people like me, they will be losing a lot of people."[16]

"The vote in the French lower house of the Parliament favoring such a step was a largely symbolic vote. But it was the fifth such gesture in two months, and arguably the most important, in what has amounted to a cascade of support for the Palestinian cause and a widening torrent of criticism of Israeli policy across Europe."[17]

For me, as a supporter of Israel's right to exist, safe and secure behind defensible borders, and for the many others who share my view, these are hard words to accept. But they should be a warning to the government of Israel and to all of its supporters in

Israel, the United States, and elsewhere: the tide of world public opinion is shifting.

Another danger, little noticed or discussed, is the divide within Israel of its Jewish and Arab citizens. The Arabs already make up over 20 percent of the population, and their growth rate is higher than for Israeli Jews. Growing along with their numbers is their disaffection. There is rising concern among many Israeli leaders about the serious adverse effects on their society of this internal division.

Some in Israel and the United States are concerned that a Palestinian state might fail and be taken over by Hamas. That's a valid concern. But many others believe, as I do, that the collapse of the Palestinian Authority and a takeover by Hamas is more likely in the absence of an agreement with Israel than as the result of such an agreement. One of the adverse consequences of the 2014 fighting in Gaza is the extent to which it has adversely affected the political standing of President Abbas and the Palestinian Authority among Palestinians and other Arabs, making a negotiated agreement even more difficult than it was before — not least because cease-fire agreements made with Hamas as the result of violence increase public support for the movement and erode confidence in the potential of reaching a political settlement through negotiations alone.

Of course, there is no policy decision that is free of risk. But finding the middle ground is the only way to open up the possibility of movement toward normalization of relations between Israel and other countries in the region, many of whom share Israel's deep concern about the threat from Iran and the extremist groups now menacing the region.

The Palestinians also face serious hurdles, particularly the indefinite continuation of an occupation under which they do not have the right to govern themselves and therefore lack the dignity and freedom that come with self-governance. In 1947 the United Nations proposed a plan to partition the area and create two states. Israel accepted it; the Arabs rejected it. And the next year brought the first of several wars, all of them won by an increasingly strong Israel.

Every sensible Arab leader today would gladly accept that 1947 plan if it were still available. But it is not — and it never will be available again. The circumstances on the ground have changed too dramatically. Since then serious Israeli negotiators have come to the conclusion, whether they admit it publicly or not, that the two-state solution will ultimately be based on the 1948 armistice lines, also known as the 1967 lines, with land swaps to be agreed by both parties, to accommodate large Israeli population centers.

But as I told both Yasser Arafat during my first tour of service in the region and, later, President Abbas, there is no evidence to suggest that the end game is going to get any better in the future. The interests of the Palestinian people would be best served if their leaders participated in and stayed in direct negotiations to get the best deal they can, even if it's not 100 percent of what they want. They must bring the occupation to an end. They've got to get their own state and build on it. They will achieve neither by staying out of negotiations.

When he was prime minister of the Palestinian Authority, Salam Fayyad tried to lay the foundation by building the institutions needed for a viable, independent state. But Fayyad resigned in 2013, and his state-building efforts cannot be sustained in the absence of any progress on the political side. They are inextricably linked; there must be concurrent progress on both.

For a quarter century the policy of the United States has been to encourage direct negotiations between Israelis and Arabs as the only feasible way to reach agreement on the issues that divide them.* As a necessary complement to that policy, the United States has consistently opposed any action by either side that could have the effect of predetermining those issues prior to negotiations. That is why the United States opposes Palestinian efforts to achieve recognition as a state at the United Nations, just as it opposes Israeli settlement construction. The United States contends that those issues, and all others that are contested, should be resolved in direct negotiations between Israelis and Palestinians, not by unilateral action on either side.

* At the Madrid Conference in 1991 the United States devised a formula to overcome Israeli objections to meeting directly with the PLO by accepting a joint Palestinian-Jordanian delegation whose liaison committee was led by Faisal Husseini. Though his lineage and family profile tied him to Jerusalem (he was the grandson of a former grand mufti) and the fight against the Zionist groups in 1948 (his father was a chief commander of the Arab forces), the Israelis could point to the fact that he was born in Baghdad rather than explicitly or implicitly acknowledge any historic Palestinian claim to Jerusalem.

From the Palestinian (and Arab) perspective, however, the problem is that the United States has been more successful in opposing their efforts at the UN than it has been in restraining Israeli settlement construction. During the nearly seven decades of its existence, Israel has had the strong support of the United States. In international forums the United States has at times cast the only vote on Israel's behalf. Yet even in such a close relationship there are some differences. Prominent among those is the U.S. government's long-standing opposition to Israel's policies and practices regarding settlements. As Secretary of State James A. Baker III commented on May 22, 1991:

Every time I have gone to Israel in connection with the peace process, on each of my four trips, I have been met with the announcement of new settlement activity. This does violate United States policy. It's the first thing that Arabs — Arab Governments, the first thing that the Palestinians in the territories — whose situation is really quite desperate — the first thing they raise when we talk to them. I don't think there is any bigger obstacle to peace than the settlement activity that continues not only unabated but at an enhanced pace.[18]

The policy described by Secretary Baker, on behalf of the administration of President George H. W. Bush, has been, in essence, the policy of every U.S. administration since Israel captured the West Bank and East Jerusalem in 1967.

As far back as 1967, in the Johnson administration, an internal communication noted, "There can be little doubt among [government of Israel] leaders as to our continuing opposition to any Israeli settlements in the occupied areas."[19] In July 1969 President Nixon's representative to the UN said, "The expropriation or confiscation of land, the construction of housing on such land, the demolition or confiscation of buildings, including those having historic or religious significance, and the application of Israeli law to occupied portions of the city are detrimental to our common interests."[20] President Ford's UN ambassador asserted in March 1976, "The presence of these settlements is seen by my government as an obstacle to the success of the negotiations for a just and final peace between Israel and its neighbors."[21] On March 21, 1980, Secretary of State Cyrus Vance, speaking on

539

behalf of the Carter administration, stated, "U.S. policy toward the establishment of Israeli settlements in the occupied territories is unequivocal and has long been a matter of public record. We consider it to be contrary to international law and an impediment to the successful conclusion of the Middle East peace process."[22] On September 1, 1982, President Ronald Reagan announced what came to be known as the Reagan Plan for the Middle East: "The immediate adoption of a settlements freeze by Israel, more than any other action, could create the confidence needed for wider participation in these talks. Further settlement activity is in no way necessary for the security of Israel and only diminishes the confidence of the Arabs that a final outcome can be freely and fairly negotiated."[23] At a press conference on December 16, 1996, President Bill Clinton stated, "It just stands to reason that anything that preempts the outcome [of the negotiations] . . . cannot be helpful in making peace. I don't think anything should be done that would be seen as preempting the outcome." Asked if he viewed the settlements as an obstacle to peace, Clinton replied, "Absolutely. Absolutely."[24] In an April 2002 Rose Garden speech, President George W. Bush

declared, "Israeli settlement activity in occupied territories must stop, and the occupation must end through withdrawal to
secure and recognized boundaries."[25] Two
months later, on June 24, Bush unveiled his
"Roadmap" for peace. Phase 1 of the Roadmap not only had Israel "freez[ing] all
settlement activity (including natural growth
of settlements)"; it also called on Israel to
"immediately dismantle settlement outposts
erected since March 2001."[26] The Bush
administration secured full international
backing for the Roadmap, including through
the UN.

While the stated policy of the government
of Israel favors a two-state solution, the
government's actions on settlements are at
times inconsistent with that policy.[27]

The fighting in Gaza between Israel and
Hamas ended on January 18, 2009, two
days before Obama took the oath of office.
A few days later I landed in the region for
the first of many visits. In the fighting,
somewhere between 1,166 (the Israeli
figure) and 1,400 (the Palestinian figure)
Palestinians were killed. Thirteen Israelis
died (ten soldiers and three civilians). Massive destruction occurred in Gaza.
Thousands of rockets had been fired into
Israel from Gaza. Emotions were raw, hostil-

ity high. In Israel Prime Minister Ehud Olmert had announced his resignation, and a close, hotly contested election campaign was drawing to a close. It would be two months before a new Israeli government took office, so even if the prospects had been less gloomy there was no possibility of an early resumption of negotiations.

In that difficult circumstance President Obama sought to create a context within which the tensions could subside sufficiently to permit a resumption of direct negotiations at some point in the future. To encourage the parties to move in that direction, each of them was asked to contribute something: the Palestinians were asked to act more aggressively to prevent any acts of violence against Israel and to reduce incitement in its schools and mosques; the other Arab states were asked to take steps toward normalization with Israel, including, for example, reopening of trade offices, permitting commercial air overflights, or opening lines of communications by mail and telephone; Israel was asked to freeze settlement construction.

We tried hard to persuade each of the parties to make appropriate contributions to this approach, including a real effort to revive the Arab Peace Initiative of 2002. By the time the new government of Israel was ready to talk substantively with us, in May 2009, I had visited fifteen Arab countries and met with virtually every Arab ruler and foreign minister. Without exception they insisted on a full settlement freeze as a necessary first step.

None of our requests was intended to be a precondition to negotiations, although that is how they were widely portrayed. While the policy itself is legitimately subject to debate, and indeed was debated within the Obama administration, what in retrospect seems to me not debatable is that we did not do a good job in announcing, explaining, and advocating for that policy, one of several mistakes we made. As a result, at least in the media in Israel and the United States, attention focused almost entirely on the request for a freeze on settlement construction. Obama was criticized for seeking a freeze, including by many who were silent when President George W. Bush made the identical request a few years earlier, when he included a full settlement freeze in his Roadmap.

Abbas came to Washington and unhelpfully told the *Washington Post* that he had not been asked to do anything, and besides, there was nothing for the Palestinians to do, it was all up to the Israelis.[28] That elicited a strong negative reaction from the Israelis, who soon made it clear that they would not agree to a total freeze on settlements, nor would they agree to include East Jerusalem in our discussions.* The Arab states said that they could not take even the most modest steps until Israel agreed to the freeze. The Palestinians were equally adamant that anything less than a total freeze that

---

* Prior to the 1967 war, Jerusalem was a divided city. East Jerusalem was controlled by Jordan. It was a relatively small area of just over six square kilometers, including the Old City. After that war Israel added all of Jordanian-controlled East Jerusalem to West Jerusalem, which it had controlled prior to 1967. Israel subsequently expanded Jerusalem's boundaries in all directions by including some of its own sovereign territory and sixty-five square kilometers of West Bank territory. *East Jerusalem,* then, is a political more than a geographic term and refers to the part of Jerusalem earlier controlled by Jordan and then expanded by Israel to the east, north, and south, using West Bank territory. Neither the United States nor any other country has ever recognized these Israeli annexations. So the dispute between Israel and the Palestinians over Jerusalem includes disagreement over its boundaries.

included East Jerusalem would be unacceptable to them. So the effort to help create an atmosphere in which meaningful negotiations could take place did not succeed. Attitudes hardened, and like the illusion of an oasis in the desert, the prospect of meaningful negotiations drifted further and further away from us.

In addition to the issue of settlements, other aspects of the president's effort to achieve an Israeli-Palestinian agreement were criticized; some of the criticism was valid and constructive, but some of it was unfounded. An example of the latter was the allegation that Obama blundered by not resuming negotiations in 2009 on the basis of the Olmert-Abbas discussions of 2008. This line of criticism appeared, for instance, in an article by the *Washington Post* columnist David Ignatius. On October 16, 2011, he wrote that Olmert had offered Abbas a "miraculous package" and that "in one of President Obama's biggest mistakes, he decided to start negotiations all over."[29] If true, this indeed would have been a serious mistake by the president. But it is not true; it is contradicted by the facts, most of them a matter of public record.

There appears to be little doubt that Abbas and Olmert did have serious discussions and that both felt they had made significant progress. But, unfortunately, they never reached an agreement. Their talks were held under the principle, agreed in advance by both sides, that nothing is final until everything is final. And nothing was final. "Saeb Erekat, a Palestinian negotiator, said the proposal was never written down and left too many details unsettled."[30]

The talks were hampered by Olmert's legal problems, which ultimately led to his departure from government. Abbas was concerned about Olmert's ability to obtain approval of an agreement based on their discussions. He later felt his concern was validated when, after Olmert made the substance of their discussions public just before the Israeli elections, Netanyahu repudiated them and no major candidate for prime minister supported them. "Less than a week before Israeli voters pick a new leader, the candidate most involved in the negotiations with the Palestinians [Tzipi Livni] is on the defensive over newly reported details of an interim peace accord offered months ago by outgoing Prime Minister Ehud Olmert. . . . [T]he disclosures last week prompted [Netanyahu] the hawkish front-runner to accuse her of agreeing to 'surrender' parts of Jerusalem for an independent Palestinian state. . . . Netanyahu seized on Israel's proffered concessions to portray Livni as 'weak on security.' His party has plastered that slogan on buses and billboards in recent days."[31] The Olmert-Abbas negotiations ended abruptly, without agreement, when violence erupted in Gaza in December 2008.

I met with Olmert at his official residence in early February 2009; he told me about his discussions with Abbas, just before he made them public.[32] Shortly thereafter I met with Abbas, and he related his version of those discussions. There were important differences in their recollections, especially on the issue of borders. Although it was not featured in the Israeli election campaign, as were security and Jerusalem, it is, of course, important to both sides. Olmert said he showed Abbas a map that included an offer by Israel on boundaries. Olmert wanted Abbas to agree and sign the map, then and there. Abbas wanted first to consult with his advisors. Olmert thought it unreasonable for Abbas not to promptly accept what Olmert felt was a fair, even generous offer. According to Olmert, Abbas promised to return the next day with experts, but he did not return. The Gaza conflict then broke out, and the discussions ended without a

Palestinian reply to the offer.

Abbas agreed that Olmert showed him a map and asked him to sign it, and that Abbas wanted to take it with him to study and to consult with his aides before signing. Abbas thought it unreasonable for Olmert to expect him to reach a binding agreement on the boundaries of a new Palestinian state on the basis of a single viewing of one map, without the opportunity to discuss and consider it with the other members of his leadership team. After Olmert refused his request and took the map back, Abbas left and met with his aides and tried to re-create the map from memory. He and other Palestinian leaders told me they then sent Olmert a typewritten list of questions seeking clarification on the map and other issues. According to Abbas, he never received a response to his questions. The Gaza conflict then broke out, and the discussions ended without an Israeli response.

The criticism of Obama also completely overlooked the crucial fact that Prime Minister Netanyahu, who succeeded Olmert, was clear, in public and in private, with me and with others, that he was strongly opposed to the substance of Olmert's discussions with Abbas and would not resume negotiations on that basis. As noted above, that position was part of his election campaign, and he has never deviated from it.[33] Indeed when Netanyahu and Abbas later met in person, in September 2010, the only substantive issue Netanyahu would discuss was Israel's security demands, and what he said to Abbas then went far beyond what Olmert had said two years earlier. In particular, Netanyahu regarded as dangerous for Israel that Olmert did not insist on a long-term Israeli military presence along a Palestinian state's eastern border with Jordan. Whether one agrees or disagrees with Netanyahu, there can be no doubt that on this issue his position has been consistent and unchanging. There never was any chance that he would agree to resume negotiations on that basis, because he feels strongly that those earlier discussions were inadequate on the issue of security and wrong on Jerusalem. To blame Obama for the fact that negotiations did not resume on the basis of the Olmert-Abbas discussions is thus wholly unfounded and unfair.

My discussions with the Israelis on settlements began at a meeting in London, after Netanyahu took office. We spent the summer months in negotiations. They would not agree to a total freeze, but by September we had reached agreement on a moratorium on new housing construction starts; it was to take effect in November and last ten months. It was much less than what we had asked for, but it was a very significant step. When the moratorium was announced, I held a press conference and was forthcoming about its shortfalls. I urged the international community to

> look at this issue in a broader context, particularly how it affects the situation on the ground and how it can contribute to a constructive negotiating process that will ultimately lead to an end to the conflict and to a two-state solution. [The moratorium] falls short of a full settlement freeze, but it is more than any Israeli Government has done before, and can help move toward agreement between the parties. . . . For the first time ever, an Israeli Government will stop housing approvals and all new construction of housing units and related infrastructure in West Bank settlements.[34]

During the ten months of the moratorium the Israelis were permitted to complete work on buildings that were already under construction, and East Jerusalem was not included. Just before the moratorium announcement, in a meeting in New York at which I and other American officials accompanied President Obama, Saeb Erekat, the Palestinian's chief negotiator, criticized the moratorium on those two points. In the presence of President Abbas, he told President Obama that the moratorium was "worse than useless."

By the spring of 2010 we had been unable to persuade the parties to resume direct negotiations, despite an intense effort. To try to establish some traction we suggested, and the parties agreed, that we conduct "proximity talks," in which I would meet separately with each side to discuss all relevant issues. There was no expectation that any issues would be resolved during these talks; rather they were to serve as a transition process that would lead to direct negotiations. Our hope was to get a clear understanding of the parties' current positions on each of the major issues, which would enable more meaningful discussions as soon as we made the transition to direct negotiations. The Israelis agreed reluctantly because they preferred to go immediately to direct negotiations. The Palestinians, on the other hand, continued to refuse direct negotiations in the absence of a full settlement freeze and were more enthusiastic about the proximity talks. It enabled them to gain a bit in the never-ending public relations battle and in what I came to describe as the document dispute. It was a minor issue, notable only because it illustrates how both sides vigorously contested every aspect of the process, always (understandably) with a view toward the political effect at home.

From the beginning to the end of my tenure as special envoy, the Israelis took the public position that they wanted direct negotiations. Privately they insisted that those negotiations be entirely oral, with nothing in writing and no exchange of documents. They were reluctant, for example, to agree to adopt further terms of reference for the negotiations, terms that would have defined the issues to be resolved (itself a very contentious task).* The Palestinians regarded this as evidence that the government of Israel was not serious about negotiations; they believed the Israelis said they wanted negotiations only to placate the United States. So the proximity

---

* Israel's view appears to be that prior agreements that defined the issues and referenced UN Security Council Resolutions 242 and 338 provide sufficient terms of reference.

talks evolved into a one-sided affair in which the Palestinians provided me with detailed position papers on every disputed issue, while the Israelis, up to and including the prime minister, said little and made clear their disdain for the whole notion of proximity talks. On one occasion, for nearly an hour a midlevel Israeli official read aloud to me a document that his government had submitted in the previous round of negotiations (during the George W. Bush administration) and which I already had in my possession.

Needless to say, this was unproductive. But I understood that the Israelis were making a point. Almost all of the many documents the Palestinians handed me were identical, or very nearly identical, to those they had submitted to the Israelis in earlier rounds of negotiations or had sent to other governments in the international community. And most of the positions the Palestinians took in the documents did not stray from their publicly stated positions. The Israelis already had all of those documents and knew the Palestinian positions; they didn't want any documents in this round of talks, and certainly not copies of documents they already had in their possession. Just as the Palestinians felt the Israelis were play-acting in demanding direct negotiations, the Israelis felt the Palestinians were play-acting on the subject of documents.

The document dispute reached a climax at a meeting in New York. Erekat insisted on handing the Palestinian position papers directly to Yitzhak Molho, Netanyahu's trusted personal lawyer and the lead Israeli negotiator. Molho refused to accept the documents, or even to touch them. After holding them out at arm's length for a few seconds, Erekat laid them on the table around which we sat. Both then turned to me to figure out what to do about the documents. I asked Molho to explain why he refused to accept documents that set forth the demands of the Palestinians on each of the relevant issues. All previous negotiations had involved exchanges of documents; surely the government of Israel could not expect to negotiate and reach a peace agreement with the Palestinians if nothing were ever written down. Molho replied that there were several ministers in the Israeli cabinet who were opposed to negotiations with the Palestinians, in part because they regarded the positions taken by the Palestinians to be so extreme that it was pointless to engage on them. If he came into possession of these documents in these discussions he would, if asked, have to turn them over to any minister who requested them. He knew what was in the documents; they were virtually identical, in some cases precisely identical to those that the government of Israel had received in the earlier negotiations (except that the dates were changed from 2008 to 2010).* Now, Molho argued, if the opposition ministers saw that the Palestinian positions were unchanged, it would confirm their view of Palestinian unreasonableness, and they would demand an end to these and any other negotiations. It was, as presented, a somewhat complicated argument, but I thought Molho was arguing that by not accepting the documents now he was keeping open the possibility of later direct negotiations in which the two sides could engage seriously.

It is an understatement to say that Erekat was not persuaded. He rejected Molho's

* But that was the previous government, under Prime Minister Olmert. As noted above, Prime Minister Netanyahu, to the contrary, strongly opposed, in public and in private, before and after his becoming prime minister, the discussions on security and Jerusalem by Olmert and the Palestinian Authority in those earlier negotiations.

argument as an example of the Israeli tactic of saying in public that they wanted direct negotiations while in private erecting insurmountable barriers to any serious negotiations. Since it was obvious that Molho was not going to accept the documents no matter what I or anyone else said, I told them that I would take all of the documents into my possession and decide how they could be most effectively used at an appropriate time in the future. The problem wasn't that the Israelis didn't know the Palestinian positions or the contents of the papers. The problem was that they did know the positions and regarded them as unacceptable, and they didn't believe the Palestinians were willing to negotiate in a way the Israelis regarded as serious; it was the mirror image of the Palestinian belief that the Israelis were not serious about negotiations.

In several interviews, Abbas claimed he could not understand why the Israelis had not received the documents. To buttress his argument he insisted that the current Israeli government had never presented him with "a map" setting forth proposed boundaries. I shook off the bickering and criticism as part of the highly charged political process in which we were engaged.

In March 2010 Vice President Biden visited Jerusalem. We had been assured by Israeli officials that there would be "no surprises" during his visit. But on the very day of his arrival, the government announced the approval of 1,600 housing units in East Jerusalem. A storm of controversy ensued, then abated, but it had an effect.

By the summer it was clear that the proximity talks were not going to yield progress. In July Netanyahu traveled to Washington to meet with the president and the secretary of state. He strongly urged the United States to press Abbas to enter into direct negotiations. Netanyahu told the president that if he and Abbas could speak face-to-face, without the burden of negotiating terms or gestures, he thought he could convince Abbas of his desire to end the conflict and the two could reach enough common ground for meaningful negotiations. The president agreed to try. The moratorium, while far from perfect, had resulted in some reduction in settlement construction activity. More significant, although no formal or public decision had been made by the government of Israel, in the aftermath of the Biden visit there was very little new housing activity in East

Jerusalem; in fact for months there had been almost no new actions.

On instruction from the White House and the State Department I met with Abbas and his leadership team and urged a resumption of direct talks. An intense effort followed, in which we received invaluable assistance from President Mubarak of Egypt and King Abdullah of Jordan. Abbas liked and trusted both. They not only urged Abbas to attend; they themselves promised to join him, and they did. Finally, although with obvious reluctance, Abbas agreed. But he had a significant condition. The moratorium had gone into effect the previous November and was due to expire at the end of September. He would meet with Netanyahu but would continue beyond September only if the moratorium were extended. That, he said, was "absolutely necessary." I never received from Abbas or Erekat an explanation of how, in less than nine months, the moratorium had gone from "worse than useless" to "absolutely necessary."

They met four times: once in Washington, twice in Egypt, then the fourth and last time at the prime minister's residence in Jerusalem. Except for a brief period during their first meeting, when Netanyahu and Abbas were alone, Secretary Clinton and I accompanied them in all of the meetings. The first meeting, in Washington, was largely ceremonial; the next two, in Egypt, were general in nature. Abbas wanted to launch immediately into the specifics of their disagreement on borders, a subject he had discussed with Olmert two years earlier. Netanyahu insisted on discussing security issues first. He did so, finally, in the fourth meeting, in Jerusalem. It was my intention to put borders on the agenda for the fifth meeting, so that each side would have had a substantive discussion on an issue of their choice at the outset of what we hoped would become a serious and sustained negotiation. But we never got to a fifth meeting.

Abbas had begun and ended each of the four meetings by saying that he could not continue meeting beyond September if the moratorium was allowed to expire. In a separate discussion we tried hard to persuade the Israelis to agree to an extension, but they refused our request as politically impossible. Netanyahu believed that they had not received sufficient international credit for the first moratorium nor any real political benefit in their dealings with the Palestinians. The Israelis were highly aggravated that Abbas had waited until the ninth month of a ten-month moratorium to agree to direct negotiations.

The fourth and last meeting was, as noted earlier, devoted to the issue of Israel's security. Netanyahu read from a long typewritten statement, in which he insisted that Israel Defense Forces would have to be stationed within any Palestinian state, along its eastern border, "for many decades." He repeated that phrase several times, with increasing emphasis. Abbas categorically rejected the proposal. He said that IDF forces could remain within the Palestinian state only during a transition period, which he first said could be "two to four years" but later described as "one to three years." He added, however, that he would accept on the Palestinian state's boundary an international force for an indefinite period, and that force could be stationed around the entire boundary, not just along the Jordan River in the east.

In this meeting the second climax of the document dispute occurred. Netanyahu repeated the Israeli position that no documents should be exchanged. This obviously angered Abbas, who immediately reached into his briefcase, pulled out a full set of the Palestinian position papers, and extended them to the prime minister. For a brief, silent moment, Netanyahu hesitated. Abbas, arm extended, looked directly at him, and their eyes locked; Secretary Clinton and I silently watched. Then Netanyahu reached out, took the documents, and laid them on the floor next to his chair. Later, when the meeting concluded, we all stood and shook hands. Abbas went into the next room, where he joined Erekat and the other members of his entourage who were waiting. They all walked out the front door to their waiting cars. Thus ended the direct talks, the moratorium, and the document dispute. I never learned what happened to the documents on the floor.

Over the next few months the process sputtered to a close, and the Arab world fell further into disarray. My two years were up, and as winter came to a close I decided to leave. On April 5, 2011, I submitted my resignation to Secretary Clinton and to Denis McDonough, then the principal deputy national security advisor and now the president's chief of staff. He asked me to stay briefly to effect a smooth transition, and I agreed. On May 19, I returned to my family and to private life.

Of course my interest in Middle East peace remains high, and I continue to search for reasons for hope.

The Palestinians' internal divisions are a

complicated matter that keeps getting even more complicated. In 2014 the Palestinian Authority and Hamas announced that they had agreed to form a unity government and schedule elections. These discussions had been going on for several years; similar announcements of reconciliation were made in 2011 and 2012 and had subsequently collapsed. The 2014 round was interrupted by Israeli opposition and the fighting in Gaza, and by a change in government in Egypt, where the current regime is hostile to the Muslim Brotherhood and Hamas. As of this writing it appears that the latest agreement on reconciliation also will fail. But the effort may be resumed. That could provide a political opening for Hamas to move away from its prior positions as well as open an avenue for meaningful negotiation.

When Hamas won the Palestinian parliamentary elections in 2006, the United States joined the United Nations, the European Union, and Russia in a statement calling for Hamas to commit to nonviolence, to recognize the state of Israel, and to accept previous peace agreements. Hamas has so far shown no inclination to accept or even move toward these principles, and there is no assurance it ever will. Yet, as happened in South Africa and Northern Ireland, and with the PLO itself, persistent efforts to wean such groups from armed resistance and into a political process has, on occasion, succeeded. And, Hamas has consistently reaffirmed its willingness to accept any agreement that Abbas were to conclude with Israel, provided that agreement is approved in a referendum of the Palestinian people.

The interim Palestinian government proposed in 2014 was composed of technocrats, all of whom reportedly were committed to President Abbas's position on nonviolence. It was accepted by the Quartet — the United States, the European Union, Russia, and the United Nations — but rejected by Israel. Israel has every right to be wary, but the government of Israel itself has a long history of negotiating with Hamas through intermediaries, including when Israel secured the release of the captured soldier Gilad Shalit and in cease-fire negotiations. The situation is complex, and the odds may be long, but the door to peaceful political negotiation should not be forever closed.

I had many meetings separately with Prime Minister Netanyahu and President Abbas, and, as noted, I was present during the four meetings between the two leaders in September 2010. I also had many discussions with other officials, on both sides, about the two leaders. From those experiences I reached the conclusion that Netanyahu does not believe that Abbas has the personal or political strength necessary to gain approval of an agreement with Israel. Abbas believes that Netanyahu is not sincere or serious about getting an agreement with the Palestinians and does only as much as he deems necessary to placate the United States. Since both men assume that negotiations will not succeed, neither has any incentive to take the political risks that will inevitably be required to make possible a peace agreement.

If this analysis is accurate, the reluctance of the leaders is understandable. But it does not serve the immediate or long-term interests of the people they represent. I believe those interests — on both sides — will be served best by an agreement that accepts Israel's existence and provides Israelis with reasonable and sustainable security behind defensible borders and at the same time creates a sovereign, independent, viable, demilitarized Palestinian state. That has been the basis for and objective of U.S. policy for many decades. I believe in and support that policy.

Rebuilding trust is a daunting challenge, not only between political leaders but also between two peoples with a long and bitter history of conflict. But the long-term interests of both societies are jeopardized by their continuing inability to reach agreement. It makes no sense for Israel to continue in a virtual state of war with most of its neighbors in a region where population and turmoil are increasing. It makes no sense for the Palestinians to spend the next sixty years as they have spent the past sixty, under occupation without the freedom or dignity that comes with self-governance. Both have much to lose in the absence of an agreement and much to gain if they can live side by side in peace. And it is in the best interests of the United States to help them succeed.

The process in which I engaged as U.S. envoy to the Middle East was largely contentious and disappointing, one quarrel and setback after another. In Northern Ireland there had been a few rays of hope and then a final burst of success. In the Middle East there was neither. From beginning to end it was an unsuccessful effort to bring together two leaders who share a deep, mutual mistrust. At the same time, I believe it is becoming increasingly clear to the leadership on both sides that the current situation is not sustainable and that both societies will be better served if they reach an agreement. To wait until another costly outbreak of violence impels them to act would be a tragic and unnecessary delay.

The Israeli-Palestinian challenge will continue to confound American leaders in the coming years, as it has for many decades. As much as I wish it were otherwise, it appears unlikely to be resolved in the immediate future. Indeed, there are ominous signs that both societies are on the brink of giving up on the pursuit of a two-state solution, or any other form of agreement. Among Palestinians and other Arabs, Abbas and the Palestinian Authority are increasingly seen as out of touch and ineffective; in the absence of any progress toward a state, support is crumbling for their approach of nonviolence and peaceful negotiation. They are therefore likely to concentrate on seeking international support for an independent Palestinian state. That almost certainly will draw a rebuke from the United States and retaliation from Israel, driving the parties even further apart, at least in the short term. The Hamas alternative is armed resistance. But a full-scale outbreak in the West Bank would be highly destructive for the Palestinians and a military and political nightmare for Israel.

In Israel, the recent rain of rockets from Gaza and the growing sense of isolation have generated frustration at the perceived inability of others, especially the Europeans, to comprehend the difficulty of their situation and the righteousness of their cause. The consequence is a political context that is increasingly conducive to the settler movement and its allies, who steadily push the government toward actions that make any agreement with the Palestinians less likely, and ultimately impossible.

Failure to make progress will be a disappointment for President Obama, who, despite the doubts on both sides, tried twice to bring about peace. Yet we must continue the effort because it is in our national interest and because, despite many failures of the past, this conflict, like every conflict, must inevitably end.

But it will take more than U.S. effort. As difficult and distant as it now seems, given current trends, Israelis and Palestinians themselves must cultivate constituencies for peace. Both societies need leaders who are able to convince their people that compromise is not a weakness but a virtue

567

necessary to secure the well-being of future generations; leaders who will act boldly to halt and reverse the descent into a new round of violence that will be terribly harmful to both societies and could spread into a wider regional conflict. Over a very long period of time both societies have endured fear, anxiety, many deaths, and much destruction. While they have many differences, they should have in common an overriding desire to avoid such negative and destructive consequences in the future. Israelis and Palestinians may not be able to live together but they should be able to live separately, side by side, in peace. Over time, hopefully, they may come to see each other not as enemies but as shared custodians of stability and of a potentially vibrant regional economy where both societies and cultures can thrive.

Part of the answer must come from ordinary Israelis and Palestinians. Will they, like the people of Northern Ireland and elsewhere, eventually tire of fear and anxiety, death and destruction? If and when they do, we must encourage them to make their desire for peace clear to their leaders. And we then must provide all the assistance necessary for them to achieve the greatest

gift of all: peace to those who for known only war.

THE SCHOLARS

Stephanie Littlehale had a rough childhood, growing up in a dysfunctional family in a small town in Maine. At the age of seventeen she found herself alone and homeless. Many of her nights were spent in the back of her 1992 Mazda in the parking lot at a nearby Walmart. Luckily some nights were spent on couches in the homes of friends. She always had big dreams of what her life could be one day; she wanted to change the world. But in the real world she wasn't sure if she had enough gas to get to school in the morning or enough money to buy a bagel. She later described the feeling as "suffocating." It was hard for her to even think about college when questions like "What will I eat?" and "Where will I live?" raced through her mind. She still had all those childhood dreams, but they were now hidden behind a fog of uncertainty, and they were slowly drifting away.

One of the great things about living in Maine is the sense of community. Mainers protect their own. Stephanie had big dreams, but she lived in difficult circumstances. She needed support and direction, and her community delivered. Her high school guidance secretary paid for the dress Stephanie wore on the day of her high school graduation. Her English teacher comforted her when she came to her class in tears, worrying about the month's rent. Anonymous gift cards were left for her in the front office of her high school so she could buy groceries and supplies. Most touching, however, was when one of her teachers and her husband invited Stephanie into their home to become a part of their family. As Stephanie later put it, "With the support of my community I am here today. I'm lucky. I was saved." Stephanie graduated from college and now attends the Georgetown University Law School in Washington, DC.

Eric Haskell grew up on Deer Isle, which is one of the most beautiful and isolated places in the state. After visiting the area, John Steinbeck wrote, in *Travels with Charley,* "One does not have to be sensitive to feel the strangeness of Deer Isle." Today it remains predominantly a fishing community where most of Eric's family continues to live and work. When Eric was growing up, his grandfather was a proud lobsterman who loved the sea. Eric later recalled standing on a milk crate at the helm of his grandfather's boat, the *Margaret Lee,* trying his best to steer between the brightly colored lobster buoys. Unfortunately the sea claimed his grandfather's life on a gusty August day when Eric was seven. That changed Eric's life. It was thus and forever made clear that he and his siblings would forge their paths with their minds and not their hands. This was instilled by his parents, both high school graduates who aspired to a higher education but never were able to achieve it. They wanted a better and easier life for their children. Eric became the first in his family to earn a college degree, going back nine generations from one tiny island. He is now a physician who cares for families in southern Maine at Family Medicine and Maine Medical Partners.

When Jessica Boyle was born, her mother was eighteen, still in high school, unmarried, and she wasn't ready to care for a child. Growing up, Jessica and her mother moved often, to towns large and small across central Maine. Every few months she was the new student, with a new teacher and a new home. They moved for a variety of reasons, mostly financial. As she got older, Jessica made many moves on her own, to group homes and to friends' spare bedrooms and couches. By the time she was sixteen, she had moved out of her mother's care, and at seventeen, she was officially considered an unaccompanied homeless youth.

She attended Bangor High School. That gave her access to life-changing teachers: her yearbook advisor teamed up with the school social worker and found her a housing program for homeless youth; her honors chemistry teacher made sure she applied to Colby College, where she ultimately enrolled. They helped her pay for admissions tests and gave her rides to college interviews. They were there to help her with the little things that would have otherwise been insurmountable obstacles. Through all of this, though, she was still very much on her own. She graduated from high school in a class of over four hundred, many of whom she felt were more deserving of the Mitchell Scholarship. But she was chosen.

As she later said, "At Colby — I'll be blunt — I was in no way prepared for the world I encountered when I arrived on campus. I brought a very unique

573

background to a place that is otherwise fairly homogenous. And as I got to know my peers, sharing certain things became uncomfortable. Talking about our parents' professions, for instance, or comparing where our summer homes were located, quickly became a minefield through which I had to carefully navigate — not so much because I was embarrassed to share my story, but because of the way my peers reacted when I told it.

"I believe that all high-performing students deserve the opportunity to attend a great school, and I wanted to make sure that low-income and first-generation college students at a small, predominately upper-middle-class school like Colby got the support they needed to successfully navigate that challenging environment. So I began chipping away at policies that hindered success and creating and building programs that would promote it.

"This effort evolved from a personal project to a student government task force, and led to many leadership opportunities on campus that allowed me to ensure these changes would live beyond my tenure as a student. By the time I graduated, the First Generation Program was in place, complete with funding."

Jessica is a now a development coordinator at the Massachusetts Institute of Technology (MIT) where she works with first-generation students.

Stephanie, Eric, and Jessica were recipients of college scholarships from a program I established when I left the Senate. Its origin can be traced back to my appearance at a conference called The Aspirations of Maine's Youth, held at the University of Maine. What began as a single speech at the university grew into appearances at each of Maine's 140 high schools. I learned a lot from that experience, much of it valuable, some of it humorous. For example, the length of a graduation ceremony is usually unrelated to the number of graduates; from a low of three graduates to a high of several hundred, each I attended took about two hours. I simply got to know a lot more about the three than I did about the hundreds. I also learned about the vast financial differences in our state (and society). I recall vividly two graduations that I attended on successive days. One was in a rural, poor area; there were twenty-one graduates. When the college scholarship awards were announced they were for amounts ranging from $25 to $100. I was astonished. At best the recipient could buy a few books! At the other graduation, in a better-off suburb of Portland, several of the awards were in the thousands of dollars.

In late 1992, two years before my second full Senate term was due to expire, I met with my campaign team to plan for my reelection effort. After much discussion we set a fundraising goal of $2 million. It was a trivial amount by national standards but substantial in comparison to prior campaigns in Maine. I knew I could raise much more than that. Since I was now Senate majority leader, I knew the money would flow quickly, unlike in my first Senate campaign. But I was determined not to be drawn into an endless money chase, which would go far beyond my immediate campaign needs. Leadership PACs are widely used vehicles for the promotion of individual congressional leaders. Despite being urged to do so, I refused to create one. As expected, I met the target quickly. I ended 1993 with a full campaign war chest.

Then, early in 1994, I decided that I would not seek reelection. That raised many questions, one of which was, "What should I do with the $2 million?" The idea of a scholarship program had been on my mind for a long time. After verifying that the funds could legally be used for that purpose,

I decided to create one. I knew that I would not do anything without the consent of those who had contributed to my campaign. They had contributed for one purpose; they would have to agree to any other purpose. So I wrote to each contributor and offered a choice: they could get their money back or they could leave it to be used for college scholarships for needy Maine high school graduates. In dollar terms they split evenly: about $1 million was returned, an equal amount retained.

To get the scholarship program off to an even better start I organized two fundraising events. One, in Washington, was attended by President Clinton; it produced about a half million dollars. The other, in Portland, raised far less money but generated a lot of enthusiasm for the program.

Because of its modest size the program was set up as a donor-advised fund at the Maine Community Foundation. From 1995 to 1998 that foundation invested the funds and administered the program. The Mitchell Scholarship was a one-time award of $2,500. During those four years 101 scholarships totaling just over $250,000 were awarded.

A foundation grant in 1999 enabled me to establish the Mitchell Institute. Our scope was broadened, adding career and personal support programs for our Scholars, and a research component. The mission of the Mitchell Institute is to increase the likelihood that young people from every community in Maine will aspire to, pursue, and achieve a college education. It is my intention that no Maine student with the qualifications and ambition to pursue a college education should be denied that opportunity due to limited financial resources.

The number of scholarships awarded each year has increased; as a result a Mitchell Scholarship has been awarded to a graduating senior from each of Maine's 130 public high schools every year since 1999.

From the beginning the three scholarship criteria have been academic potential, community service, and financial need, with a focus on first-generation college-goers. Eligibility was expanded to include students enrolling in two-year degree programs; between 5 and 10 percent of Mitchell Scholarships each year are now awarded to students entering community colleges and other two-year degree programs.

The amount of assistance to students has increased gradually as we struggle to offset the rapid rise in the cost of college education. It is now $7,000, and we hope to get it to $10,000 in the very near future.

Roughly 1,300 students apply for the Scholarship each year, about 9 percent of all Maine graduating seniors and 15 percent of the roughly 8,500 who enroll in college. With 130 new Mitchell Scholars named annually, over five hundred are attending college in any given year. Well over 1,500 Mitchell Scholar alumni are now in graduate school or the workforce, and that number grows with each graduating class.

Since the program began our Scholars have received more than $11 million in direct financial aid and the number of students who have received assistance is nearly 2,300.

The scholarship program is designed to make a difference for college students and to have a positive impact on the state. The unique approach of awarding scholarships statewide, providing career and personal support, and conducting research on outcomes has proven to be a powerful combination leading to outstanding results. Ninety percent of our Scholars earn all As and Bs in college. Eighty-five percent complete college and earn a degree, compared with about 50 percent of entering college students nationally. Together our Scholars and alumni contribute over thirty thousand hours each year to community service.

These accomplishments are particularly impressive in light of the Mitchell Scholars' modest backgrounds. More than 60 percent are the first in their family to earn a bachelor's degree; 65 percent come from families with incomes below the state median, and 24 percent are from families with annual incomes below $20,000; the vast majority work during the school year in high school and during the college academic year.

Over the past few decades I've met and talked with thousands of students. I learned about them and about myself, including a personal revelation: over and over again I saw in their eyes and heard in their words mirror images of myself at that age. Enough intelligence to show promise, but often obscured by anxiety and insecurity and a lot of feigned indifference. At first I thought, "I can help these kids." Gradually that changed to "I have to help these kids." I thought about some of those who had helped me: Elvira Whitten, Hervey Fogg, Bill Shaw, the Morrell family, Ed Muskie, and most of all my parents. I came to believe that I, who had benefited from so many helping hands, have a duty to use whatever ability I possess to see that no child in Maine who wants to go to college is without a helping hand. It is, of course, a huge aspiration, perhaps unattainable in a precise, mathematical sense. But just trying to meet that aspiration on every remaining day of my life can do so much good for so many of our young citizens.

I've done a lot in my life. I've never done anything better or more meaningful.

THE ART OF
NEGOTIATION

THE ART OF NEGOTIATION

I had no formal education in the art of negotiation. What I know came from the trial and error of experience as an army officer, a practicing lawyer, a state and federal prosecutor, a federal judge, a U.S. senator, Senate majority leader, chairman of the peace talks in Northern Ireland, the special envoy for Middle East peace, and a mediator of private and public disputes. The earliest and most obvious lesson I learned is that no two negotiations are the same, whether a public conflict involving nation-states or a dispute over money between private companies or individuals; each is specific to the people and the circumstances involved. Each requires a particular resolution.

But if the facts are unique, the methods used to gain resolution are often strikingly similar. Over the past three decades I have been asked thousands of questions, none more often than "How do you negotiate?"

It is definitely not a science or math. It is very much an art, requiring knowledge, skill, judgment, and humility. Especially humility.

THE SOUND OF
YOUR OWN VOICE

The weeklong trip began in Rumford, Senator Muskie's hometown in western Maine.
There was an active Italian American community in Rumford, and Muskie had accepted an invitation to speak at their annual
gathering. Following that he was to travel
across the state, meeting constituents,
speaking each evening in a different town.
For Muskie, and for most elected officials,
it was a familiar routine. But it was a first
for me, a new member of the senator's staff,
and I was excited. Muskie had asked me to
draft a speech for the Rumford event and
for another of that week's speeches. More
meaningful to me was that he asked me to
travel with him, to serve as his driver,
staffer, advance man. I was born and raised
in Maine but was embarrassed to admit that
I was not familiar with much of my state's
geography. "Don't worry," Muskie told me,
"I know every road in Maine and I'm sure

you'll learn them soon enough."*

The hall was packed, the crowd friendly and enthusiastic. They loved him and he returned their love, with an emotional speech that drew frequent applause. I had done a lot of research on the role of Italian Americans in the development of our nation. It is an amazing and emotional story, not well enough known even among many younger Italian Americans. Muskie weaved it into a broader lecture about the benefits and responsibilities of citizenship in a free, democratic society. At six feet four inches, slightly stooped, he was frequently compared physically to Abraham Lincoln. Unlike Lincoln, however, he had a huge head with a long, lantern jaw and a powerful speaking voice. Most important of all, he had a quick and brilliant mind. Today, two decades after his death, I can repeat what I said often during his life: he was the smartest person I ever met. Of course he had his faults. But not before or since have I encountered anyone better able to grasp and retain information, sort out the es-

* He was right. When I retired from the Senate three decades later, I had visited almost every town in Maine, many of them several times, and I had traveled almost every road.

sential from the nonessential, and use his intellectual and physical talents to impose his will on others.

In the few months I had been on his staff, I had seen him use those talents in the Senate. On this trip I watched as he used them with his constituents. It quickly became obvious that he liked them and they liked him. The statistics confirm the observation: he ran for statewide office six times, twice for governor and four times for the Senate, and he won every time, mostly by comfortable margins. When he left the Senate in 1980 to accept President Carter's appointment to secretary of state, he was undoubtedly the most popular public figure in Maine.

Every aspect of life is of course much different today than it was in the 1960s. As we traversed the state (on this and future trips) Muskie and I often slept at the homes of friends of his, occasionally at a small summer camp he owned on China Lake in central Maine, or in motels where, to save money, we frequently shared a room with two single beds. I saw close up how he gained respect by giving it, how he never acted in a condescending manner to those he met, how he weaved integrity into every aspect of the political process, how he won over opponents by the force of reason, logic, and effective presentation. I also saw close up his faults, one of which was that his speeches were almost always too long; once he got started he often found it hard to stop.

I noticed it that first night in Rumford, and then saw it each night thereafter, whether he had a prepared text or spoke extemporaneously. For the first twenty minutes he gave an informative and humorous speech. Then, just as he got to what should have been the end, he went back to the beginning and essentially repeated the speech, in summary fashion. Then, to my amazement, he went back at it a third time. The crowd was enthusiastic the first time through, somewhat less enthusiastic the second time, and quietly exhausted by the third, although they roused themselves to a long standing ovation when he did finish.

Six nights later we left Calais, in the far east of Maine, and headed down what is known as the Air Line Road to Bangor. It is a hundred-mile stretch of two-lane road through a heavily wooded, sparsely populated area. On that night the sense of isolation was heightened by alternating spurts of driving rain and heavy fog. By any measure it had been a successful week. Muskie had met, talked with, answered questions, and received a warm reception from thousands of Maine citizens in several towns across the long middle belt of the state, much of it staunchly Republican. When we left Calais we were both very tired.

As I drove slowly through the rain and fog there was none of the friendly banter of the earlier part of the week. After several minutes he asked, in a low, flat voice, "What did you think of my speeches?" I hesitated. I sensed that he liked me, but I had been on his staff for only a few months. I admired him, indeed was in awe of him, but I had seen firsthand his explosive temper and was a little afraid of him. In that week, and before, I had seen how just about everyone he met complimented him, often lavishly. I had yet to hear anyone offer a critical comment. But I also sensed that he expected the truth from me and that he was not unaware that his speeches were too long. So I decided to tell him the blunt truth. I was generally positive about the week but added that I thought there was one major problem with all of the speeches. Then I focused on the Rumford speech, describing it as I have just done. After I finished there was a very long and ominous silence. The rain splattered on the windshield, and the wipers rhythmically swept them clean; the car moved slowly down the Air Line. My eyes were fixed on the road so I could not see him, and I didn't dare turn to look. My imagination took hold and I braced myself for what I thought would be at best a tirade, at worst a pink slip, maybe even being thrown out of the car many miles from any human structure. Then a hopeful thought: maybe he's fallen asleep.

Finally he broke the silence. His voice was low and soft, devoid of anger. "You're a smart young man. I think it's likely that someday you'll be in elected office, giving speeches like I have this week. When you do you'll find that there's nothing in the world like the sound of your own voice." I knew he was right, but I said nothing. We rode in silence all the way to Bangor and the next day flew in silence back to Washington.

Eighteen years later I stood on the floor of the Senate, raised my right hand, and took the oath of office as a U.S. senator. In that moment I thought of Ed Muskie, whose seat I would now occupy, of how much I respected, admired, loved him. I thought of how much I had learned from him, what a challenge it would be to fill his big shoes. I recalled specifically that long dark ride down the Air Line Road. Often since then, when I've gone on too long in a speech, when I've struggled to bring it to a close, I've thought of him. Even the smartest man I've ever known succumbed to the temptation of talking too much. It took me a long time, but eventually I learned to spend less time talking and more time listening.

Although I didn't realize it at the time, when I served in the Senate I was being prepared for the Northern Ireland peace talks. There I spent hundreds of hours listening. By doing so I earned the confidence of the delegates to the talks; I learned what their concerns were; I ultimately figured out where the common ground was. The result was a peace agreement that ended a brutal long-standing conflict.

In Northern Ireland and elsewhere I learned some of the qualities and approaches needed for successful negotiation. They include learning to listen, patience, a good sense of timing, and a willingness to take risks when justified.

LEARN TO LISTEN

Learn to listen: that is the most important lesson of my political life. I've talked a lot in my life, especially during my years in the Senate: speeches, statements, press conferences, debates, committee hearings, marking up bills, conference committee deliberations, Senate Democratic caucuses over which I presided. I can't possibly estimate the number of words, but surely it must be in the millions. And in all that time, as all those words flowed out of my mouth, the only certainty I have is that I learned little while I was talking. Learning has come from listening, from reading, from observing, from doing. The product of my learning has, hopefully, helped others to learn and has improved some lives. But it was not my talking that did it. Rather it was what I learned when I was not talking.

Although these thoughts crystallized while I was in the Senate, and especially in my last six years, most were based on earlier events, including Muskie's words on the Air Line Road. And, as I'd noticed early in life, most people like to talk about themselves. That's one reason why I've never had a problem striking up a conversation with a stranger. Simple questions usually get them talking: Where are you from? Where are you heading? The answers then permit more personal questions: Where did you grow up? What do you do? Invariably some word, phrase, or fact in the answers opens up lines of follow-up questions, and in a short time I've learned something about another person's life that distinguishes him or her from everyone else I've met.

I also observed early in life that it is common in social conversations for people not to listen carefully to what others say. Rather it is often the case that a person speaks and then thinks about his or her next statement rather than intently listen to what others are saying; that is especially true of public figures who meet, usually briefly, large numbers of people. By the time you get to shake a person's hand, your eyes and mind often are already on the next person in line. Too many persons in positions of authority become accustomed to deference, develop excessive self-confidence, and are incapable of showing respect to others, especially those with whom they disagree. These attitudes demean the position and lessen the person's ability to perform his or her duties. I've been fortunate to receive many kind compliments in my life, none more so than "Thank you for listening to me." The simple gesture of maintaining eye contact and concentrating on what another person is saying is not only a source of information and learning. It also is a sign of respect.

This approach served me well in the Senate and the Northern Ireland peace process. I was not an especially good listener when I entered the Senate. By definition the job requires a lot of talking, and for my first eight years as a senator I worked hard to live up to the definition. Becoming Senate majority leader called for more talking, not less, and in the early years I achieved that. But one crucial difference led me to change. As a senator most of my advocacy was public: in the campaigns for election, in public speeches, during debate in the Senate, in televised interviews and press conferences. There were, of course, some occasions that called for private advocacy. But after I became majority leader the balance shifted. While still plentiful the public appearances declined in significance in relation to my most important objectives. The real advocacy, the real work, increasingly was in small groups or frequently one-on-one.

There was not a single moment or event when I suddenly grasped the value of good listening. It was rather a gradual process of awakening to the startling reality that in my dealings with other senators my persuasiveness grew the less I talked. It was a combination of factors: as I listened more and better, I gained insight into the views and needs of the senator with whom I was engaged. That enabled me to be more precise in my arguments, which in turn enhanced my ability to persuade and, in a beneficial ripple effect, improved my standing when the next round of advocacy began, as it inevitably does for the Senate majority leader.

It's a simple concept, in other circumstances called learning on the job. I did a lot of it as majority leader, as one evolution led to another. So it was that learning to listen led me to become more patient and more effective. However, most good things come with a cost. While I gained much from learning to listen, I also lost a lot of time because much of what I listened to was not worth the effort. Stated another way, it was important and helpful to become a good listener, but that in turn required me to become more patient. To get to the wheat you have to endure a lot of chaff.

Patience Is a Muscle

After I retired from the Senate I often said that as majority leader I had developed the best and strongest patience muscle in Washington. That muscle was sorely tested in the Senate and in Northern Ireland. The Senate is a great institution and a harsh teacher. In my first few years as majority leader I made many mistakes. More than once I lost my temper and with it control of the situation. On other occasions I made indiscreet comments in what I thought were private conversations, only to have them become public, or worse. Once, angry at a senator's failure to follow a well-established protocol in handling legislation on the Senate floor, I rebuked him directly, in strong language. That was bad enough; a short time later, in what I thought was a private conversation, I unwisely answered fully another senator's question about what had just happened. Of course I should have known better; he promptly reported my remarks to the first senator, who, already angry at my private rebuke, was justifiably outraged that I would tell someone else about it.

I was initially unable to control my frustration at the seemingly endless talk, delay, and obstruction that characterize the Senate. By the time I became majority leader I had been in the Senate for seven years, so I was aware of its frustrations, but I had not been responsible for dealing with them. Now I was, and it was extremely difficult to accept. Gradually, through trial and error, necessity, and force of will, I adapted. The long and painful process that led to enactment of the Clean Air Act amendments in 1990 and the protracted budget struggles in both the Bush and Clinton administrations taught me the value of patience and perseverance. By the time I left the Senate I had learned to deal with and even come to appreciate some of its quaint rules and archaic practices. And what I learned there was later immensely helpful to me.

The negotiations in Northern Ireland involved thirteen parties: two governments, the United Kingdom and Ireland; ten political parties from Northern Ireland; and the independent chairmen.* On the first day, in a large conference room packed with nearly a hundred people, in a moment of overconfidence I told them, "I'm a product of the United States Senate which, as you know, has a rule of unlimited debate. Any Senator can stand up, at any time, and talk for as long as he or she wants. So I've listened to a sixteen-hour speech, a twelve-hour speech, and lots of other very long speeches. I can and I will sit here and listen as long as any of you can talk. I can take anything you throw at me."

I was trying to reassure them that their concerns would be heard because I was aware that their history was not one of listening to each other. To the contrary, they routinely refused to listen to each other, and the dramatic walkout was a staple of their politics. But, as became clear in retrospect, I went too far in my opening statement, and over the next few years I paid a heavy price. Although there were no twelve-hour speeches, there were many long monologues. Most of all there was eye-

* I was assisted by two distinguished colleagues: Harri Holkeri, the former Prime Minister of Finland, and John de Chastelain, the former Canadian Ambassador to the United States.

glazing, mind-numbing repetition. Over and over and over again, for month after month, then year after year, for what in the aggregate must have been hundreds of hours, the same people made the same speeches. It took every bit of patience I had, and more, to sit there and listen, but I did. I didn't prohibit any delegate to the talks from speaking, although I could have and perhaps should have. But I knew that if I was ever able to get them to agree, the result would be in some respect painful to each of them. I did not want anyone to have the excuse that he or she wasn't heard or didn't have the chance to argue a position.

It became especially difficult for me in the last few months of the main negotiation, roughly from February to mid-April 1998. As the end neared tensions rose within the negotiations and throughout society. So too did the number and specificity of threats. One day I received a visit from security officials who wanted to discuss those threats. They had reviewed my travel schedule, my day-to-day movements, and had come to recommend changes. For roughly the first year and a half the negotiations had been conducted on Monday, Tuesday, and Wednesday of each week. The delegates, almost all of them elected officials, had tended to their other duties on Thursdays and Fridays. My schedule varied widely, but in the first year or so, if there had been a "normal week," it would have started early on Sunday morning, when I left New York to fly to London; there I connected to a flight to Belfast, arriving at my hotel at about eleven o'clock in the evening. We met from Monday morning through Wednesday evening. After three long days of negotiations I often left on Thursday to fly from Belfast to London and then to Washington. I spent Friday working in my law office there, then flew to New York that evening. On Sunday morning the cycle began again. As the negotiations became more intense I often remained in Belfast an extra day, Thursday, to hold informal meetings with delegates, to brief government ministers, and to plan for the next week. This meant that I was spending four nights a week in Belfast.

The security officials reassured me that the venue for the negotiations was heavily protected. However, they warned me that my vulnerability to a personal attack was highest in the morning, when I traveled from my hotel to the building in which the talks were held, and then in the evening, when I made the return trip. One response to that was to change hotels frequently, sometimes every day, which I had done from the beginning. Another was to vary the time of departure and the route by which I was driven from the hotel to the talks venue and back; I usually waited until I got into the car to decide which route to take that day, so no one could possibly have advance notice. Still another, which they now strongly recommended, was that I reduce the number of nights I stayed in Belfast from four to two. Instead of leaving New York on Sunday morning and arriving in Belfast that evening, I was to leave New York on Sunday evening, fly overnight, arrive in Belfast on Monday morning, and go straight from the airport to the negotiations. On Wednesday evening, instead of staying overnight in Belfast, I was to fly to London, stay overnight there, then fly to New York on Thursday morning. I liked the fact that I could spend a little more time with my family each week, but I dreaded the prospect of beginning each week flying overnight from New York to London to Belfast, then going directly to the negotiations. I knew that I would be exhausted.

With apprehension I accepted their recommendation. It turned out to be even worse than I had anticipated. The several

Mondays I went through this routine were among the worst days of my life. I found it difficult to listen, to focus, to even stay awake. Fortunately the last two weeks involved little travel. I stayed in Belfast as the negotiations extended through the entire week and ultimately around the clock. Somehow I got through it, although by the time the Peace Agreement was reached, on Easter weekend, I was more tired than I have ever been, before or since. But the result was worth it, and, as an added bonus, my patience muscle had survived its greatest test.

RISK

Since listening and patience are cautious pursuits, it may seem paradoxical that another important lesson of my life is a willingness to take risks. At several turning points in my life I took chances that seemed imprudent at the time. These included leaving the security of a federal judgeship for a temporary appointment to the Senate and declining an appointment to the Supreme Court as I was leaving the Senate for an uncertain future. Those were large and obvious risks. To leave the security of being a federal judge, a job I truly loved, for the insecurity of a Senate seat, especially for just a short time, was difficult. So was the decision to turn down an appointment to the Supreme Court. But I was confident of my ability to properly evaluate the risks and rewards, to rationally prepare a personal cost-benefit analysis. Most of all, whatever my decision, I was reasonably well-assured of being able to continue to successfully engage in important and productive work. In neither case was money a factor. My experience prior to each decision had bred in me confidence that I could earn enough to take care of my family's needs.

Another risk that, in the context in which it occurred, was significant for me took place much earlier. Although to most people it will seem trivial, not risky at all, my decision to attend Bowdoin College seemed to me at the time to be very risky. By the time I accepted appointment to the Senate I was a mature man who already had been reasonably successful in life; that was even more true when I declined President Clinton's offer to appoint me to the Supreme Court. But in the spring of my senior year in high school, I was a confused, insecure, sixteen-year-old boy who had not accomplished anything. Most of my school classmates were older and bigger and seemed more mature and wise. My lack of athletic ability, in comparison to my brothers, had generated in me a massive inferiority complex, and the trauma of my father's unemployment had a devastating effect on him and on me. Although it was only a year it seemed like a lifetime. My emotions swung back and forth from love and sympathy to shame and hostility; he wallowed in despair and I reacted badly. I loved him, but I was ashamed of him; that made me ashamed of myself. In that situation I should have seen Bowdoin as a chance to escape, especially since there was no obvious alternative. But in my confusion I saw it as just the opposite: as a challenge I was unprepared to meet. I was overwhelmed by fear that I would fail.

When I met with Bill Shaw, the director of admissions at Bowdoin, I told him that my family didn't have any money for my education, but I was too ashamed to tell him that my father was unemployed. On my return to Waterville I told my guidance counselor at Waterville High School about my trip to Bowdoin. She encouraged me to talk with the principal and took me to his office. To my surprise, he urged me to forget about Bowdoin. You won't fit in, he told me, the boys there are from different backgrounds. He wasn't more explicit. He didn't have to be. I knew little about Bowdoin, but I understood his message: given my background I wasn't good enough for the place. I was nervous when I entered his office; when I left I was shaking with anxiety, inadequacy, and anger.

That weekend at home was long and painful, the peak of my inner turmoil and the nadir of my relationship with my father. I was angry at him, at the principal, at myself. I also was consumed with self-pity: I couldn't do anything, couldn't be anything. I had no one to talk to. My brothers were away at college. I felt that neither my sister nor my mother would understand what I was going through. So I spent the weekend alone with my thoughts. I cried often on the inside, occasionally on the outside. Gradually the anger dissipated, the self-pity lifted, the tears dried up, and I began to see that I had a chance to change my life. I would show them! "Them" included the principal, the high school basketball coach, my brothers, and my father. He wanted me to go to Bowdoin, so it is a measure of my confusion that somehow I felt that by going I would be showing him — what? When I received the formal letter of acceptance from Bill Shaw I didn't tell anyone. I simply sent back a short thank-you letter. I've made a lot of consequential decisions since, involving people's liberties and lives. Although many were far more difficult and consequential, none seemed it at the time. That I made it through Bowdoin was, to me, at that stage in my life, a huge accomplishment. It gave me the confidence to take the next important steps in my life.

I also took a risk when I accepted the invitation of the governments of Ireland and the United Kingdom to serve as chairman of the Northern Ireland Peace Negotiations. The conflict was ancient, fueled by religious and other differences, and marked by extraordinary brutality. Previous negotiations had failed; there was no reason to believe that these would be any different. But I felt that I could somehow help them find a way through their many differences. I knew there was a substantial risk to my life and personal safety, but I managed to submerge my doubts and fears by concentrating on my work. By far the greatest risk I took in the negotiations themselves was when I established the firm and final deadline of midnight on April 10, 1998. That was regarded by some as a desperate and dangerous move. Some British civil servants opposed the deadline; they had been engaged in trying to manage the Troubles for many years, and they feared that an abrupt end to the process would trigger an immediate return to violence more savage than ever. I shared their concern. But, I argued, without a final deadline the process was ultimately more likely to fail, producing the very result they feared. Just a few months earlier, on

December 27, Billy Wright, a prominent Unionist paramilitary leader, had been murdered while in prison by a group of Republican prisoners. That touched off a brutal round of tit-for-tat reprisals. In the early months of 1998 violence rose, threatening the negotiations. Two parties were expelled from the talks because of their relationships with paramilitaries, although they later returned. Two other parties had earlier walked out, never to return. The process was now in danger of a final collapse. To avoid that, I believed a dramatic change was necessary, so I proposed an early, unbreakable deadline, just prior to which there would be an intense, final two-week push for an agreement.

The British and Irish governments accepted my assessment and my recommendation. But I was deeply worried, all the more so because I respected the civil servants who urged rejection of my proposal. The prospect of renewed conflict, which virtually everyone assumed would be more violent and brutal than what had occurred before, hung heavy on me for the last few months. Although I tried to project an air of calm confidence, inside I was anxious and fearful. It was close, but it ended well, to my enormous relief. I had taken a huge risk and it paid off.

As a young man I wanted to teach history at Bowdoin, but ended up in military intelligence in Berlin. I wanted to practice law in Maine and did for a while, but ended up in politics in Washington. I wanted to be a federal judge and was for a short time, but ended up in the U.S. Senate. When I left the Senate I wanted a private life, but ended up in public positions in Northern Ireland and the Middle East. Not in my wildest early dreams did I imagine that I would ever write a book, but at the age of fifty-four I wrote one; this is my fifth.

A central lesson of my experience (and that of many others) is that life is not lived in a straight and predictable line. It zigs and zags, goes sideways and backward, and lurches forward suddenly and in ways that cannot be foreseen. Around every corner there is risk. A willingness to confront it, at times to go against the odds, is an important part of success in life.

CHANCE

On November 4, 1979, fifty-two Americans were taken hostage in Teheran by Iranian revolutionaries. The televised images of mobs swarming the U.S. Embassy and of blindfolded American diplomats being led through hostile crowds aroused public opinion in our country. Each night, as the newscasts reminded Americans of the length of their captivity, the pressure mounted on President Carter to do something. Overriding objections from his secretary of state, Carter authorized a military rescue mission. It proved to be a disastrous failure. When Secretary Vance resigned in protest, Carter turned to Ed Muskie for his replacement. Less than a year earlier, at the age of forty-six, I had been sworn in as a federal judge. I did not, indeed could not then have imagined that by the time I turned forty-seven I would be a U.S. senator.

Viewed objectively, filling Muskie's seat

was a huge risk not worth taking. I loved being a federal judge and I was assured (if I maintained good conduct) of lifetime security. Most of those whose advice I sought urged me to stay where I was. One very good friend, a Portland lawyer, pointed out, "If you stay on the bench you'll almost certainly get the chance to move up to the First Circuit,* and then you'll have a good shot at the Supreme Court." The possibility that I would someday be offered appointment to the Supreme Court seemed very remote and unrealistic to me. I later joked that so many of the friends I called for advice urged me to decline that I stopped calling. Instead I made the decision on my own. I was able to do so because my vision was no longer clouded by inadequacy, insecurity, or fear. I had been a partner in a small, good law firm, working with men I liked and admired. I was confident that even if I accepted appointment to the Senate and was defeated at the next election I could return to a successful law practice in Maine. Twenty years earlier that had been my principal goal in life. A few years earlier I

* One seat on the U.S. First Circuit Court of Appeals, based in Boston, is traditionally held by a judge from Maine.

had lost an election and discovered that the world didn't end, for me or anyone else. I felt I had acquitted myself well as U.S. attorney and was confident that I also would have done so had I remained a federal judge; I had developed the habit of working hard to prepare myself for every task I undertook. While I knew accepting the Senate seat was a risk, I decided it was worth taking. I was influenced in part by the reality that while judges play a crucial role in our society, they are involved only in disputes that others choose to bring to them; they have virtually no independent authority to act on their own initiative. Elected officials, by contrast, and U.S. senators in particular, can initiate action on any issue they deem important enough to address.

Cy Vance was a man of integrity. I had gotten to know him well. When I saw him for the first time after entering the Senate, I thanked him for making it possible for me to become a U.S. senator. He laughed and replied, "Well, I'm glad some good came out of it."

Entering the Senate was a major turning point in my life, and it was due largely to chance. In many other instances — some large, some small — chance has intervened to alter the course of my life, usually for the better. I believe that to be true of all other human lives as well. Life is unpredictable and random; we are unable to fully control it against the vagaries of chance. So we should anticipate chance, even without knowing when and how it will occur, and view it as offering an opportunity that might otherwise not be available. Chance can offer an escape from tedium, from a dead end, from failure; it can offer redemption from error; in some dramatic cases it can offer a new life, as it did for me.

MOUNT DESERT ISLAND

There is, of course, no one most beautiful place on earth. The judgment is entirely subjective. But for me, Mount Desert Island is that place.

I write these words on a late August day. What I call the summer symphony is in full swing as the incoming tide pounds steadily against the rocky coast, the bell buoy in the harbor clangs, and the ocean breeze swishes softly through the trees.

The sky is a light, cloudless blue. The temperature will reach the seventies this afternoon and dip to fifty tonight. The trees and plants, nourished by a wet spring and summer, are deep green. The cold ocean changes from gray to green to foaming white as it nears then crashes against the granite blocks on the shore. The air is clean and pungent with the odor of Maine: salty ocean mixed with spruce and fir trees. The forests, the mountains, and the ocean meet in a rugged beauty that pleases the senses and refreshes the spirit.

Long before the white man, the Indians of the Penobscot tribe summered on the island they called Pemetic, or "Sloping Land." In 1524 the explorer Verrazano called the region Acadia, apparently after a place in ancient Greece. The name Mount Desert came from the great French explorer Samuel de Champlain, who landed there in 1604. Viewed from the sea the granite outcroppings on the tops of several of the island's mountains could be confused for patches of desert sand. Thus the name "the Island of the Mountain Deserts." As I look out my window I try to imagine a French sailing vessel captained by Champlain, gliding slowly toward the island, just as it did almost 410 years ago.

Champlain could not have missed the island, as it is by far the largest along the Maine coast. Indeed it is the third largest off the coast of the continental United States, being exceeded in land area only by Long Island and Martha's Vineyard.

Like other places in Maine and eastern Canada, Mount Desert Island was the scene of conflict between the French and British. Although many of its landmarks bear French names, reflecting their early presence, it, like most of the rest of Maine, was eventually controlled and settled by the British. As one historian noted, the French brought Jesuits to the New World, while the British brought guns, so the outcome was inevitable. The island's early growth centered on shipbuilding and fishing. Around the middle of the nineteenth century its cool, clear weather and beautiful scenery began to attract summer visitors.

Soon the island was "discovered," and the rich and famous of their day came and built large mansions, which, no matter how pretentious, were always described as "cottages." They created a lively (if class-conscious) social scene. One commentator described the period between 1880 and World War I as "the golden days," which were ended by "the servant problem and the income tax." Although perhaps not golden, the island continued as a preserve for the wealthy. Two things changed that: the great fire of 1947 and the creation of Acadia National Park. From May to October 1947 there was no rain. Forests across the state were the driest in centuries, and many areas suffered from extensive fires. One of them was Mount Desert Island. About a third of the structures in Bar Harbor, the island's largest town, were destroyed, as were large portions of the island's forests. Many of the most elegant mansions were never rebuilt. To be sure, there remain many large, attractive, and expensive homes on the island, but the gaudy, golden age was over, never to return.

Charles W. Eliot set in motion the events that led to the creation of a national park on Mount Desert Island. Then president of Harvard, Eliot, a summer resident of the island, took two steps in 1901 that were to prove decisive. He and a group of like-minded people obtained a state charter for a "public reservation" society to acquire land in the area for public use, and he recruited George Dorr to run the society. A lifelong bachelor whose consuming passion was conservation, Dorr inherited a fortune and spent it and his life acquiring land on Mount Desert Island for public use. Tireless, persistent, considered by many egocentric, Dorr gave of his own land and bought more with his funds and those donated by others.

In 1913 he had to confront and defeat a bill introduced in the state legislature to annul the Public Reservation charter. The experience unsettled him and convinced him that the only way to preserve the area that had been acquired was to create a national park: the state might undo what he did, but it could not undo an act of the federal government. After three years of effort by Dorr and others, President Woodrow Wilson signed a proclamation on July 8, 1916, creating the Sieur de Monts National Monument area. Soon thereafter it was converted into a national park, eventually to be known as Acadia. It was the first national park to be created east of the Mississippi River, and the only one created entirely by private donations of land to the government.

Dorr was helped immeasurably by John D. Rockefeller Jr., who had come to the island at the turn of the century. He liked it and built a hundred-room "cottage" here. He also built fifty-seven miles of roads (now called carriage paths because when built they were intended to be used only by horse-drawn carriages, not motorized vehicles), which traverse large portions of the island, providing scenic hiking, biking, and horseback-riding opportunities. Rockefeller also provided much needed funding for further acquisition by Dorr. Today his son David and several members of his family maintain summer homes on the island and continue their family's impressive legacy of philanthropy and conservation.

Acadia is one of the most-visited national parks in the country, even though it is one of the smallest. Millions of people come each year, rich and poor alike, to enjoy the island's beauty. I became involved with the park when, as a U.S. senator, I wrote and obtained enactment of legislation establishing for the first time a permanent boundary for the park, resolving other contentious issues, and ending nearly a quarter century of conflict between the park and the surrounding towns. It took me six years and required many trips to the island, where I had dozens of meetings with local and national park officials. I negotiated many land swaps between the park and the towns and encouraged some private landowners to donate, then or at a future date, some of their property to the park. That experience instilled in me a love for the island and its people that has grown over the years.

That feeling has been enhanced by many humorous events. One of my favorite stories is about a visit to the Jordan Pond House. It is a restaurant that has existed for decades within the park. It is a lovely setting, the restaurant on a ridge above a long lawn that slopes down to the heavily forested shores of the small, picturesque body of water known as Jordan Pond. The original structure burned down in the late 1970s. When I entered the Senate I helped obtain funding to complete the rebuilding, and it has since been one of my favorite stops on the island.

One warm August day early in my Senate tenure, I agreed to meet two close friends there. One of them, Don Peters, a builder and contractor from Portland, arrived just as I did. We waited for a long time for our mutual friend, Marshall Stern. Frustrated, we decided to call Marshall to see if he was in fact coming. We walked to a spot near the restaurant's men's room where we knew a pay telephone was located. A man was standing at the phone, on which he had propped up a card with several phone numbers written on it. He was having trouble getting the pay phone to work. As he pumped in quarters without response he started banging the side of the phone box with his open hand and cursing. To his wife standing next to him he unleashed a torrent of criticism in which he made clear that he, from Boston, didn't care much for the "yokels" in Maine who didn't even know how to properly maintain a pay telephone. Gradually the line grew, and the small crowd watched and listened in embarrassed silence. Suddenly the man standing behind me tapped me on the shoulder and said, "Excuse me, aren't you Senator Mitchell?" I acknowledged that I was, and he extended his hand toward me, saying, "I'm Bob. I'd like to shake your hand." We did, then he asked, "Are you working or are you on vacation?" I told him I was there on vacation and had just stopped to have lunch with a couple of friends. Then, since it seemed like the polite thing to do, I asked him the same question.

"Oh," he said, "I'm working."

"What do you do?"

"I'm a telephone repairman."

It took me a moment to digest that, then he added:

"When that fella from Boston runs out of quarters I'm gonna fix that phone."

He then leaned forward and said to me, in a low and conspiratorial tone, "Senator, if I was you I'd go downstairs and use the phone there. I know it's working 'cause I just fixed it."

We went downstairs and called Marshall. He eventually arrived and we spent a pleasant hour laughing over the telephone story.

The wily and resourceful Mainer who outsmarts the big-city slicker is a staple of Maine humor. Another story I like to tell makes that point. Two smart young men graduated from Harvard during the Great Depression. Unable to find work, they took an old printer and rebuilt it so that it produced counterfeit twenty-dollar bills. This enabled them to live comfortably, and one of them bought a small summer cottage in Maine. One summer day the machine malfunctioned and produced a batch of eighteen-dollar bills. One said, "We'll never be able to pass these, so I'll destroy them."

"No," said the other, "I'm going to Maine next week. I'll get them past the old guy at the country store near my cottage." When he got to the country store he asked the old man if he'd had a good winter.

"No problems," the old man answered. He then told the old man he needed a favor.

"No problem," the old man answered.

"Can you change this eighteen-dollar bill?"

"No problem," the old man answered again, "you want two nines or three sixes?"

Out my window the Cranberry Islands, and other islands beyond them, stretch like stepping-stones to the east, across the cold gray waters of the North Atlantic Ocean. Over the horizon lies Europe and beyond that the Middle East. For a half century I traveled to those and other distant lands where I met, talked, and worked with people of many languages, religions, races, and colors.

It has been a long way home. But no matter how far from Maine I went, I was at all times rooted in the place of my birth, my upbringing, my family, and my values. Fate and hope carried my mother and my father's parents many thousands of miles, from Lebanon and Ireland to Maine. Here my parents lived lives that were very hard, but meaningful. They had neither wealth nor status, but they achieved their goal and their efforts were validated by their children. Because of them I have been fortunate beyond measure, for I have lived the American Dream.

In Northern Ireland I chaired three separate but related negotiations over a five-year period. In the Middle East I completed two tours of duty over three years. In one the result was a peace agreement. In the other conflict continues.

Both were long, difficult, and draining, physically and emotionally. The separation from my family, especially after Andrew and Claire were born, was especially hard. A parent's love for his or her children cannot be understood until it is experienced. But, ultimately, both were rewarding because I was able to serve my country, in and from which I have received more than my share of benefits.

It is pure coincidence that my mother was born in Lebanon and my father's parents were born in Ireland. But traveling to and working in Ireland and the Middle East enabled me to learn about my parents' heritage: to walk the land of my ancestors; to meet the people among whom they lived; to learn of their hopes, fears, aspirations. It helped me fill an inner void that I didn't know existed before I travelled to Ireland and Lebanon. All this I came to regard as an extra benefit from serving my country.

On the hundreds of long flights to and from Ireland and the Middle East, I tried to imagine my mother's early life: what was it like for a young girl growing up in the hills of southern Lebanon? What was her parents' life like, Arabic-speaking Christians living in a Muslim-majority land? I asked the same questions while daydreaming about my father, who never knew his parents and went from a Catholic orphanage in the center of Boston to the cold forests of northern Maine where, as a boy, he worked among men. I wondered about his parents: much has been written about the Irish immigrants who succeeded in the new land, little about the many who failed. Their lives often were as hard and barren as the huge rock formations of the west coast of Ireland. Had that been the fate of my grandparents and their parents?

On a recent flight across the Atlantic, I saw the sun rising in Dublin as the plane touched down. I was drowsy but my mind was awake with thoughts, dreams, fantasies, about those whose blood is now mine. I thought of stories of Ireland and Lebanon that always make me smile when they come to mind.

I was at a reception in my honor at a resort hotel just below the border between Northern Ireland and Ireland. A bridge between them had been destroyed during the Troubles. It had been rebuilt and was now to be called the Peace Bridge and named after me. The large and friendly crowd of well-wishers peppered me with questions about my father and his family. Most reacted with surprise and disbelief when I answered that I really didn't know much about his family history; to them, history is a living part of the present. A couple of them suggested that I retain them, both in the business that specializes in genealogy, mostly for wealthy Irish-Americans. With a twinkle in his eye and a sly smile on his face, the host of the event, a local official said, "Senator, if you pay them enough they'll connect you to Brian Boru" (an ancient warrior-king well-known in Irish history). We all laughed. In other words, it's all hokum!

On the other hand, maybe it's not. The other story is about my mother. When we were growing up she often said to her children, softly and with nostalgia, "You should see Lebanon. It's so beautiful. The air is pure, the water is clear, the mountains, the forests, even the flowers smell better. Oh Lebanon, my Lebanon." After arriving in the United States at the age of eighteen, she returned to Lebanon only once, late in her life, after my father died. My sister Barbara accompanied her as they returned to the village of Bkassine, where they attended a reception and dinner with relatives and friends in the house in which my mother had grown up. Late in the evening my mother was asked to say something. According to Barbara, my mother stood, paused, looked out at the large, happy crowd, and, with great emotion and a broad smile, said, "You should see America. It's so beautiful. The air is pure, the water is clean, the mountains, the forests, even the flowers smell better. Oh America, my America."

She had little formal education; she couldn't read or write English and spoke it with a heavy accent; she worked her entire adult life on the night shift in a textile mill; but she was generous and loving, strong and wise, and she understood clearly the meaning of America.

To me, no one has ever said it better.

Oh America, my America.

NOTES

The Senate Years

1. Michael D'Antonio, "Senator for a Year, Mitchell, Still Unknown at Home," *Maine Sunday Telegram,* May 17, 1981.
2. William S. Cohen and George J. Mitchell, *Men of Zeal: A Candid Inside Story of the Iran-Contra Hearings* (New York: Viking, 1988).
3. Ibid., 183–93. One of the many ironies that emerged in the hearings was that North justified lying to Congress because he "had to weigh in the balance the difference between lives and lies," and Congress could not be trusted with sensitive information. But in one of the examples he cited, the terrorist seizure of the cruise ship *Achille Lauro* in 1985, North himself was reportedly the source of the leak (183–86).
4. Ibid., 169–72.

5. Robert McFarlane, national security advisor, four misdemeanor counts of withholding information from Congress; Oliver North, National Security Council staff, three counts of accepting a gratuity, aiding in the obstruction of Congress, destroying documents; John Poindexter, national security advisor, two counts of false statements, two counts of obstructing Congress, and conspiracy; Richard Secord, head of the enterprise, pleaded guilty to one felony count of false statements to Congress; Albert Hakim, head of the enterprise, pleaded guilty to giving money to North; Thomas Clines, businessman in the enterprise, guilty of underreporting earnings and stating falsely on tax returns that he had no foreign accounts; Carl Channell, fundraiser, pleaded guilty to conspiracy to defraud the United States; Richard Miller, fundraiser, pleaded guilty to conspiracy to defraud the United States; Clair George, CIA deputy director for operations, two counts of making false statements and perjury before Congress; Duane Clarridge, CIA European Division chief, indicted on seven counts of perjury and false statements; Alan Fiers Jr., CIA Central American Task Force chief, pleaded guilty to two counts of withhold-

ing information from Congress; Joseph Fernandez, CIA station chief in San Jose, Costa Rica, four-count conspiracy indictment issued in Virginia, dropped because of failure of attorney general to mandate disclosure of information relevant to defense; Elliott Abrams, assistant secretary of state for inter-American affairs, two counts of withholding information from Congress; Caspar Weinberger, secretary of defense, indicted on five counts of perjury, making false statements, and obstruction.

6. McFarlane, North, Poindexter, Secord, Hakim, Clines, Channell, Miller, George, Fiers, Abrams.
7. Abrams, George, Fiers, McFarlane.
8. Weinberger and Clarridge.
9. David Johnston, "The Pardons: Bush Pardons 6 in Iran Affair, Aborting a Weinberger Trial. Prosecutor Assails 'Coverup,' " *New York Times,* December 25, 1992.
10. Ibid.
11. Too much deference for some. See Seymour M. Hersh, "The Iran-Contra Committees: Did They Protect Reagan?," *New York Times Magazine,* April 29, 1990.
12. Nationally televised speech from the White House, March 4, 1987.
13. Richard E. Cohen, *Washington at Work:*

Back Rooms and Clean Air (New York: Macmillan, 1995), 27–48.

14. Ibid., 62.
15. Helen Dewar, *Washington Post,* March 25, 1990.
16. *Congressional Record: Senate,* March 29, 1990, 5861.
17. Paul A. Gigot, "Clean-Air Game: Green Machine Routs Bush Team," *Wall Street Journal,* April 6, 1990; Matthew L. Wald, "Industry Wary of Clean-Air Bill," *New York Times,* April 5, 1990.
18. Cohen, *Washington at Work,* 174.
19. Ibid., 176.
20. Environmental Protection Agency, *Our Nation's Air,* 2012 Report. The amounts of reduction were significant: ground-level ozone 17 percent, particulate pollution 38 percent, lead 45 percent, nitrogen oxides 45 percent, carbon monoxide 73 percent, sulfur dioxide 75 percent.
21. "Portland Girl Given Little League Rights," Associated Press, *Lewiston Daily Sun,* May 28, 1974.
22. 132 Cong. Rec. 14336 1986.
23. 132 Cong. Rec. 14341 1986.
24. "White House Shores Up No Tax Stand," *Washington Post,* May 10, 1990.
25. John Robert Greene, *The Presidency of*

George Bush (Lawrence: University Press of Kansas, 1999), 37.

26. A copy of the original document, with my handwritten changes, is included at the end of these notes.

27. Statement by the president, August 19, 1982.

28. "The Budget Agreement," *New York Times,* October 2, 1990.

Northern Ireland

1. George J. Mitchell, *Making Peace* (New York: Knopf, 1999), 187.

No Time for Retirement

1. Ashley Dunlak, "Tigers' Scherzer on Steroid Scandal: 'We're Tired of Cheaters,' " CBS Detroit, August 6, 2013.

2. Stephen Lorenso and Christian Red, "Mike Trout Wants Players Caught Using Steroids and PEDs Thrown Out of Baseball for Life," *New York Daily News,* August 13, 2013.

3. Mike Cardillo, "Diamondbacks Pitcher David Hernandez: Throw PED Cheats Out of Baseball," *Big Lead,* June 7, 2013.

4. Peter Abraham, "Dustin Pedroia OK with Hiking PED Penalties," *Boston Globe,*

March 4, 2013; Bryan Curtis, "Q&A: Angels Pitcher C. J. Wilson on Steroids, Screenplays, and Star Wars," *Grantland,* March 11, 2013.

5. Associated Press, "All Star SS Peralta, Cardinals Reach 4-Year Deal," November 24, 2013.

6. Bill Madden, "MLB Players Association's Michael Weiner Says Some Players Would Welcome Tougher Bans for Positive Drug Tests," *New York Daily News,* February 25, 2013.

7. Statement by Major League Baseball and Major League Baseball Players Association, March 28, 2014.

8. Ibid.

9. Mark Fainaru-Wada and Lance Williams, *Game of Shadows: Barry Bonds, BALCO, and the Steroids Scandal That Rocked Professional Sports* (New York: Gotham, 2006).

10. The history of baseball's efforts to confront drug use is summarized in George J. Mitchell, *Report to the Commissioner of Baseball of an Independent Investigation into the Illegal Use of Steroids and Other Performance Enhancing Substances by Players in Major League Baseball,* December 13, 2007, 18–137.

11. *Report of the Special Bid Oversight Com-*

mission, United States Olympic Committee, March 1, 1999.

12. Mitchell, *Report to the Commissioner of Baseball.*

13. Report of the International Commission on Violence in the Middle East, April 30, 2001.

14. U.S. Department of State, Remarks by Senator George J. Mitchell, Appointment of Special Envoy for Middle East Peace and Special Representative for Afghanistan and Pakistan, Washington, DC, January 22, 2009.

15. Naftali Bennett, "For Israel, Two-State Is No Solution," *New York Times,* November 5, 2014.

16. Stephen Castle and Jodi Rudoren, "A Symbolic Vote in Britain Recognizes a Palestinian State," *New York Times,* October 13, 2014.

17. Dan Bilefsky and Maia de la Baume, "Symbolic Vote in France Backs Palestinian State," *New York Times,* December 3, 2014.

18. Testimony before the U.S. House of Representatives Committee on Appropriations, 102nd Congress, May 22, 1991.

19. U.S. Department of State, airgram to the Embassy in Israel, April 8, 1968. See http://history.state.gov/historicaldocuments

/frus1964-68v20/d137.

20. UN Security Council, Statement by Charles Yost, U.S. Permanent Representative to the United Nations, July 1, 1969. See Foundation for Middle East Peace, "Report on Israeli Settlements in the Occupied Territories," Special Report, February 1994, p. 6.

21. United Nations Security Council, Statement by William Scranton, U.S. Permanent Representative to the United Nations, March 23, 1976. See Foundation for Middle East Peace, "Report on Israeli Settlements in the Occupied Territories," Special Report, February 1994, p. 6.

22. U.S. Department of State, Statement by the Secretary of State, March 21, 1980.

23. White House, Statement by the President, September 1, 1982.

24. White House, Statement by the President, December 16, 1996.

25. White House, Statement by President George W. Bush, April 4, 2002; White House, "President Bush Calls for New Palestinian Leadership," June 24, 2002, http://georgewbush-whitehouse.archives.gov/news/releases/2002/06/20020624-3.html.

26. United Nations, "A Performance-Based

Roadmap to a Permanent Two-State Solution to the Israeli-Palestinian Conflict," July 2002, http://www.un.org/News/dh/mideast/roadmap122002.pdf.

27. Thomas Friedman, "The Last Train," *New York Times,* October 26, 2014.

28. Jackson Diehl, "Abbas' Waiting Game on Peace with Israel," *Washington Post,* May 29, 2009. Abbas's view, that others are resonsible for the plight of the Palestinians, is widely shared in the region among Arabs, and also in Turkey and Iran and other non-Arab countries. It is often expressed more broadly to included the plight of the entire region. See Tim Arango, "Turkish Leader, Using Conflicts, Cements Power," *New York Times,* November 1, 2014.

29. David Ignatius, "The Mideast Deal That Could Have Been," *Washington Post,* October 26, 2011.

30. Richard Boudreaux, "Olmert's Peace Efforts Put Livni in Tight Spot," *Los Angeles Times,* February 4, 2009.

31. Ibid.

32. Much later, in an interview, Olmert described those discussions in detail. Greg Sheridan, "Ehud Olmert Still Dreams of Peace," *Australian,* November 28, 2009.

33. Richard Boudreaux, "Olmert's Peace

Efforts Put Livni in Tight Spot," *Los Angeles Times*, February 4, 2009.

34. U.S. Department of State, Briefing by Special Envoy for Middle East Peace George Mitchell, November 25, 2009.

APPENDIX

STATEMENT BY THE PRESIDENT

I met this morning with the Bipartisan leadership — the Speaker, the Senate Majority Leader, the Senate Republican Leader, the House Majority Leader, and the House Republican Leader — to review the status of the deficit-reduction negotiations.

It is clear to me that both the size of the deficit problem and the need for a package that can be enacted require all of the following: entitlement and mandatory program reform; tax revenue increases; growth incentives; discretionary spending reductions orderly reductions in defense expenditures; and budget process reform — to assure that any Bipartisan agreement is enforceable control. The Bipartisan leadership agree with me to these points

The budget negotiations will resume promptly with a view toward reaching substantive agreement as quickly as possible.

ACKNOWLEDGMENTS

Writing is personal, but publishing a book is a collaborative process. In that process I have been helped immeasurably by many people, foremost among them Jonathan Karp, the publisher of Simon & Schuster. Jon encouraged and guided me throughout. Without him my notes would have remained just notes. I also thank at Simon & Schuster in Editorial Megan Hogan, Publishing Assistant; in Publicity Cary Goldstein, Vice President and Director of Publicity; Maureen Cole, Senior Publicist; in Marketing Richard Rhorer, Vice President and Associate Publisher; Stephen Bedford, Marketing Manager; in Managing Editorial Irene Kheradi, Executive Managing Editor; Gina DiMascia, Associate Managing Editor; Ffej Caplan, Assistant Managing Editor; in Art and Design Jackie Seow, Vice President and Executive Art Director of Trade Art; Christopher Lin, Associate Art Director; Joy O'Meara, Design Director; in Production Lisa Erwin, Senior Production Manager; and Lisa Healy, Senior Production Editor.

My assistant, Ann Ungar, was invaluable in the preparation of the manuscript — and in nearly every other aspect of my life! She is attentive to both detail and nuance.

While serving in public office I was fortunate to have help from many talented persons on my staffs. Not all are mentioned in this book, although all deserve my gratitude for their contributions to the causes I served. In the Senate I was ably assisted by, among others, Rich Arenberg, Jan Welch Barrett, Bob Bean, Donna Beck, Larry Benoit, Tom Bertocci, Sandy Brown, Judy Cadorette, Paul Carliner, Bob Carolla, Jim Case, Gayle Fitzgerald Cory, Kelly Currie, Bob Davison, Diane Dewhirst, Tom Gallagher, Steve Hart, Mike Hastings, Beverly Bustin Hathaway, John Hilley, Kelly Riordan Horowitz, Charlie Jacobs, Anita Jensen, David Johnson, Kate Kimball, Charles Kinney, Margaret Malia Kneeland, Estelle Lavoie, Mary Leblanc, David Lemoine, Clyde Macdonald, Sandy Vigue Martin, Mary McAleney, Sandy Moore, Gary Myrick, Lisa Nolan, Brett O'Brien, Janie

O'Connor, Marty Paone, Jeff Peterson, Martha Pope, Jeff Porter, Grace Reef, Bob Rozen, Abby Safold, Pat Sarcone, Sarah Sewall, Diane Smith, Charlene Sturbitts, Sharon Sudbay, Regina Sullivan, Kim Wallace, and Chris Williams. Anita, Larry, and Bob Rozen were also helpful in reviewing portions of this book.

Martha Pope joined me in Northern Ireland, where I was also assisted by Kelly Currie and David Pozorski. Kelly was also with me on my first tour of duty in the Middle East, along with Jim Pickup and Fred Hof. Fred returned for my second tour in that region, where I was also helped by several able officials in the State Department and in the Executive Office; they include Jeff Feltman, David Hale, Gloria Hubbard, Payton Knopf, Prem Kumar, Janice Neal, Julia Reed, Mara Rudman, Alon Sachar, Jonathan Schwartz, Dan Shapiro, and Jake Sullivan.

Throughout my life I have benefited greatly from a close and loving family. It began with my parents and siblings; how much they meant to me is clear from the early pages of this book. It continues today with my patient and supportive wife, Heather; my children, Andrea, Andrew, and

Claire; and my grandson, Ian. I love and thank them all.

Mount Desert Island, Maine
2014

ILLUSTRATION CREDITS

Numbers in roman type refer to illustrations in the inserts; numbers in *italics* refer to book pages.

Courtesy of George J. Mitchell Papers, Bowdoin College Library, Brunswick, Maine: *v,* 4, 5, 7, 8, 9, 10, 17
Author's collection: 1, 2, 3, 6, 11, 12, 13, 19, 20, *631*
Official White House Photo: 14, 15
© PETER FOLEY/Reuters/Corbis: 16
State Department Photo by Michael Gross: 18

ABOUT THE AUTHOR

George J. Mitchell served as a U.S. attorney and a U.S. district court judge before entering the U.S. Senate in 1980. In 1989 he became Senate majority leader, a position he held until he left the Senate in 1995.

In 1995–99 he chaired successful peace negotiations in Northern Ireland, for which he received numerous awards and honors, including the Presidential Medal of Freedom, the highest civilian honor the U.S. government can give; the Philadelphia Liberty Medal; the Truman Institute Peace Prize; the German (Hesse) Peace Prize; and the United Nations (UNESCO) Peace Prize. At the request of President Bill Clinton and Israeli and Palestinian leaders, Senator Mitchell served in 2000–2001 as chairman of an international fact-finding committee on violence in the Middle East. At the request of President Barack Obama he served in 2009–11 as the U.S. special envoy for Middle East Peace.

He was chairman of the board of the Walt Disney Company and chairman of the International Crisis Group, a nonprofit organization dedicated to the prevention of crises. He also served as chancellor of Queen's University of Belfast, Northern Ireland.

In 2008 *Time* named him one of the one hundred most influential people in the world.